CHARLOTTE

Searching for Soul in a
Booming Southern City

by Robert L. FitzPatrick

FitzPatrick Management Inc., Hot Springs, North Carolina

© 2025 Robert L. FitzPatrick, All Rights Reserved

ISBN: 979-8-218-61869-8

Library of Congress Control Number: 2025903226

robertfitzpatrick@mac.com

Cover Image designed by Cindy Cash

CHARLOTTE: monochrome, towers of glass and steel,
sky and nature blocked by the logo of capital, proudly
wearing a golden crown of commerce

Other books by Robert L. FitzPatrick

*FALSE PROFITS, Seeking Financial and Spiritual
Deliverance in Multi-Level Marketing and Pyramid
Schemes (with Joyce K. Reynolds)*

*PONZINOMICS, the Untold Story of Multi-Level
Marketing*

DIRECT SELLING, A Nonfiction Fable

Acknowledgments

There are writers with the fortitude to spend years producing a book of a type or in content for which there is no prior example and which no one requested and no publisher accepted and that will almost certainly produce no financial return. I am not one of those. For this book, I needed a lot of support and encouragement, even some unpleasant coaxing to keep me going.

I am grateful to my spouse and soulmate, Terry Thirion, who perhaps draws on her own deep well of inspiration to produce beautiful paintings and drawings—which, fortunately, many people do request and purchase. Without her support and coaching I would never have finished this book. She patiently listened to my endless complaints and long-winded discoveries and analyses, my tedious thought-processes to connect historical events with current trends and my nagging doubts about the wisdom of the project.

My search for Soul in Charlotte's arts community benefitted greatly from the experience and insights of intrepid artists Peggy Hutson and Bunny Gregory, providing me with both historical perspective and a glimpse into future directions.

I thank my men friends in the Barney Offerman-inspired coffee group who consistently lent encouragement and ideas. Same for some of my family who also lived most of their lives in Charlotte, thought deeply about how it affected their perspective, and shared their feelings with me. Also, I extend gratitude to long-time friends who offered their impressions based on years of living in Charlotte. They confirmed to me that there is an enormous font of original ideas, humor, truthful observations, and fresh hopes for a more open, free and multi-dimensional Charlotte. That creative font has been stifled by the visionless vision of a small group of business oligarchs, bankers and Babbitts. I hope this book validates their fresh views, gives voice to their unrecorded frustrations, and adds to the possibility of a future shaped by a wider range of people in Charlotte.

I am grateful to my editor, Sarah Veeck of Santa Barbara California, for shortening and clarifying some of my sentences and helping me get to points more directly and concisely. I also appreciate her wise suggestions that I leave out some obscure literary and historical references and to further explain others she saw as useful. Her assurances that my analysis of Charlotte has meaning and value far beyond the city limits have been encouraging.

This book spans Charlotte mostly from the 1960s forward but also includes earlier events. Without the current and past documentation of the *Charlotte Observer*, *Charlotte News* (where I once worked as a reporter), *Charlotte Post*, *WFAE*, *Charlotte Business Journal*, *Charlotte Magazine*, *Queen City Nerve*, *Axios Charlotte*, and other local news organizations, this story could not have been told. The ability to cite local stories and archives should make all of us think about what is lost when local news media disappears or is replaced by national chains focused more on ideology and advertising than local, fact-based documentation.

Claims and Rights

It is customary for authors to make certain disclaimers that limit or personally disavow views presented or facts and events referenced in the book. I want to do the opposite—to lay claim to the views expressed and facts presented and to humbly assert my qualifications.

Charlotte has a long history—I have personally experienced it—of invalidating and discrediting alternative voices and views, especially those that challenge the dominant Profit, Growth and Status ideology.

I have heard the voices, *"Who are you to make a critique of Charlotte's Soul? What is your education? Whom do you represent?* More recently is added, *"An older White male, you have no right to speak about the "soul" of Charlotte. You cannot know of the experience of racial minorities, women, or others that are marginalized and unprivileged!"*

I lay claim to having relevant knowledge and experience to speak—imperfectly and with great limitations—to the issues addressed in this book and to the civic right to speak to the social character of Charlotte.

My claims and rights come partly from being a native Charlottean and an observant, and engaged long-time resident, which turn out to be rare qualifications in Charlotte. My family on both my mother's and father's sides has been in the Charlotte area more than 100 years. My maternal grandfather owned and operated one of Charlotte's most popular restaurants in the 20s, 30's and early 40s, the Barbecue Lodge on Wilkinson Blvd. My father's father designed, built and managed a mercerizing textile plant for its owners in Mount Holly, just west of Charlotte, a major advancement in the quality of Southern textiles. My parents lived and worked in Charlotte their entire adult lives. I attended

Catholic schools in Charlotte and Belmont Abbey College just west of the city.

My claims and rights also derive from unique life and work experience in Charlotte in which I engaged deeply in a wide range of civic issues. In several chapters of this story, I refer to my years of work as a professional community organizer, trained in Chicago by the renowned Saul Alinsky. This work plunged me into the most basic elements of civic life—zoning, neighborhood preservation, mass transit, parks, public school funding, equitable city services, road planning, location of emergency healthcare, and the most basic of all, the ability of all people, regardless of social status, to have a voice and power over their lives.

The perspective I gained in every issue was shaped by the views, the daily needs and life experience of ordinary people, not developers, city planners, bankers, or politicians. I was in a rare position to observe and test the claims, promises and pretenses of those in power by how they affected most people and future generations in tangible, measurable ways. Most instructive of all, I had a special vantage point from which to see how those in power responded when local people presented petitions, challenges or alternative views.

As further noted in the book, I left Charlotte for nearly two decades to live in South Florida, returning often for short visits throughout the 1980s early 90s. When my wife and I moved (back for me) to Charlotte in the late 90s to take care of my mother, following my father's death, I overlaid my previous professional experience and insights on to the explosive transformation Charlotte was experiencing. Growing up in the Jim Crow era and later witnessing the traumas inflicted on thousands from urban renewal, in addition to civic education I gained as a community organizer, provided a foundation for examining Charlotte's sprawl, destruction and redevelopment of downtown, widening income gaps, and re-segregation of schools.

On retuning to Charlotte and now able to speak Spanish, I was able to engage with Charlotte's growing new population of Latinos. My wife became a leader in Charlotte's art community and launched a successful career as a fine artist, giving us a special view into how non-commercial, creative expression–Soul–thrived or withered in Charlotte.

Moving back to the very neighborhood where I grew up, I once again led efforts to preserve Freedom Park, Charlotte's most revered public park, which, incredibly, was once again threatened with commercial development. As a homeowner, I closely observed and experienced the new forces of gentrification and Charlotte's "world class" branding campaign.

By Charlotte standards, these are unorthodox and probably inadmissible credentials. I let the history, facts and observations that follow speak for themselves in the search I made for Soul in Charlotte.

Contents

EXILE

"Honest and earnest criticism from those whose interests are most nearly touched—criticism of writers by readers, of government by those governed, of leaders by those led—this is the soul of democracy and the safeguard of modern society."

— W. E. B. Du Bois, *The Souls of Black Folk*

Hank and I are about the same age. He is African American, a New Yorker by birth, and a longtime Charlotte resident; I am White and a Charlotte native. We take occasional drives together through various parts of Charlotte, each time speaking to each other as if we are seeing the city for the first time. Our drives feel dreamlike due to a sense, more like a status, that we know we share with many others, yet so seldom spoken of in Charlotte that it has no name.

I have come to identify it as "exile." We feel exiled from the city we call home—not physically, of course, but, for lack of a better term—soulfully. A connection is broken, the past erased, and we are left with little or no stake in the city's future. Home was taken away, imbuing our city tours and discussions with a sense of trespass and sedition.

I hold a suspicion that this feeling of exile accounts for much of America's rising angst and anger. My purpose in making a deep inquiry into Charlotte is to find for myself, and maybe also for those who barely know of Charlotte, the source of that shared discontent. Until we do, we shall search for "home" in sham substitutes. As this story uncovers, Charlotte and America produce these substitutes in abundance.

To be exiled is to be forced to live away from your home. It was an official method of punishment in imperial Rome. Home meant Place—generational residence where life and identity were attached and sustained. To be forcefully separated from your home city or country was to be made not just homeless and stateless, but a nonperson. It was an extreme punishment, just short of the death penalty. The sentence of exile was given for political opposition, exposing corruption, and sedition or treason. Exile was the penalty for challenging, or even just failing to enthusiastically support, the forces of status quo. Exile is now regarded as a violation of human rights on par with arbitrary arrest and detention without charge.[1]

Modern exile is separation from home while still residing in it. This is what Hank and I acknowledge on our driving tours of Charlotte. It is felt as isolation, bewilderment, and alienation, as exile has always caused people to feel. But exile is now utterly impersonal in its execution. It is carried out by forces said to be invisible, inexorable, and infallible. Resistance is foolish and futile.

The mysterious forces that have reshaped Charlotte—which the ordinary people of Charlotte have little to nothing to do with—give our drives their otherworldly sense. They feel like Dante's allegorical tour of the afterworld, where he encountered leaders and residents of his beloved home-city, Florence. Dante Alighieri wrote his famous *Divine Comedy* while in exile.

Dante passed extreme moral judgment upon revered historical figures and famous contemporary people. On a terrifying tour of the Inferno of hell as well as purgatory, limbo, and paradise, Dante saw where the souls of the powerful and humble resided for eternity, some enduring unspeakable agony for their roles in civic affairs of Florence.

He also passed judgment on what today might be called "the general public" and their prevailing values. Florence in Dante's time was an economic powerhouse, growing at such a rate it had to annex surrounding land to expand city walls. It was "world class," notable for extravagant displays of wealth and high culture. Yet in Dante's view, Florence had lost its soul:

> *Florence, rejoice, now that you have such fame,*
> *And over land and sea you spread your wings!*
> *The whole Inferno's ringing with your name!*

Dante's vivid and haunting depictions of the "levels" of the Inferno have resonated through the ages and are readily mapped onto modern life. He placed perpetrators of fraud and treachery, types who are surely dominant in today's politics and market, in the lowest depths of hell. Only a little above were those obsessed with wealth.

Charlotte, North Carolina, is undergoing an amazing economic and demographic shift and expansion. It is, as journalists and boosters constantly say, "booming." What Charlotte's leaders passionately seek is recognition, status, a Place in the world, and for the city to be known, admired, and envied. Such glory has mostly been won. In the eyes of its leaders, Charlotte is now a Renaissance city. From the shame of obscurity, once often confused with Charleston or Charlottesville, it has become, almost overnight, according to the *New York Times*, "a center of the New South." From Charlotte's airport, passengers "can fly directly to Europe." Charlotte is notable for a "cultural life considerably richer than many other comparable cities."[2]

In 2024, Charlotte was ranked No. 5 in America on a list of "Best Places to Live" by *US News and World Report*.[3] The following explanation (excerpted) was given for its ranking:

> A charming yet sprawling Southern city, Charlotte is a
> pleasant urban area . . . the second-largest banking hub
> in the U.S. behind New York City . . . takes pride in its
> cityscape . . . diverse neighborhoods and suburban ar-
> eas . . . Southern charm . . . generally temperate weather,
> relative affordability . . . NBA and NFL . . . museums,

parks and an exploding brewery scene . . . downtown free from trash and graffiti . . . adorned with large, old trees . . .

The city has undergone a massive, physical redevelopment on a scale and at a pace with a post-war reconstruction or a Maoist-style Great Leap Forward. In front of our eyes, under our own feet, our city disappeared and a new one emerged. This development has no local precedent and few can comprehend it, yet it is almost universally described, without qualification, as triumphant advancement.

Associating this triumphant advancement in any way with loss, alienation, and powerlessness—the classic response of the exiled—is forcefully and immediately dismissed in Charlotte as sentimental attachment to the past, or an incapacity or unwillingness to accept change. As Charlotte is a Southern city, critics can be cast as favoring the old world of homophobia, apartheid, and white patriarchy. These critics can then be dismissed as relics, racists, or reactionaries, guilty of moral offenses worthy of cancellation.

A longing for restoration of the old order does not at all characterize our sentiments on our driving tours and is not a motive of this inquiry into Charlotte's social character, its Soul. Hank and I have few illusions about earlier decades. We were among those who fought to tear down old walls of prejudice and oppression. Our sense of exile, and that of millions more, is not due just to growth or rapid social change. We are both well-traveled, have lived other places, own property, and are financially secure. We don't fear the future.

In the tradition of Dante in exile, this book makes judgments on the social values and the methods used by those in power. These are not the kind of moral judgments that cast individuals into the Inferno or carry them in chariots to paradise, like those that Dante made. They are about life here and now, recognizing that something extraordinary happened in Charlotte—and to some degree in many cities and maybe to America as a whole. This book engages with questions that are seldom raised in Charlotte. It explores whether something has been lost that is more important to people than growth, towers, status, "luxury" condos and sports stadiums.

In this story, I call it "Sense of Place" and "Soul." Sense of Place is not recorded, documented, or calculated. It is not included in any official measurements. Yet, the stories and analysis about Charlotte that follow, I suggest, identify the source of feelings, spreading across the land, of being uprooted, left out, voiceless, and perhaps even primed for sedition.

For making my home city of Charlotte the exemplar of what is lost, I don't fear Charlotte's well-honed treatments of ostracism, dismissal, or cancellation. I am already in exile.

---

[1] The Universal Declaration of Human Rights, Article 9, states, "No one shall be subjected to arbitrary arrest, detention or exile."

[2] "Spreading the Wealth; As a Booster of the Arts, One City Proves a Model," by Stephen Kinzer, *New York Times*, Nov. 12, 2001

[3] https://realestate.usnews.com/places/rankings/best-places-to-live?src=usn_pr

HOME

In the first paragraph of chapter 1, you will read that a Sense of Place, rooted in where we live or have lived, is a basic and universal component of a quality life.

This is unprovable. Yet, until very recently, almost no one would have thought to dispute it. It was beyond question that home, hometown, place of birth, and places where we live or have lived that are cherished and hold meaning, are as necessary to the Soul as food is to the body. Searching for Soul in the town of your birth and where you lived most of your life would have reflected only upon the searcher, not the hometown.

Home is where we gain a shared identity. Home is where most of us first learn love and belonging, as well as where we first encounter failure, rejection, and even abuse, all experiences that shape the Soul. It was presumed that these places would imprint themselves upon us and, in most cases, would deserve our protection. It would have been considered utterly abnormal not to experience sorrow if these places were lost or destroyed or, in their absence, to feel a deep yearning, a cosmic orphanhood.

Until . . . well, precisely when this changed is not so much the point. It is enough to know that it *has* changed, and within the memories of some of us. So, my quest for Soul in my hometown, Charlotte, is not just—or even mostly—personal. I stand in for all who experience this loss and who may also be searching.

My own awareness of this cultural change, causing loss, even disappearance of home and a Sense of Place, was felt not so much as a personal misfortune but as an experience of being a witness to something strange and new—a force so righteous and blind to its damage that its emissaries always wore a smile. News photos from the 1960s show grinning Charlotte leaders christening the demolition of entire neighborhoods condemned to allow for "urban renewal" and happily voting to implode old hotels and other city landmarks. Beaming city planners stand over maps of new roads that will split communities and mow over parks.

Long before "facts don't matter" came to describe national politics, Charlotte sought to make history not matter as the city transformed from a Place to a brand. The city's humble mercantile roots as a place where mundane goods like textiles and tobacco were bought, sold, and shipped, were deemed negative to the adopted brand of a world-class financial center. In the new narrative, the brief and largely unknown era of gold mining in the 1830s was implausibly resurrected as the predestined harbinger of Charlotte's glorious future in banking.

Charlotte's retail-based center city serving local residents and thousands from nearby mill villages had to be replaced with glass and steel towers, faux historic statuary, and gigantic but incomprehensible frescos. These replacements were fit for an imagined city where, like Seahaven, the hometown of Truman Burbank, played by Jim Carrey, *"It's all real. Nothing here is fake. It's merely controlled."*

Charlotte's role in the slave trade and slavery-based agriculture were erased, along with the acknowledgement that much of Charlotte's wealth was gained from the unheralded textile mills that ringed the city. Charlotte's decades under Jim Crow were replaced with a self-invented "Charlotte Way," whereby racial conflict—and, indeed, all conflict—had always been resolved fairly and amicably to everyone's satisfaction.

The force behind all this destruction, replacement, and mythmaking, I came to see, was not foreign, not "Yankees," but homegrown. When I traced this force's native roots, I found they were religious in nature. Nothing short of fundamentalist faith could sustain such a campaign of elimination, conversion, and righteous reinterpretation. It all had to be for a higher, divine purpose.

As my inquiry shifted from investigating economic and political conditions and the physical transformation of the city to exploring how these changes affect us personally, I suddenly grasped the meaning of Orwell's statement that "Who controls the past controls the future: who controls the present controls the past."[1] As Charlotte's past, where Sense of Place had been evident and honored, was erased and reinvented, public perception shifted compliantly to the view that Sense of Place had never been significant. The disappearance of Sense of Place could therefore be seen as being of no consequence. Far from a social sustenance, it was a negative and restrictive yoke to be thrown off.

More than a few friends and colleagues expressed doubt about my thesis that Sense of Place is a basic and universal component of a quality life. They told me Charlotte's New South identity, even if contrived, and regardless of what was lost as it was imposed, is an unquestionable advancement. They pointed to ethnic restaurants, glittering towers, night clubs, and luxury condos in the new uptown, though they admitted they seldom, if ever, went there themselves.

Others told me that they personally have no connection to any place in particular, including where they were born or grew up, and do not feel any longing, beyond mild preferences, for any special geography or climate or traditions. These friends suspected that this was more the American norm today. Families are dispersed or members alienated, making "hometown" an anachronism, I was told. What connection they might have to place comes from *current* friends, which may change over time as moves occur. Others said where people live today is mostly a matter of making a living or other mundane circumstances which can quickly change, such as the location of children and grandchildren or even proximity to shopping or medical services. History, tradition, and attachment play no significant role.

The Soul I was searching for in Charlotte was not just missing. It was extinct and irrelevant, like typewriters, spittoons, and corsets, these friends told me. It is missing in Charlotte because it is irrelevant to modern American life, they said, though they seemed a little surprised to hear themselves asserting it.

It is indisputable that facets of modern life do reduce the power of Place. Many places are now almost identical—thanks to franchises, glass towers, strip shopping centers, Lowes, Costco, big banks, packaged local news formats, and so on. What is called "social mobility" has become so crucial to what is defined as a successful life that some even forgo home ownership for the agility to seize fleeting job opportunities in some other city ahead of others.

What if Sense of Place were an anachronism, like handwritten letters? Even so, who would argue that career advancement, amenities, and entertainment equate to the benefits of Home: security, identity, and a reference point from which to see the larger world? If Place no longer means Home and offers no attachment, sense of history, or group identity, what else does?

Today the ubiquitous substitute for Place and Home is cyberspace: Facebook, LinkedIn, Substack, Zoom, X, Instagram and YouTube chats, communities, and "rooms." These "spaces" are phantoms governed for commercial ends by invisible algorithms. These platforms have no history, change at an incomprehensible rate, and boast of "disruptive" impact—precisely opposite characteristics of Place and Home.

Millions also seek identity and quenching of the soul in brands and pop culture, celebrity worship, and art and music "scenes," which also dispense with history in order to change quickly and inexplicably. Related to brands and "scenes" are the luxury amenities that are now the main features of major cities—ethnic restaurants and fine dining, endless varieties of beer and coffee, high-end shopping, luxury residences, museums, high art—all requiring substantial incomes and therefore reserved for the very few.

Perhaps confirming these offerings as sham, millions are turning to cultic religions, which enigmatically promise both prosperity and safe haven. I have spent two decades in research, consumer education, and as an expert witness in court cases related to the phenomenon of economic cults, called "multi-level marketing" (MLM). Tens of millions dedicate their lives, at least for a while, to MLMs' utopian promises of wealth and happiness. These pyramid selling schemes are led by authoritarian figures who assume roles as gurus and models of "total success." These self-serving characters are mirrored in political movements in America and abroad. In the end, I have come to see the force behind these frauds and false prophets is the great quest for Home.

Other Americans are withdrawing into the walled social space of the patriarchal nuclear family, shielding children from discomforting history or differing sexual identities. More expansive and oriented toward connection, but still part of the search for Soul, are the quests for a lost ancestry and DNA-based connections.

The simplest and most conclusive testimony to the significance of Place did not come from examining destructive public policy or the empty substitutes that have proliferated in the wake of destruction. I found it in an honest yet seldom acknowledged observation made by the poet Deborah Tall. In *From Where We Stand: Recovering a Sense of Place,* she writes:

> Avoidance of ties to a place . . . allows us to be indifferent to our towns and cities, to ignore their human

and environmental plights, to say but this isn't mine. To cling to the right of mobility with all the freedoms it bestows is ultimately to contribute to destruction.[2]

Home and Sense of Place are not only natural to our lives, they are also essential to our survival. The national and local figures that separate us from these basic connections and offer in their place amenities, lifestyle and status—as well as leaders who promise security in return for total loyalty or compliance—are ultimately seeking control for their own purposes. Far from sentimental illusion or a cultural anachronism, Home and Sense of Place are foundations of personal freedom.

---

[1] From George Orwell's famous novel, *1984*: "Past events, it is argued, (by the authoritarian Party leaders) have no objective existence but survive only in written records and in human memories. The past is whatever the records and the memories agree upon. And since the Party is in full control of all records, and in equally full control of the minds of its members, it follows that the past is whatever the Party chooses to make it."

[2] *From Where We Stand*, by Deborah Tall, Syracuse University Press, 1996, Kindle Edition, p. 80

I. No There

"There is no there there."

– Gertrude Stein in *Everybody's Autobiography*

Just a few decades ago . . .

Somebody:	*Oh, yes, Charlotte. Beautiful town. So historic! Civil War, the canons, I love the old architecture.*
Me:	*Sorry, no, that's Charleston in South Carolina. I'm from Charlotte.*
Somebody:	*Oh, right, yeah. But I love Charlotte too. Monticello. The university.*
Me:	*No, actually that's Charlottesville, in Virginia. I'm from Charlotte.*
Somebody:	*I think I've been through the airport. What's there?*

This book is about Sense of Place, a basic ingredient of a quality life, and it's about Charlotte, North Carolina, a city that has largely eradicated Sense of Place. How and why this happened in Charlotte and how the spirit of Place is yet maintained by some might also be relevant to where you were born or live now.

As this story seeks to affirm, Sense of Place is a timeless and fundamental need that transcends disruptive events. It is often powerfully held by immigrants, victims of foreclosure, the highly mobile, and even the unhoused.

What is robbing many of us of Home is denial of the very reality of Place in favor of commercial substitutes. This can occur even as we live in the city of our birth, as I did for many years. Staying is no longer a remedy to homesickness.

Charlotte, North Carolina, is popularly perceived as pleasant, prosperous, and mildly progressive. As will be shown in the following pages, behind that constantly boosted image, deeper, contrary traits prevail that eat away at Sense of Place. This story examines those deeper traits, their effects, their causes, making Charlotte a study of Loss of Home, wherever it occurs, and how people maintain a Sense of Place in their lives without institutional support.

Charlotte offers special illumination in its *radical inattention* to Place. Ironically, the neglect and destruction of what is local, characteristic, historical, established, and treasured is routinely justified by the city leaders as necessary to make Charlotte *recognizable*.

Charlotte is the sixteenth-largest city in the U.S, with a population of nearly one million souls. In some years Charlotte claims to be the country's "fastest growing city," competing with about twenty others for this presumably laudable status. A popular claim is that over one hundred people are moving to Charlotte each day of the year. The figure leaves out how many move away.[1]

Charlotte has long been a *work-based* destination and a good place to locate *a business*. The workforce is proudly characterized as nonunion, productive, and cooperative, sometimes implying a positive contrast with troublesome workers in other cities. The pay scale is also lower than the national average. Charlotte's government website boasts of Charlotte's No. 1 position in "employee engagement," according to *Forbes*. This is described as "employee willingness to go the extra mile . . . intent to stay . . . and the employee's willingness to brag about their workplace."[2]

Median income in Charlotte is $68,367, versus $74,580 for the country. The numbers reflect lower pay, which would be good for employers. But this figure does not communicate the related data most important for employees—income distribution. Charlotte's income distribution is polarized and getting wider. The attractive median figure and the acclaimed worker "engagement" also obscure the stark color line that corresponds to income disparity. There are vast swaths of White Charlotte where a person of color will virtually never be seen by residents unless they are doing low-paid service work. How this pattern of extreme color separation developed in Charlotte, even greater now than the days of the old Jim Crow laws, is shown in later chapters.

A *Charlotte Observer* study of census data showed a top 10 percent tier of census tracts with median incomes triple those of the bottom 15 percent. The article noted that the dominant financial industry in Charlotte is delivering more wealth only to the small sector of the population that is already affluent, resulting in an ever-widening gap.

As will also be shown, the White working class largely emigrated from the city years ago due to racial fears exploited by blockbusting realtors and a lack of affordable properties within the city limits. They now live in a diaspora in surrounding small towns and rural areas. Their African American counterparts are currently facing even worse affordability conditions and, ironically, a reverse form of blockbusting. Affluent Whites are moving into predominantly Black areas, demolishing homes, and building McMansions and "luxury" condos.

The *Charlotte Observer* analysis featured one predominantly African American neighborhood called Grier Heights. The median income in this neighborhood is $21,000. Literally just across a four-lane road is the ultra-affluent White community of Eastover, which has a median income of $250,000. Now, the separating line is being breached.

The story quoted a local historian and an attorney specialized in combatting evictions who said that "change is coming" to Grier Heights. "White residents have moved into many of the new houses" on the edge of Grier Heights, and a local shopping district is getting a "makeover" including its first Starbucks and Chick-fil-A. The eviction attorney predicted that soon this historically Black community "most likely will be a neighborhood that's unaffordable for someone who's not making a six-figure income."[3]

Many younger working people and families are faced with cheaply built, but remarkably high-rent apartments in dense complexes. These apartments are owned by private equity funds that impose restrictions or added costs based on credit scores or ratings of individual tenants.

Though costs and congestion are on a trajectory to match the places people are leaving, Charlotte is a climate heaven to those from Buffalo, Rochester, Maine, and Michigan. For now at least, it is less crowded than urban New Jersey or Los Angeles; safer, in most neighborhoods, than Detroit or Cleveland; and has lower cost of living, including lower taxes, than New York. "Nothing could be finer," as they say often in Charlotte.

Today, millions pass *through* Charlotte's enormous hub airport, one of the busiest in the world and, though this is pertinent mostly to local residents, one of the most expensive in the country to fly to and from.[4] Some of the millions that come to the airport also visit the city for events, meetings, conventions, or social and personal reasons. Few people today would have to add *North Carolina* as a reference to know *where* they are, but few can associate Charlotte with anything memorable, unique or definitive, including the airport. They can't say *what's* there.

An Extreme Statement

To support my story about Place and how this has diminished in Charlotte I quote sociologists, poets, historians, philosophers, and anthropologists, but this does not claim to be an academic treatment. I cite news articles, novels, and short stories but also have no pretense that this is an objective, journalistic analysis. Some of the story is my own direct experience as a native son, a citizen activist, and many years ago, a Saul Alinsky-trained community organizer in the city for over five years.

Like Henry David Thoreau, who wrote about our loss of connection to Nature, I want to make, to borrow his terms, an "extreme statement" about loss of Place and about Charlotte. Defending his "extreme" statement on the vital importance of nature to our lives, Thoreau noted that there were already enough "champions of civilization." Accordingly, there are already more than enough champions of commercial substitutes for Place, and Charlotte is abundantly supplied with boosters and brand managers. Though vastly more powerful today, they are the same "champions" that Thoreau countered—merchants, realtors, advertisers, financiers, and land developers. The most important modern "champions" belong to the priesthood of economists, exalted especially in Charlotte whose main industry is the very face of economics—banking. The economists' assumed intellectual and moral authority imbues destruction of Place with the mystical work of the Invisible Hand, always supposed to be serving a higher purpose.

Thoreau's prescription for reconnecting to Nature was to walk or, in his words, to "saunter," a term, he explained, derived from walkers in the Middle Ages traveling to the *sainte terre*, the Holy Land. And so, Thoreau viewed walking in Nature and learning to view ourselves "as an inhabitant of Nature," as a crusade for human freedom.

As this story seeks to reveal, loss of Place in Charlotte, or anywhere else it occurs, is also loss of freedom and individuality. Defense of Place, or even its remembrance, is also a crusade, and, like Thoreau's, it is a lonely one against forces appealing to conventional wisdom, economic necessity, and historical inevitability. Like many pilgrimages, this one begins with a recognition that something is lost or is missing, and reclamation occurs along the way. There is no need to call out this story as biased, prejudiced, and imbalanced. It is all of that. It must be.

---

[1] The real net increase average is about 40 people per day. From 2000 to 2022 (8,030 days), Charlotte's population increased by 320,323 (https://www.neils-berg.com/insights/charlotte-nc-population-by-year/)

[2] See: "The 10 Cities With The Best Employee Engagement" by Jacquelyn Smith, *Forbes*, Apr 18, 2013 (https://www.forbes.com/sites/jacquelynsmith/2013/04/18/the-10-cities-with-the-best-employee-engagement/?sh=598d75dd3f52)

[3] "In Mecklenburg, One Side of this Street Earns $230,000 More than the Other Half" by Gavin Off, *Charlotte Observer*, December 26, 2023. Read more at: https://www.charlotteobserver.com/article283184818.html#storylink=cpy

[4] Currently, Charlotte is ranked the #4th most expensive airport in America to fly from but there is less than a $10 difference between Charlotte and the #3 and #2 ranked most expensive airports, Salt Lake City and San Francisco. See: "2024 U.S. Airport Cost Rankings: See How Airfare Compares at the Nation's Busiest Airports" by Josh Koebert, edited by Mindy Woodall, *FinanceBuzz*, May 30, 2024 (financebuzz.com)

II. Searching Downtown

When you're alone, and life is making you lonely
You can always go Downtown.

-1968 song sung by Petula Clark

My search for Charlotte's Sense of Place, its Soul, begins at the place that identifies and characterizes most cities—the center city, traditionally the city's heart. Until the 1970s, this small but dynamic district was called "downtown," and at its core was the city's most famous place, the Square.

In the early decades of the twentieth century, Charlotte grew into one of the largest centers of textile manufacturing on earth at the time. This manufacturing zone mostly surrounded Charlotte as distinct towns and "mill villages." Some of the mills, however, were located within the city. Textile mill operators came to the Carolinas to find cheaper, nonunion workers, some of whom were recruited in remote mountain villages. For the owners of one of these new mill companies, my Irish immigrant grandfather, Thomas Bernard FitzPatrick, designed and opened a mercerizing plant in the town of Mount Holly, just west of Charlotte. He personally recruited workers out of those mountain towns.[1]

The mills came to the Charlotte area to escape labor organizing and to tap into cheap and abundant energy. It was for these same reasons that textile plant owners later left Charlotte for Asia and Mexico. Charlotte's textile-based wealth had been transferred from New England, just as New England's was gained from England, and so it goes.

At the core of Charlotte, in the middle of this manufacturing dynamo, was downtown, an exciting and memorable destination for thousands of residents from those nearby small towns and for all of Charlotte's own people. Downtown Charlotte was not architecturally significant, though there were some remarkable buildings. It was not beautiful, but every street and every building had a history and held meaning for generations of people.

Historically, the center of downtown, called the Square, had been a trading crossroads carved out of the forests by Native Americans. It was a Place before Charlotte became a Place. Officially, the Square is now called Independence Square to commemorate the Mecklenburg Declaration of Independence, a mythical document and signing event that local officials claim preceded the famous Declaration in Philadelphia by nearly a year. Credible historians say that this document is apocryphal and that the signing event never occurred. Regardless, the name "Independence Square" honors the spirit of personal freedom and the quest for self-rule.[2]

During my youth and for many years before, the Square was a landmark, a place of orientation, and a meeting spot. To say you were at the Square was meaningful and exhilarating. It was the most public of public places in Charlotte.

Downtown Charlotte was vibrant, crowded, exciting, and diverse. Reflecting the city's history of Jim Crow segregation, cotton and tobacco farming, and low-paying textile production, it was both prim and seedy, socially stratified yet spatially mingled. Not far from formal department stores, there were pawn shops and pool halls. Unpretentious diners sat near the Manufacturers Club. Local residents of every income level mixed with mill village shoppers.

All city bus routes passed through and stopped at the Square, where passengers waited and transferred. Every skin color and age group met at the crossroads of downtown. Shoulder to shoulder, people walked the sidewalks and poured across intersections. These tight, unifying few blocks seemed to belong to everyone, despite legalized and strictly enforced racial segregation. We "dressed up" to go there. It was a Place, *the* Place.

Beginning in the 1960s, the city's business leaders launched an extraordinary reconfiguration of vast tracts of downtown, including the Square. The availability of millions of new dollars from the federal government for urban renewal opened the door to government seizure of vast tracts of prime property—including homes, businesses, and churches—that were obtained by classifying areas as "blighted."

The inflow of urban renewal money and the destruction it financed occurred in many cities, but Charlotte's leaders had a particularly radical vision. Their plan was not just to "renew" dilapidated housing occupied by the poor. In fact, this was not the purpose of Charlotte's redevelopment program at all, as no new housing was provided at the time to replace what was destroyed.

Urban renewal provided a pretext for the destruction of Black neighborhoods that city officials considered undesirable, or feared might become sites of social unrest. Indeed, in a 1973 interview, Mayor Stan Brookshire, who oversaw the urban renewal program, said, "I'm convinced that if we hadn't cleared Brooklyn . . . along with giving [Black people] equal citizenship rights . . . I think that we might have had such incidents here that they had in Watts."[3] Labeling centrally located Black neighborhoods as blighted and in need of redevelopment allowed city governments to opportunistically seize the desirable real estate these communities occupied, leading some people to sardonically refer to urban renewal as "Negro removal."

In Charlotte, destruction of centrally located Black neighborhoods was only one aspect of a more ambitious plan. Charlotte leaders actually planned to erase downtown and its history and identity and to erect a new center city, redefined with a new name and image. All that downtown stood for—its meaning, memories, and landmarks—was to be wiped away. Spaces that were once public and accessible to all were increasingly privatized, designed to be welcoming only for some and inhospitable to others.

Along with Charlotte's physical reconstruction, its history would be rewritten. Charlotte's roots in textiles and tobacco were largely erased and replaced by a forward-looking story about commerce, finance, and opportunity—a rebranding as purposeful and total as the "great" Jay Gatsby's. Charlotte's business and government leaders, mostly one and the same, executed a grandiose, China-style social engineering program.

How long this radical plan had been in the making is unknown. It must have incubated long enough for insiders to examine property lines and values and identify plum properties. These insiders must have negotiated among themselves the anticipated spoils after tracts were bulldozed, resold, and rezoned. Undoubtedly, there were discussions with leaders in other cities who were planning something similar using this vast new pool of federal money, and meetings with federal officials who would sign off on the funding to Charlotte. Private consultants were likely retained.

None of that was public or publicly disclosed. Secrecy was not difficult to maintain since Charlotte's political system was proudly described at the time as "run like a business" and led by businesspeople. Secrecy was called confidentiality. There were no competing forces to drive transparency or an open process: no unions, no immigrants, no blue-collar communities that were organized. The African American vote was minimal following the years of terror and lynching that suppressed voting throughout the South in the early part of the century.

The potential for private profit was enormous, but the narrative as the grand plan was gradually publicized always focused on how redevelopment would serve the public interest. The eviction of thousands from their homes, churches, and businesses was piously depicted as well-intended and benevolent.

The largest African American community of Charlotte, called Brooklyn, was obliterated without a trace. The same fate was meted out in later stages to other Black neighborhoods in the downtown area.

Not only were segregated African American communities in the inner city eradicated, a tapestry of independent, sustainable retail stores, warehouses, and office buildings was also destroyed. Businesses that had operated for generations in the city's core commercial district were later condemned and bulldozed under the same master plan.

Acres upon acres in the heart of the city became vacant grassy tracts. By the 1970s, Charlotte's downtown was clinically dead, awaiting a Dr. Frankenstein jolt of investment in the form of new hotels, office towers, government centers, and a sports stadium, as conceived by the transformative planners. The new developments, when they eventually began to arrive after more than twenty years, would be described as miraculous lifesavers for a dying center city, without reference to all that had been purposefully obliterated. A new city would be erected—taller, shinier, wealthier, more modern, more impressive—but without a heart, a Soul, a local vibe, *or a past.*

Charlotte's former, thriving downtown, a defining Place, was officially erased. Its character was demeaned as "blighted" and needing to be "cleaned up." By this point, the economic forces of suburbanization were also at work, but Charlotte's downtown merchants were never given a chance to adapt organically. Businesses were not given the opportunity to upgrade their buildings. Merchants were driven away or out of business and the structures they had occupied were knocked down. According to the revised historical narrative propagated by city officials, these businesses and the targeted African American communities were standing in the way of the destiny that the leaders believed awaited Charlotte. The destruction was only an initial chapter in the quest for greatness and a new identity, first as part of the "New South" and then as a "world-class city."

No moment of sorrow for Charlotte's old downtown and all that it stood for was ever allowed. Even as the bulldozer and wrecking ball were at work, the center city was being rechristened with a concocted new identity. Henceforth, "downtown" would be known as "uptown." The Chamber of Commerce and the local newspapers, PR writers, and urban planners adopted the new nomenclature. Some pundits claimed that the downtown name had always been inappropriate, since Charlotte's center city is at a higher elevation than the surrounding area. Decades of fond attachment to the center city by generations of residents of Charlotte and neighboring towns were erased, even as thousands of African Americans were violently displaced from their homes and social networks.

Sixty years later, as office towers and luxury condos are erected and the face of the center city is unrecognizable to any who lived before the redevelopment, city boosters applaud a miraculous "rejuvenation." These leaders speak as if a bustling center city had never previously existed in Charlotte or the entire center city had been dilapidated and declining in the years before "renewal." So extensive has been the redevelopment, and so pervasive the message that the demolitions were positive, necessary, and inevitable, that it is now almost impossible even to imagine how the city might have developed differently—retaining its character, honoring its history, and upholding a Sense of Place.

But while an alternative course can hardly be imagined, no one would ever suggest going to uptown Charlotte "when you're alone, and life is making you lonely." Where Place disappears or is taken away, anomie and "lonely crowds" increase, even if the architecture is glittering and business is booming.

Today, the center city streets of Charlotte are weirdly devoid of many pedestrians, though most of the buildings are new or under construction. At one point, the renewal plan included enormous overhead walkways, some enclosed. These structures eliminated most walking at street level, where small-town and local, rich and poor, and Black and White pedestrians might physically interact. The effect of these walkways was only to further deaden the streets below, making them unwelcoming and unsafe. The Square lost all meaning.

Charlotte's new historical narrative did not include the pain, loss, and trauma of entire communities wiped off the map. The image of a group of local businesspeople and politicians secretly poring over a map of their own city, plotting to use the power of government to seize huge sections of property and forcibly remove thousands of people was never revealed or even imagined in those terms. Views of these actions as a land grab, government overreach, or an unjust disruption of residents and businesses were virtually never referenced in any public forum. The prevailing and consistent message was uplifting, visionary, and professional. The core of Charlotte had to be destroyed in order to save it.

The greatest infusion of artificial life, the most jarring instance of replacement over renewal, and the grandest of all pretenses was reserved for the most iconic Place in downtown Charlotte, the Square. The rewriting of history through the transformation of this space would not just erase Charlotte's association with textiles and tobacco, but even the site's symbolic connection to the Revolutionary War.

History Rebranded

"Who controls the past controls the future. Who controls the present controls the past."

–George Orwell

The Square, the most familiar and visited Place, the most historic as Native-American crossroad and Revolutionary War commemoration, was included in the areas of "blight" required for urban renewal funding and inclusion in the grand plan.

At one of the Square's four corners, where local retailers once were, a hotel for conventioneers and an office tower of the city's then-largest bank, NCNB, were built. The NCNB bank tower, described as "glittering," was said to "begin the transformation of 'the Square.'"[4] At the time of its construction, it was the tallest building in the state, an achievement considered a "prize" for Charlotte, which had succeeded in "beating" competitor cities. Charlotte still holds this prize for the newer sixty-story headquarters building of Bank of America—the successor institution to NCNB, renamed in the course of its aggressive expansion through a series of mergers and acquisitions.

After construction of a new office tower on the Square, the bus transfer point which brought every social class and color into contact at the center of town was moved blocks away to an enclosed "transportation center."

The Charlotte Transportation Center, a cavernous, sunless, scary space, was spearheaded by Bank of America executive Hugh McColl in a partnership with the city. It moved the buses and their riders, who stood in sharp contrast to the bank's button-down professionals, away from the entrance of the glittering new tower. Ridership at this point was comprised almost entirely of people too poor to own cars, and the elderly and disabled. City bus fares were among the highest in the country.[5] The service was notoriously inadequate, unreliable, and inconvenient. There were few routes, meaning that reaching a destination often required multiple transfers and waiting at unsheltered stops. People avoided riding the bus unless other transportation was unavailable. African Americans were no longer forced to sit in the back of the city buses, as they had been in Jim Crow days, but were now often the vehicles' only passengers.

Regarding moving the motley bus riders away from the Square, McColl apparently had no regrets. He was quoted by a biographer as saying, "I am so damn proud of that transportation center. I'm proud of my tower, but I really think that the transportation center may be the best thing I ever did for this city."[6]

In front of the new bank tower, on arguably the highest-valued piece of real estate in Charlotte—now reclassified as "blighted"—the city created a tax-free, publicly owned but privately developed "plaza" to serve as a grand entrance to the bank building.

On this historic public space, the bank placed a work of monumental art—from Italy! This artwork, 15-feet high and weighing 6 tons, is a round disc, called *Il Grande Disco,* by Italian artist Arnaldo Pomodoro, who had never been to the city. This sculpture was installed as a "gift to the people of Charlotte" (officially a permanent loan) from the bank and the plaza's private developers, at a cost of about $2.5 million in today's dollars. As was later revealed, *Il Disco* in Charlotte, is not unique. There are nearly exact copies in four other cities.

To the question of why an Italian artist who had never been to Charlotte was commissioned, the bank benefactors explained it was based on consultations with art experts and their own preferences. However, bafflingly, the bank's president, son of a North Carolina governor, told the city council that *Il Grande Disco* "is a tribute to Mecklenburg's foresighted Revolutionary leaders, who declared independence from the British crown in 1775 . . . [at] 'The Square,' or 'Independence Square' to Charlotteans."[7]

Initially the huge coin-shaped disk spun on bearings, but the bank tower created an extreme wind draft that caused it to spin at a dangerous rate. This posed a hazard to any children who got in the way of the massive object in motion. After a few years and having been marred by graffiti, the sculpture was resurfaced and made stationary.[8]

The Italian sculpture, which no one other than the former bank CEO ever associated with "revolutionary leaders," was soon overshadowed by another addition to Independence Square. This artwork was not only more imposing and alien, but also more overt in its intent to redefine the Square's symbolic meaning. Giant five-thousand pound, vaguely Soviet-looking statues on twenty-foot-high concrete pedestals were installed at each of the Square's four corners.

The sculptor, Pennsylvania-based Raymond Kaskey, said he attempted to replicate a style of the ancient Romans and Greeks called herm, in which the bust of a god or ruler is placed on a pedestal. The actual herm pedestals also featured male genitals, carved at roughly the anatomically correct height. The name herm refers to Hermes, a Greek deity, said to be a protector of travelers, thieves, and merchants. At this famous and beloved intersection, which the common and privileged folk of Charlotte formerly defined with their own crowded presence, these enormous structures now dominate. The sculptures loom over foot traffic, now greatly diminished in volume even though city population has grown significantly.

The statues, which the public played no part in seeking, obtaining, or designing, were said to represent the "four pillars"— that is, the core values—of Charlotte. No one else knew there *were* four pillars of Charlotte. If they did exist, perhaps people might think these pillars would include Labor, Family, Freedom, Home, or maybe even Justice.

According to these private funders, the pillars of Charlotte are *Commerce, Industry, Transportation,* and *The Future.* The four giant statues were planned, financed, and controlled by a somewhat secretive group of wealthy people in Charlotte called Queen's Table.[9] Membership is anonymous. The group has no website or physical location. The Queen's Table chair of the statuary project was the wife of the owner of the company that developed an office tower on one of the corners of the Square. The Queen's Table also commissioned and financed the same sculptor to produce a life-size statue of Queen Charlotte, wife of George III of England, that sits at the entrance to parking garages at Charlotte's airport.

Commerce

Strangely, the commerce statue does not depict the city's retail and wholesale merchants who defined downtown. The Charlotte-based department store, Belk, was the largest family-owned department store chain in America. Charlotte was also the wholesale and distribution center for cotton and tobacco.

Instead, the commerce pillar honors a brief era of wild speculation in gold mining in the Charlotte region during which thousands sought to strike it rich. This was in the 1830s, preceding the more famous gold rush in California. The sculptor acknowledged that prior to starting work on this project, he did not know that this gold mining era had occurred.[10] This is unsurprising given that many Charlotte residents were also unaware of this history until it was publicized by Charlotte's boosters. The only active memorial to the period is located thirty-five miles from the Square in the little town of Midland, where one of the mines operated and the largest single nugget of gold was found.

Even more strange than how commerce was defined, the sculptor sought to connect modern Charlotte's main business, banking—which had, at least at one point, been expected to be rational, prudent, and conservative—to that wild wealth-hunting era. He achieved the strange connection through what he called a "private joke." The statue shows a gold prospector emptying his pan into the top of the head of Alan Greenspan, former chairman of the Federal Reserve.

At the time, Greenspan was popularly known as the "maestro" of the global economy.[11] The joke of the sculptor linked Charlotte's recent financial preeminence to Greenspan. The statues were dedicated in 1995, just five years before the publication of Bob Woodward's celebratory Greenspan biography. At this time, the US economy appeared to be roaring and expanding, led by rising home values that magically bestowed wealth on anyone with the initiative to apply for a home mortgage. Often, the mortgages did not even require a downpayment or good credit. The boom was ignited by Alan Greenspan's policies at the Federal Reserve, which were gleefully carried out by banks that were granted access to nearly free money from the Fed. Banks, including those in Charlotte, rose in wealth and power.

Whatever the prices of homes—which were rising rapidly—buyers were assured they could sell later for far more. If the mortgage payments were a burden, buyers were told they could always refinance later at better terms, even pulling out some cash for a vacation. Greenspan's program was a modern gold rush, with family homes transformed into speculative nuggets.

This speculative frenzy turned out to be as brief as Charlotte's gold mining era and about as commercially sustainable—hardly a pillar. Within a few years, 2008, the global economy went up in flames when the mortgage pyramid collapsed. Millions lost jobs and were evicted from their homes, unable to pay mortgages. The catastrophe spread from the US to all over the world.

Charlotte's two largest banks, now among the biggest in the country, became insolvent and survived only with a taxpayer rescue. The maestro admitted he had never imagined capital markets self-immolating. Greenspan was a faithful believer in the teachings of Ayn Rand that markets are omniscient and omnipotent, and his face now peers out over the Square, jokingly linked to Charlotte commerce.

Industry

The industry statue shows what the sculptor described as a female textile mill worker with her small child at her side, indirectly referencing child labor in the textile mills. For the child, the sculptor used his own image and face, though he never worked in a mill or had any personal experience with that industry.

The plaque states that the child represents "CHILDREN WHO LABORED ALONGSIDE PARENTS," which, like the statue itself, gives the impression that children accompanied their parents and worked with them in family units. In fact, children were separated from parents in the mills to do specialized work they could perform more cheaply than adults. As explained in a historical collection on mill workers curated by the Georgia Institute of Technology, "In some mills, the spinning rooms were even known as the Children's Department. Young boys would start out as doffers and sweepers and might eventually gain enough experience to become spinners. Spinners were mostly young girls."[12]

Transportation

The transportation pillar bears this inscription from the sculptor: "AN AFRICAN AMERICAN LABORER HONORS THE BUILDERS OF THE FIRST RAILROADS IN CHARLOTTE IN

THE 1850S, LEADING TO THE CITY'S STATUS AS A TRANS-
PORTATION HUB."

Like the industry pillar, this representation seems to cover over a harsher historical truth. It is a fact that the opening of
a railroad line to Charlotte from Columbia, South Carolina, in
1852, which was linked to the port in Charleston, made Charlotte
a "hub." However, in 1852, the African American man depicted
would not have been a "laborer," but an enslaved person working without pay and under penalty of the whip or worse. That reality is not revealed or even indicated in the image or inscription.
During the timeframe indicated by the inscription, 39 percent of
the residents of Mecklenburg Country were enslaved.

The Future

The fourth pillar, *The Future*, is the focal point of the display,
with each of the other sculptures facing toward it. This pillar replaced an originally planned statue dedicated to *Religion*. The
religion monument was supposed to reflect Charlotte's cultural
foundation in Scotch Calvinism, the religious heritage of most of
the planners and a denomination known less for sublime spiritu-
ality than for laying up treasure on earth. The private planners,
however, concluded that this highlighting of religion invited
controversy and "complication."[13]

Instead, *The Future* shows a kneeling mother holding an in-
fant aloft. The plaque explains: "A MOTHER AND CHILD SYM-
BOLIZE THE FUTURE OF CHARLOTTE." *The Future* is the only
noncommercial image, and the only one to reference anything in
nature, a tree. The sculptor did not explain how three commercially oriented "pillars"—involving a mad rush for gold, child
labor, and enslavement—might lead to mother, child, and nature. The message this work seems to assert is that commerce,
industry, and trade are the bases of life and nature, rather than
the other way around.

History Obsolete

In 2023, the southwest corner of the Square went through another transformation and revision of history. Like the plaza in front of the bank with *Il Grande Disco*, this corner had also been made public property, yielding no tax revenue. As part of urban renewal, it had been developed into a small public park, a respite for city workers.

At that time, a thirty-foot-high fountain, designed by internationally acclaimed Bulgarian architect Angela Danadjieva, was installed in the middle of a tree-shaded sitting area. At the behest of the local historical organization, this little park on the Square was dedicated to Charlotte's most famous figure from the Revolutionary War era, Thomas Polk. Polk, called the founder of Charlotte, had lived in a home located on the Square.

Polk was one of the first Scotch Irish settlers to come to what would become Charlotte. A surveyor, he purchased over 300 acres of land from a British aristocrat where downtown Charlotte would later develop. Polk led a local militia against the British and rose to become a general. He lost a son in the war. Polk fought at Brandywine. He was at Valley Forge. He helped to get the Liberty Bell out of Philadelphia to prevent British capture. Later, Polk was instrumental in establishing the Charlotte area's oldest university. Reportedly, George Washington dined at Polk's home on the Square in 1791. Thomas Polk died in Charlotte in 1794.

In May of 2023, the city announced plans to demolish and replace Thomas Polk Park, including the fountain. The new park will be named not for a historical figure, but a currently living former CEO of Bank of America, Hugh McColl. The city paid

$350,000 for the demolition, stating that the Polk Memorial was obsolete.[14]

The Polk Memorial Park, on public land, had been publicly financed and many local people were involved in its design and naming. However, the new McColl memorial on the same city land is being designed and financed with private funds from a small group of wealthy and influential figures, including Bank of America officials, calling itself the Hugh McColl Park Coalition.[15]

Retired from Bank of America, Hugh McColl is now a philanthropist and private equity investor. He officially left his position as CEO of Bank of America in 2001. Two years before his retirement, McColl was awarded a controversial compensation from Bank of America that included stock worth $1.5 billion in today's dollars at a time when the bank's stock had dropped about 17 percent. Additionally, he received stock options valued at $875 million in today's dollars. One of the bank's largest institutional shareholders protested the extraordinary pay. According to its proxy, the bank's directors granted the options and stock as a reward for increasing the bank's size, in particular, the 1998 merger of Charlotte-based NationsBank and San Francisco-based BankAmerica.[16]

McColl reportedly lost a significant part of his wealth following the banking crisis of 2007 but financially recovered with profits from the private equity firm, Falfurrias Capital, which McColl co-founded in 2006. Falfurrias buys and sells mid-size privately owned companies. It manages $850 million and has raised over $3.4 billion since inception.[17] Among its acquisitions were Bojangles fried chicken and C.F. Sauer Company that makes Duke's Mayo. The mayonnaise maker was acquired by McColl's fund, Falfurrias, in mid 2019 and sold at the beginning of 2025.

A biographer of McColl wrote he lives modestly, but McColl's "real excess" is his 40,000 acre hunting preserve in Texas, managed by a full-time staff, where McColl enjoys shooting quail.[18] McColl's private equity firm is named for the nearby small Texas town of Falfurrias, population 4,600.[19]

Hugh McColl is the most celebrated promoter of Charlotte's crusade for world-class status. In keeping with Charlotte's commercially oriented four pillars on the Square, McColl famously declared that Charlotte's "common purpose" is "to make money, build nice things, make it happen."[20]

Though he has never held any elected office, McColl boasts that he has "built" modern Charlotte in accord with his personal vision, stating, "You see our [Bank of America's] hand in almost everything. I've had more fun building a city than I have, perhaps, in building the bank."[21] McColl, as previously noted, was the person primarily responsible for moving bus passengers away from the Square and the bank's grand entrance, the site of *Il Grande Disco*.

The demolition of Thomas Polk Park was protested by the Cultural Landscape Foundation (TCLF), a Washington, DC-based nonprofit dedicated to "connecting people to places." On its website, the TCLF notes that the Square had once been the center of commerce and civic activity in Charlotte, but that, as a direct result of urban renewal, "The square became derelict." The site explains: "In the 1970s skyscrapers, connected by skywalks, were erected near the site and workers spent less time at street level, leading to its desertion."

Following the dereliction and desertion that were the paradoxical results of "renewal," the Thomas Polk Park opened in 1991 to redeem one corner of the Square. Located across from the plaza with *Il Grande Disco*, its thirty-foot waterfall drowned out noise from traffic and air-conditioning units.

Patterns on the pavement made of local red granite were de-signed to create an effect of "drawing pedestrians into the sheltered space," which, according to TCLF, was "evoca-tive of an outdoor 'living room' for the city, where people may gather."

The CEO of the TCLF, Charles Birnbaum called the demoli-tion another example of Charlotte destroying its history. "You can't know where you're going if you didn't know where you come from. And this is an unfortunate act of erasure."[22]

---

[1] Thomas Bernard FitzPatrick, my father's father, an Irish immigrant, was working in a textile plant in Lawrence, Massachusetts, when he was recruited to come to Mount Holly, NC, just west of Charlotte to set up and manage the first mercerizing plant there for the Charlotte area. This included choosing the location and building the water system for the plant and the village of homes around it. He had a deep working knowledge of mercerizing, which chemi-cally treats cotton yarn to soften and strengthen it, not from formal training, but direct experience. He arrived in Mount Holly in 1919. His son, my father, Thomas Raymond FitzPatrick, also worked in the textile mills in Mount Hol-ly from his teens to early adulthood before moving to Charlotte, where he met my mother, Kathleen Ann Frank, daughter of German immigrants on her mother's side. My mother's father, Anthony Frank, was an Italian immigrant who opened and ran one of Charlotte's most popular restaurants from the mid-1920s to mid-1940s, the Barbecue Lodge, on Wilkinson Boulevard.

[2] For a summary of the "debate," see: Ronnie W. Faulkner and Kelly Agan, "Mecklenburg Declaration of Independence" *NCPedia*, December 2021, https://www.ncpedia.org/mecklenburg-declaration.

[3] "Season of Change" by Virginia Brown, *SouthPark Magazine*, May 1, 2020.

[4] "NCNB (Bank of America) Plaza" *North Carolina Architects & Builders*, https://ncarchitects.lib.ncsu.edu/buildings/B003741

[5] Charlotte bus fares rose sharply in the 1970s. See *Charlotte News*, Nov 6, 1970, page 19 and *Charlotte News*, Jan 8, 1974, p. 1-B and *Charlotte Observer*, Feb. 21, 1974, p. 1-C

[6] *McColl: The Man with America's Money* by Ross Yockey, Longstreet Press, 1999, p.500

[7] *Charlotte Observer*, Dec. 4, 1973, p. 1-B

[8] See *Charlotte Observer*, Dec 5, 1976, Page 1-F

[9] "Sculptures on the Square, Charlotte" *Commemorative Landscapes of North Carolina*, https://docsouth.unc.edu/commland/monument/448.

[10] Oral History Interview with Raymond J. Kaskey, *Smithsonian Archives of American Art*, June 15–18, 2009, https://www.aaa.si.edu/download_pdf_transcript/ajax?record_id=edanmdm-AAADCD_oh_289311.

[11] The popular characterization was reflected in the title of the best-selling biography *Maestro: Greenspan's Fed and the American Boom*, by Bob Woodward (Simon & Schuster, 2000).

[12] *Fulton Bag and Cotton Mills General Collection*, https://exhibit-archive.library.gatech.edu/fulton_bag/.

[13] A Trifling Place, episode 8, Tasnim Shamma, host, "The Story Behind Those Big Statues On Independence Square" *WFAE*, April 9, 2013, https://www.wfae.org/podcast/2013-04-09/a-trifling-place-episode-8-the-story-behind-those-big-statues-on-independence-square.

[14] "Work Starts on Hugh McColl Park—A Makeover of the 'Obsolete' Polk Park" by Alexandria Sands, *Axios Charlotte*, May 18, 2023, https://charlotte.axios.com/329581/polk-park-demolition-construction-uptown/.

[15] For an extensive and disturbing account of how the city decided, without public input, to demolish Thomas Polk Park, including the extraordinary fountain designed by Angela Danadjieva, see https://www.tclf.org/charlottes-shame-was-polk-park-legally-razed

[16] "McColl Compensation a Target for Critics," *Tampa Bay Times*, Published April 22, 2000 | Updated Sept. 27, 2005

[17] *PR Newswire* from news provided by Falfurrias Management Partners, Dec 07, 2023

[18] *Beyond the Bank: Hugh McColl's Chapter Two*, by Howard E. Covington Jr., Lorimer Press 2021. An excerpt, "Hugh McColl's Second Act" was reprinted in *Charlotte Ledger* magazine, Dec. 5, 2020.

[19] *Wikipedia's* treatment of the town of Falfurrias, Texas states, "The biggest industry in Falfurrias is the United States Border Patrol interior checkpoint . . . on U.S. Route 281. As an indirect consequence, many migrants seeking to bypass the checkpoint by setting off across the arid land die of exposure and dehydration."

[20] "Charlotte's Power Elite Confront a New Order" by Ken Gepfert, *The Wall Street Journal*, Nov. 4, 1998

[21] Quote in "Searching for Respect: From 'New South' to 'World Class' at the Crossroads of the Carolinas" by Matthew D. Lassiter, included in *Charlotte NC: The Global Evolution of a New South City*, published by the University of Georgia Press, 2010

[22] https://www.wsoctv.com/news/local/its-heartbreaking-charlottes-thomas-polk-park-demolished/OIVSLHCDYBGVLAKMA7E5NOULD4/

III.
PLACE — BRAND — NON-PLACE

Eradication of Place and its replacement with a commercial and changeable brand identity claims an economic mandate and historical inevitability. Promoters cite the positive goals of greater wealth, higher status, innovation, and modernity. Place is destroyed in the quest for new industry, more jobs, and to escape a reputation as a city without vision. Visual sameness, social conformity, empty boosterism, and the loss of Home are accepted as a necessary price. The city must become an abstraction with a good story that can be managed. The consequences—forgotten history, the loss of Home—are not acknowledged. *There is no alternative*, it is said with finality.

Brand World Class

Charlotte's branding program is an extreme version of turning real Places with real history and connections to people into marketable abstractions. The brand is expressed in the city leaders' relentless ballyhoo about "world-class" status. The intense energy behind Charlotte's quest might be seen as only a localized expression of global capital's explosive energy, and the rising Charlotte skyline as just one of the mushroom clouds.

This explanation is an abstraction. It removes local forces and human players from history. By describing these changes as destiny—whether they are viewed as inherently positive or monstrous—this narrative closes off any critique or consideration of alternative directions.

Historian Matthew Lassiter has shown that Charlotte's intense obsession with world-class status is not driven by the faceless force of capital, which exists everywhere, but is rooted in local history.

In his essay, "Searching for Respect: From 'New South' to 'World Class' at the Crossroads of the Carolinas," Lassiter writes

that Charlotte, like other Southern cities, was haunted by stereo-
types of ignorance, backwardness, and racism:

> Few places in the United States are as obsessed with is-
> sues of civic identity, and as driven in their searches for
> both internal and external respect, as the boomtowns of
> the Sun Belt South. . . . Few places in the nation are as
> cavalier toward history and tradition, and as willing to
> destroy or deny the past.[1]

Of Charlotte in particular, Lassiter says:

> By the 1980s and 1990s, Charlotte appeared to have tran-
> scended these gothic and mythic images . . . by veering
> all the way to the other extreme . . . creating a bland
> bankers' paradise with no unique character, no true
> soul, no sense of place at all.

In Charlotte, the "world class" brand gains expression, as it
does everywhere, in more restaurants and bars, coffee shops,
major museums, sports franchises, recreational activities, and
lifestyle amenities. These are the standard substitutes for Place,
available only to those that can pay. Wealth is extravagantly displayed in the form of enormous houses and art collections.

Whatever the meaning of "world class" in terms of daily life,
it is always understood that it has not quite been achieved. It is
not here and not right now, not yet. Whatever world-class status is, though it is not currently being experienced, it is fervently
believed to be wondrously superior to whatever does now exist,
justifying constant disruption and losses in order to attain it.

The quest for world-class status was never chosen or necessarily even favored by Charlotte's citizenry. They are not con-
sulted. It is not up for debate. To aspire to world-class rank is an
article of faith, embraced by all Charlotte politicians, city officials,

and business leaders. There are no voices, no group, and no political party with a different vision.

To publicly express doubt or disdain for the mandate is seen as a sign of disloyalty in Charlotte. Those who question this mandate are smeared as in league with small-town prejudices, Bible Belt morality, and Old South stagnation. Most suspiciously, they would seem to doubt that the market's Invisible Hand always moves toward earthly perfection. It is heresy.

Those who might privately harbor doubts or consider Charlotte's developmental trajectory nonsensical are prudently quiet. No one asks for proof of the need for or value of Charlotte's quest to become world class, just as no one in a kingdom would ever ask the king, "Who gave you the right?"

Non-Place

As is the case with any single-minded and extreme belief, contradictions inevitably arise when the faith begins to turn its visionary ideal into concrete reality. Extreme commercialization of life, constant change, and the wiping out of hometown memories and noncommercial activities are the outcome of the quest for world-class status. These consequences push a city toward a fate worse than loss of global prominence or slowing growth—that of becoming a "Non-Place."

Non-Place is a concept formulated by the French anthropologist Marc Augé in his 1995 book, *Non-Places, an Introduction to Super-Modernity*.[3] A Non-Place may be filled with people. It may perform a vital civic function, have an esthetically pleasing design, or serve as a major economic driver. It is defined less by what it is than by what it is not—by what is missing.

The classic Non-Place is a major airport. Tellingly, many people know of Charlotte only from passing through its hub airport, CLT. Other commonly noted Non-Places include shopping malls, convention centers, theme parks, and waiting rooms.

For years, Charlotte bus riders met and made route transfers at the Square, a real Place. The transfer point was moved to the Transportation Center, a Non-Place. This was only one of many changes that began to transform "downtown," a Place, into "uptown," a lonely and arid Non-Place.

But Non-Place is not just a description of specific locations. It is a modern condition facing humans and producing social and psychological consequences. The forces and values that create Non-Place exert a widening influence. A discussion outline for "Non-Place" on the website of Brown University, entitled "Archeologies of Places," describes Non-Place as physical spaces in which,

> humans do not … identify with in any intimate sense … Residues from human practices do not accumulate; they are continuously wiped out … Non-Places fit well with the lifestyles of supermodernity.

Supermodernity is characterized as having "accelerated history, overabundance of events… loss of memory (and) not about identity." The study guide raised the question, "Can places re-emerge from within these bland wastelands?"[3]

Wikipedia's treatment of Marc Augé's concept recalls the work of David Reisman's *Lonely Crowd*, explaining, "(in a Non-Place) the individual remains anonymous and lonely." Places, on the other hand, "are relational, deeply historical and intimately connected to identity, both social and individual."

Seahaven

Formulated within the discipline of anthropology, Non-Place is an academic concept that describes physical locations and situations where people interact but human attachment is absent.

It fell to the world of art to provide a vivid and dramatic depiction of Non-Place as a pervasive condition encompassing the entire social sphere: the 1998 film, *The Truman Show*, with the central character of Truman Burbank played by Jim Carrey.

Truman lives in Seahaven, a technologically advanced, artificial bubble. It was modeled on and partly filmed at a real "master-planned community" in Florida called Seaside on the state's Panhandle coast.

Truman is born and lives from childbirth to age thirty, innocently and unknowingly, as a manipulated character in the Seahaven movie set. His life is orchestrated by unseen directors and producers for the benefit of commercial investors. Unknown to Truman, his everyday activities are followed by millions as TV entertainment. He is a center of attention on a global scale—a world-class figure, the star of a show that is broadcasted to the entire world.

All the people in the set whom Truman interacts with are, unknown to him, paid actors. Every word, action and show of emotion is as sincere as a sales pitch. In this world, Truman is himself a product. Truman's "best friend" in Seahaven explains, *"It's all true. It's all real. Nothing here is fake; nothing you see on the show is fake. It's merely controlled."*

The totality of Truman Burbank's life is a commodity, and in market terms, the show is spectacularly successful. *The Truman Show* is so globally popular that those who would question or criticize the show are labeled as "sick" and "political." The show generates revenue from product placements. All items in the show are available in the Truman catalog, with "operators standing by" to take orders.

A more subtle message of the story of Truman Burbank is that the millions who spend time watching his life unfold are themselves living empty, manipulated lives in the service of commercial interests. They are using Truman's life as a distraction from their own, which enriches the show's sponsors.

Until his discovery of his situation and subsequent escape, Truman has a cheery, upbeat temperament. He is married to a beautiful woman, sells insurance, and lives in a pleasant and safe suburb. Ensconced in the show's false world, Truman's "wife" defends her work in the show, which allows her barely any true personal life, as a "lifestyle."

As Truman's controlled existence illustrates, Absence of Place is a deprivation, a loss of freedom, and a restriction on human potential, but it may not necessarily evoke sorrow or protest. It is only when an alternative is discovered or even imagined that loss of freedom is recognized and true yearning is experienced.

---

[1] Essay by historian Matthew Lassiter, included in the 2010 book, *Charlotte NC: The Global Evolution of a New South City*, published by the University of Georgia Press, 2012

[2] *Non-Places: An Introduction to Supermodernity* by Marc Auge (Author), John Howe (Translator), Verso; 2nd edition, 2009

[3] https://www.brown.edu/Departments/Joukowsky_Institute/courses/archaeologiesofplace/7002.html

IV. SEARCHING FOR ALTERNATIVES

Where Place still has a strong influence on residents, discussions of preserving history and quality of life are a normal part of civic dialogue. Where Place has been deemed an anachronism, an irrelevant sentiment, or even a hindrance to a city's efforts at branding, substantive dialogue about these issues seldom occurs.

Defenders of Place must, first, prove that Place has any meaning; then, they must present comprehensive *alternatives* to the ideology of demolition and continuous rebranding. Since it is taken for granted that commercial development is the greatest priority, people proposing alternative policies that preserve Place are expected to demonstrate that these approaches will have little or no negative economic impact. And they must somehow do so in the context of a prevailing narrative that holds no alternatives to destruction in the pursuit of continuous expansion could possibly exist. As Charlotte's crusader-in-chief for "world-class" status, former Bank of America CEO Hugh McColl famously said, "You're either growing or dying. There's no middle ground."[1]

With McColl as champion of the goal of all-out growth, Charlotte is following the same script as his bank. This approach now appears to be succeeding, as it did at the bank for a while . . . until 2008. This is when the ill-fated "assets" the bank had taken on in its largest acquisition, that of Merrill Lynch, finally "broke the bank." Charlotte's leading business, closely tied to the identity and fortunes of the city, became insolvent.

The bank was deemed "too big to fail"—meaning that it is a structure so massive that if it toppled, it would crush everything in its proximity: other banks, businesses, whole cities. US taxpayers rescued Bank of America, which needed an infusion of $45 billion and an agreement that the government would help cover losses on $118 billion in "toxic assets" that the bank acquired in its frenzied expansion. In one week, Bank of America's stock price dropped by half. The Secretary of the Treasury stated he would have preferred a comprehensive remedial program for the banking industry, but said Bank of America's dire situation required immediate and special attention. He called BOFA, "the turd in the punchbowl."[2]

This catastrophe would seem to cry out for an alternative course. Yet no one could imagine a way forward that substantively altered how the bank operated, or envision a plan to untether the future of the city from that of the bank.

Alternative visions for city life that respect the importance of Place and Home—contrary to McColl's grow-or-die narrative—do exist. And, contrary to what detractors claim, they are not a call for a mythic return to an earlier era or an embrace of stagnation. In Europe, it is taken for granted that government funds should be allocated to public services that enhance quality of life. It is uncontroversial that cities should prioritize creating or nurturing noncommercial environs. And it is taken for granted that the past should be honored through the preservation of significant buildings, protection of historic neighborhoods, and celebration of local identity. These practices are so culturally ingrained as to not require any economic or social defense.

These alternative ideas and policies are not new and do not need to be extensively described in this book. Most are obvious. In fact, an alternative approach to urban planning was forcefully presented in Jane Jacobs's classic *The Death and Life of Great American Cities* over 60 years ago.

Jane Jacobs begins the book by acknowledging that approaches to urban planning that value the preservation of historic buildings and established neighborhoods lacked champions, and had not yet been clearly and forcefully stated. Jacobs sought to change that. In her words: "This book is an attack on current city planning and rebuilding. It is also, and mostly, an attempt to introduce new principles."

Jacobs's influential book was published in 1962, just as Charlotte launched its major transformation. And point for point, almost as if her book were used as a guide of what *not to do*, Jacobs's recommendations and analyses were ignored or directly contradicted in Charlotte. The poorest areas were not given support to allow them to "unslum" with their own energy and under their own direction. Instead, whole neighborhoods were destroyed by urban renewal. Swaths of the city were irreparably severed by new high-speed roads. There never was a discussion of alternative principles.

In his masterpiece, *The Unsettling of America*, novelist and environmental activist Wendell Berry offers one of the few extended statements on practical values that could underpin alternative policies that would preserve a Sense of Place. Berry approaches the challenge through an assessment of the state of agriculture. He notes a shift from agriculture to agri*business*, and he examines the implications of this shift for sustainable livelihoods, the protection of home, and care of the earth. Berry's work is a devastating critique of the policies that produced today's gigantic factory farms; mass animal slaughter; and dependency on chemicals, antibiotics, hormones, pesticides, and genetic engineering. He argues that modern agriculture is unsustainable and risks catastrophe.

Berry's critique of agriculture looks beyond production to longer term social, human and environmental consequences. This perspective can be extended to urban policies that destroy communities, drive out working people, wipe out history. He quotes Montaigne: "Who so hath his minde on taking, hath it no more on what he hath taken." Berry acknowledges that the "dominant tendency" in American history has been to take, to exploit, to use up, and to move on. But he also reminds us that there has also always been another opposing tendency: "to stay put, to say, 'No farther. This is the place.'"

This tendency has been less successful, but it is older, Berry notes. It was dominant among the Native Americans who revered the earth as home, making destruction of its life-forms and resources unthinkable. Yet even during the aggressive expansion of European settlement, "every advance of the frontier left behind families and communities who intended to remain and prosper *where they were.*"

Berry discusses Native Americans not just to express admiration for their culture, though he does this, but to point out that the principles and values that destroyed the homes and communities of Native Americans were eventually turned against those who displaced them. The destructive process, he explains, "did not stop with the subjugation of the Indians but went on to impose substantially the same disasters upon the small farms and the farm communities, upon the shops of small local tradesmen of all sorts, upon the workshops of independent craftsmen, and upon the households of citizens."

Berry wrote his treatise nearly fifty years ago, just as the corporate system began to eradicate small farms, gut smalltown economies, and deindustrialize Midwest and Northeast cities. In the cities, this was followed by corporate downsizing and outsourcing, wiping out previously sustainable corporate-ladder careers. More recent economic changes put the country's youth into debt dependency even before they enter the job market and have closed off their access to home ownership.

The people who are the beneficiaries of earlier waves of appropriations, or who passively stand by as others are displaced, often eventually become victims of later cycles of accumulation through dispossession. Berry would see similar destructive logics at work in Charlotte's wiping out of Brooklyn and what later became of lower-middle-income White residents in the era of White flight. Exploiting the racism of White homeowners, blockbusting real estate agents persuaded people in White districts that Black families were planning to move to their neighborhood and that the value of their property would soon plummet, persuading White families to sell their homes at below-market rates. Many White families lost life savings as they sold in a panic and scattered to small towns and rural areas. To paraphrase Yeats and the Coen Brothers film title, "Charlotte is no town for lower-and mid-income families."

Parallel trends have made retail space increasingly unaffordable. Urban renewal drove out older retail from "uptown." More recently, retail space throughout the city has become increasingly inaccessible except to large chains and franchises.

This self-destructive cycle will be presented in the pages of this book, showing that the bulldozing of the city's largest and best-established African American community was only the first salvo in destruction of Place. Black neighborhoods were deemed inconsequential and their residents, churches, and businesses dispensable. The urban renewal ideology soon came to see many other sectors of the city in the same manner.

Wendell Berry noted that agribusiness boasted enormous gains in productivity, measured by the smaller number of people needed to work larger acreages of farmland. But what were the consequences of driving millions of people off the land? What happened to them, he asks? So, too, Charlotte's self-promotion of its "tallest" tower, luxury condos, and massive stadiums pretends a one-sided ledger, one that does not account for losses.

Today, there are many more areas at the receiving end of a wrecking ball of rezoning, real estate speculation, and frenzied land development. All of this is justified, just as urban renewal was, by claims of inevitability and a higher purpose.

The *New York Times* has reported that, nationwide, corporate speculators "own 3.8 percent of the country's single-family rentals, but in Charlotte, they own 20 percent." In 2022, 17 percent of all homes sold in Charlotte were purchased by corporate buyers, in all-cash transactions.[3]

Officially, Charlotte is economically booming and growing in size. Yet home ownership, small businesses, the arts, volunteer associations, and the hopes of lower-income youth for a better future *where they live*—bedrocks of Place—are in decline. They are replaced with what is touted as something much better, a great "lifestyle."

Lifestyle

Songs and poems pay homage to Place and Home. The loss of Place and Home is lamented in novels and dramas. *Lifestyle*, on the other hand, is a term that is constantly used but it is never venerated or mythologized, hinting at artificiality or even sham.

Lifestyle is described in various ways—relaxed, family-oriented, casual, active—but the thing itself is never directly defined. I suspect this is deliberate, since lifestyle was born as a term of marketing, not from life experience. It is part of the secret code of commercial persuasion. It did not enter the language until the 1950s. It is a term drawn from what sociologist Jules Henry called advertising's dictionary of "pseudo-truth."

"Pseudo-truth in advertising," Henry writes in *Culture Against Man*, "is a false statement made as if it were true but not intended to be believed *literally*." Its validity is not based on actual experience that could be verified, remembered, or compared. It is suggestive, ephemeral, a facsimile of real life like a theater set. Its validity, Henry explains, "is that it sells merchandise."[4]

Lifestyle is shown to be primarily about what can be purchased. As a marketing term, it is intended to convince the consumer that purchasing goods and services will satisfy deep, authentic, and universal human needs—including the need for Place. The goods and services can be so comprehensive and interconnected as to constitute a "way of living."

Philosopher Theodor Adorno is one of the few to closely examine the modern term "style." In Adorno's view, "style," like "lifestyle," is a term of the "culture industry" that promises— but actually obstructs—individuality, creativity, and personal freedom. The main effect of style, Adorno argues, is to impose conformity. It is a form of domination. The real purpose of style, Adorno warns, and as is well-understood by commercial users of the term, is to instill ever more need for the culture industry's goods and services.

Where lifestyle is sold as a replacement for the comforts, pride, and security of Place and Home, the overriding ideal is called *growth*. Growth is a metaphor taken from nature, making it appear "natural," but its meaning is only commercial. The term *growth* belongs to the glossary of boosterism and actually entails the exploitation of nature.[5]

Growth is the unending obsession of Charlotte's leaders. In the end, growth just means *more, always more*. The ideal implicitly cheapens what already exists for what could be gained later. The path to *more* is narrow and rigid. The "world class" quest looks the same wherever it dominates.

Gaslighting Ourselves

The broad denial that Place has any significant meaning and the lack of a coherent, well-articulated alternative lead many of us who experience loss or sorrow in response to the changes in our cities to question our grip on reality, to gaslight ourselves. In Charlotte and elsewhere, this self-doubt serves to silence debate and make it appear that universal consensus exists, satisfaction prevails, and all parties were heard. In Charlotte, this supposed consensus is called "the Charlotte Way." The Charlotte Way only goes in one direction.

In America at large, a longing for Place or any voice against its destruction is so invalidated or ignored that there is not even a term to describe it. The term *nostalgia* is often used, which carries a connotation of whimsy or futility.

In *From Where We Stand*, a memoir of her own search for a sense of place, the poet and scholar Deborah Tall explained that "nostalgia" originally meant *homesickness*. So powerful—and presumably so natural—was human connection to Place in earlier times that homesickness was treated as a serious physical malady that often involved anorexia and palpitations. Loss of Place was taken as seriously as loss of nutrition or any other fundamental human need. Medical books through the late 1800s described this longing for home as a potentially fatal infirmity, with symptoms of melancholy, indifference, "obstinate silence," and rejection of food. Especially beset were soldiers on long expeditions and young women sent to distant cities to do service work. During World War II, the Surgeon General described this malady as contagious.[6]

By the end of the 1800s, coinciding with small towns and provinces becoming less isolated and improvements in communication technologies, the meaning of nostalgia started to shift, according to Tall. Rather than a real malady born of physical dislocation, nostalgia was increasingly understood as a personal psychological state "rooted in time." The longing for the customs and connections of earlier times was soon further demeaned as "regression," a psychological disorder characterized as an unwarranted yearning for childhood.

Today, the dismissive term "sentimental" is often applied to the longing for Place. Those who might question policies or actions that destroy local identities, traditions, buildings, or landscapes are labelled "sentimentalists" and seen as engaging in "a useless longing for something no longer possible."

Tall recovered her own Sense of Place in the Finger Lakes region of upstate New York, where she and her husband had moved, by learning and reflecting on the area's rich and tumultuous history, including its brutal treatment of Native Americans; by growing her own garden in that fertile soil; and exploring the region with her children, connecting whatever they discovered to their own lives.

She concluded that "social mobility," the ideal most often cited to diminish respect for Place, is mostly misused. "The deliberate avoidance of ties to a place . . . allows us to be indifferent to our . . . cities, [and] ultimately to contribute to [their] destruction," she wrote. "A full life involves both venturing out and returning," which must include caring and being attached to a Place.

Tall quoted T. S. Elliot:

We shall not cease from exploration
And the end of all our exploring
Will be to arrive where we started
And know the place for the first time.

Anomie, Conformity, and Soul

Though it's barely referenced in popular culture, academic literature does recognize the yearning for Place that is absent or has been destroyed as a social pathology termed *anomie* or *alienation*. These terms were not in use in Thoreau's day, though loss of freedom, which is the underlying factor, and its effects were arguably better understood then than now. "I think that they (who sit in shops all day and don't spend time in nature) deserve some credit for not having all committed suicide long ago," he wrote in his famous essay, *Walking*.

In modern usage, anomie and alienation is often thought to occur at the margins of society or seen as an abnormal or unusual response experienced only by overly sensitive souls, the maladjusted, or grieving purists. This minimization is not dissimilar from the evolution of *nostalgia*, which was first viewed as a painful, potentially fatal, response to loss of Place but is now seen as merely a form of today's diminished and disrespected concept of sentimentality.

It is rare to see alienation and anomie described as a *norm*, affecting huge numbers of people, as Thoreau did with his famous statement: "The mass of men lead lives of quiet desperation." Only a few well-known works have argued that anomie is a prevalent experience in modern America, or even part of the modern American character. One of the earliest and best-known works with this perspective is *The Lonely Crowd* by David Riesman, published in 1950. Riesman saw American society "driving great numbers of people into anomie," in which "they lose their social freedom and their individual autonomy in seeking to become like each other."

Writing in the early 1990s, sociologist Christopher Lasch viewed *anomie* as an integral part of the "social character" of modern America, which he described as a "culture of narcissism."

Lasch defined narcissism as a personal response to *loss of power* or fear of loss. Paradoxically but also tellingly, the term narcissism is now associated with those at the pinnacle of material acquisition, oligarchs and billionaires who seemingly have everything, yet desperately need more.

One of the earliest uses of the term *anomie* was by French sociologist Emile Durkheim in his study of suicide published in 1897. Durkheim described anomie as increasing when there is a large discrepancy between popular myth and what people experience. This is a useful description of what people feel about their actual lives as measured against a hyper-promoted *lifestyle*.

More recently the term *solastalgia* entered the language to describe "homesickness," a sense of being cast adrift, or feeling like a stranger even while never leaving home. In cities, this can refer to feelings brought on by gentrification, sprawl, or rapid population increase, but it can also refer to the disruption of landscapes or climate, producing "ecological grief."

Nostalgia and solastalgia are well-documented modern forms of discontent but to experience either requires having once lived and appreciated Place. The focus of this book is *absence of*—not just the loss of or the longing to return to—Place. Absence of Place leaves us bereft. Yet, because it is such a profoundly unnatural condition and the loss of Place is not broadly recognized, we struggle to explain or describe what we grieve for. We are like the children diagnosed with "nature-deficit disorder" who have never known, and therefore could not describe a longing for, the joy of play in the outdoors.

---

[1] "Breaking the Bank," *PBS Frontline*, June. 16, 2009, full transcript at https://www.pbs.org/wgbh/pages/frontline/breakingthebank/etc/script.html

[2] The data of bailout in the forms of federal loans and guarantees and Henry Paulson's scatological reference to Bank of America are from *Banktown: The*

Rise and Struggles of Charlotte's Big Banks by Charlotte author, Rick Rothacker, John F. Blair, Publisher. Kindle Edition, 2010.

"In the earnings conference call, Lewis calmly detailed the damage ... He also detailed an aid package that boosted the bank's TARP loans to $45 billion... Treasury and the FDIC were also providing protection against "unusually large losses" on the pool of $118 billion in assets."

During the bailout, there was much public confusion as to what was direct subsidy, what was a "loan" and what "protection against losses." The "loans" were officially called "Troubled Asset Relief Protection."

[3] "What Happens When Wall Street Buys Most of the Homes on Your Block?" by Ronda Kaysen and Ella Koeze, *New York Times*, Sept. 16, 2023

[4] *Culture Against Man* by Jules Henry, Random House (Vintage Books); First Edition, 1963

[5] *The Culture Industry: Selected Essays on Mass Culture* (Routledge Classics) 2nd Edition by Theodor W. Adorno (Author), J. M. Bernstein (Editor), 2001

[6] *From Where We Stand: Recovering a Sense of Place*, by Deborah Tall, The Johns Hopkins University Press, 1996

V. What's The Matter With Charlotte?

If I have put enough substance on Place to redeem it from useless sentimentalism, and if I have given credible indicators that Charlotte offers useful clues to how and why Place is disappearing in American cities, there remains one more challenge: establishing Charlotte North Carolina, out of all other cities, is the prototype of Eliminator of Place. What, in particular, is the matter with Charlotte?

So many other instances of destruction of Place could be cited over many years in so many cities, including some that have received national attention, that it would be pointless and futile to catalogue them. It is, as Wendell Berry noted, the "dominant tendency" in American history to take, use up, and discard.

In the opening pages of her classic book on the death and life of big cities, Jane Jacobs recounts how a group of clergy had assessed civic and social conditions in Chicago. Their report read:

Could Job have been thinking of Chicago when he wrote:

"Here are men that alter their neighbor's landmark . . . Reap they the field that is none of theirs, strip they the vineyard wrongfully seized from its owner."

If so, he was also thinking of New York, Philadelphia, Boston, Washington, St. Louis, San Francisco and a number of other places.

So, can undistinguished, mid-size, and prosperous Charlotte truly serve as the exemplar for this national—indeed, global—force that is shaping not just our cities but the substance of our inner lives as well?

Some readers likely know little of Charlotte beyond its hub airport or are dimly aware of it only as it is depicted by boosters. Charlotte is promoted as a fast-growing metro and yet also an oasis. It is known as moderate and inoffensive in culture and weather, like a predictable, family-oriented franchise restaurant.

Yet there is another feature of Charlotte that contradicts this mild image. *Charlotte, North Carolina, is a cauldron of fierce commercial aggressiveness.*

Charlotte is the second largest financial center of the United States. Not Philadelphia, Chicago, Los Angeles, Dallas, or Boston, but Charlotte. It is the global headquarters of Bank of America and East Coast headquarters of Wells Fargo. Its homegrown electric utility, Duke Energy, founded upon tobacco fortune, has grown and made acquisitions to become the largest electricity provider in all of America. The locally owned nonprofit hospital in Charlotte, Atrium, is the seventh largest hospital in America. Belk, based in Charlotte, was the largest family-owned department store chain in America. It was sold to a private equity firm in 2015 for $3 billion and today employs over 10,000 with 300 retail locations. Charlotte is the location of the very first Family Dollar store, and the home of the founder, Leon Levine, who grew it to an 8,000-store chain. Family Dollar was sold in 2015 for $9.5 billion.

As earlier noted, Charlotte's hub airport, CLT, is one of the largest in the world in terms of plane traffic. And though the city or the region has no history with major league sports, it now has NBA and NFL franchises.

How did Charlotte achieve this national, even global stature? Charlotte's current status as a commercial powerhouse and urban magnet has puzzled many analysts. It has no notable geographic features: It's not located on a coast or a river. It has no claim to unique scenery, and an unremarkable, though moderate, climate. Its earlier sources of wealth—textiles and tobacco—are nowhere to be found in Charlotte now, and their significance to Charlotte's history is downplayed by city boosters. Charlotte is not a notable technology center or epicenter for research. It has no leading university or major medical school. It has little historical significance, no interesting architecture (anymore), and no military base or military fame, not even from the Civil War. While nineteenth century immigrants brought an entrepreneurial spirit and left a cultural imprint on places such as New York, Boston, Honolulu, and San Francisco, Charlotte was not historically a haven for immigrants.

Charlotte's sudden and dramatic population increase, massive office tower and apartment construction, and airport enlargement have been nationally noticed. Charlotte's court-ordered school desegregation and anti-immigration policies also received national media attention. But what really distinguishes Charlotte, North Carolina, from other cities that might account for its financial ascendancy and population growth is seldom even considered.

To the contrary, modern Charlotte is lauded for its lack of any special character or distinction. It is like an agile and versatile retailer with no legacy culture and no pensioners, able to appeal to new and multiple customer groups with seemingly incompatible promises. The *Charlotte Observer* proudly reported a regional author's characterization of Charlotte as "just constantly changing and deciding to be something else," considering this high praise.

For decades, Charlotte has elected Democratic local officials and a Republican to represent it in Congress. Charlotte comfortably hosted the Democratic convention to renominate Barack Obama in 2012 and then the Republican national convention to renominate Donald Trump in 2020. Each of those conventions was polarizing, especially the 2020 event, but the arguments for hosting them were identical—to gain recognition. It's good for business.

US News named Charlotte one of the 10 best cities to live, describing Charlotte, *impossibly*, as "charming, yet sprawling" and "Old South, and modern cosmopolitan."[1]

Charlotte maintains these contradictory depictions in both promotions and policies without showing need for justification or explanation. Tearing down elements of Place "to be something else" is dogmatically advocated on the claim it bestows greater social mobility and higher standard of living on all residents, even those displaced or whose businesses are destroyed. Doubting universal benefit is considered "negativity" in Charlotte.

On the official website of Charlotte's tax-funded PR website, three neighborhoods are featured to "explore." Each of the three is a recently created replacement of an actual neighborhood that was effectively eliminated, or a gentrified version of a neighborhood that now has a new name, erasing the identity and history of what had existed. They are products of real estate marketers. The website's name is the city's official promotional slogan, the supremely inoffensive and generic: "Charlotte's Got a Lot."[2]

No Satire

It might be imagined that imposition of policies aimed at making Charlotte "world class" and the destruction of local culture and character would spawn a unique local humor in Charlotte. One might imagine that the sense of humor that would develop would be a biting, rueful, satirical take-down of the conceits of hypocritical, business-obsessed leaders. This sort of humor is a way that people everywhere find relief from powerlessness, as a subversive act of protest.

Officially, Charlotte does not laugh at itself. Brands are not self-deprecating. What is authentic, historical, and traditional is fair game for humor, but not the paid-for narratives of boosterism.

No famous comedians come from Charlotte. There's no local or regional humor—e.g., New York irony, Boston sarcasm, redneck self-mockery—associated with Charlotte and no ethnic humor either.

There is a kind of *official comedy* in Charlotte. It is a production that occurs once a year, always by the same actors, singers and writer. It is called, strangely, "Charlotte Squawk." A squawk means a loud protest. But the event is actually a tribute, a good-natured ribbing. It can be genuinely funny but does not bite. There's no anger in it. No one takes offense. It is light parody, not satire. It is produced as a musical, putting everyday Charlotte places and events into famous or dramatic show tunes.

Rarely has Charlotte been targeted for genuine humor or satire expressing hidden or forbidden truths. Almost nothing substantive has been written about the character of Charlotte since W. J. Cash's scathing and hilarious critique of the city in the 1930s.[3] In an essay in H. L. Mencken's *American Mercury* magazine, Cash infamously mocked Charlotte as a "Calvinist Lhasa," a "citadel of bigotry and obscurantism," worshipping a Presbyterian God "impossible to match anywhere in the South." This was back when Charlotte was still a Place. Places laugh at themselves.

A quarter century after Cash's mockery, a very different kind of writer took a casual swipe at Charlotte along similar lines. Famed civil rights activist and intellectual James Baldwin visited Charlotte in 1959. He wrote, "I had spent several days in Charlotte, North Carolina. This is a bourgeois town, Presbyterian, pretty—if you like towns—and socially so hermetic that it contains scarcely a single decent restaurant."[4]

James Baldwin's visit to Charlotte was prompted by a nationally publicized event in which a young Black female student was harassed and threatened when she attempted to enroll in one of Charlotte's all-white high schools. Baldwin skewered Charlotte's claim to racial harmony, which has long been part of Charlotte's brand. "I was also told, several times, by White people, that 'race relations' there were excellent," Baldwin wrote. "I failed to find a single Negro who agreed with this."

Today, even when Charlotte is lightly mocked, few residents, as they are overwhelmingly from other places, take the jab as directed at them. One can hear a local strain of mockery among some blue-collar workers and a few people within the arts community, but it is judiciously confined to private conversations. One local artist angrily announced a plan to write a new play about Charlotte, entitled *World Class, My Ass*. Of course, no such work was ever produced. Such murmuring is locally dismissed as nattering.

The *New York Times* punctured Charlotte's pretenses in 1996 when the local theater company scheduled a production of Tony Kushner's Pulitzer Prize-winning play about gay life during the HIV plague, *Angels in America*. Some Charlotte church and political leaders mobilized to block the play, threatened cast members with arrest, and organized protests in front of the theater, claiming the play included "indecent exposure."[5]

The condemned scene involved a patient with HIV disrobing frontally for a nurse's humiliating and fearsome exam for lesions. Charlotte's sales-guy mayor, Pat McCrory, weighed in with a business-like proposal to the show's local producers that the play be modified, just for Charlotte, so the patient showed his backside to the audience instead. A judge eventually cleared the way for the production in its original format, but local political leaders slashed funding across all of the arts for the next year. Funding was later restored, but the theater company that directed and presented the play permanently closed down a few years later.

To the horror of Charlotte's brand managers, the *Angels* incident got the city labelled a "Bible Belt town" in Section A of nation's foremost newspaper. "Bible Belt" is one of the vestiges of Place that Charlotte's visionary leaders seek to eradicate, though, as we shall see, Christianity remains woven into the town's social fabric. In Charlotte, the term "Bible Belt," like references to cotton mills and tobacco, is anathema to the "world class" brand.

Thanks to the achievements of Charlotte's world-class crusaders, a rising skyline began to light up the night, the airport became an international hub, banks based in the city gained national stature, and a new "coliseum" was erected to host Charlotte's first NBA franchise. However, soon after the city was transformed by these triumphs, an embarrassing short story appeared in *Harper's Magazine*, entitled "Charlotte."[6]

Written by Tony Earley, an award-winning, North Carolina-based novelist and short story writer, the story is set in a faux-Irish pub that used to attract bleached-haired, pumped up professional wrestlers. The bar's manager in the story feels that crowd had been truer to what Charlotte is. But now that Charlotte is becoming "world class," the wrestlers don't come in anymore. The wrestling alliance that organized their matches was sold and moved to Atlanta.

Now, the bar manager laments,

> Everyone in Charlotte tries to be something they are not. . . . Our lives are small and empty, and we thought they wouldn't be, once we moved to the city. . . . How do you tell somebody from Polkville . . . not to let the beauty of the skyline fool them? Charlotte is a place where a crooked TV preacher [Charlotte-based evangelist Jim Bakker] can steal money and grow like a sore . . . by simply promising hope.

Earley's story was discussed in the *Charlotte Observer* by the book editor, Dannye Romine. She wrote, "The story, fiction with recognizable characters and landmarks, doesn't flatter us. In fact, *Charlotte* makes us look like a homogenized hick town of superficial overreachers."[7]

Charlotte's Terrible Truth

Far more concerning than rare episodes of derision or parody, the greatest hit to Charlotte's brand in recent years was delivered by a 2014 study on social mobility. The report refuted the claim that the city's quest for global greatness is the surest support for the future of all residents. A terrible truth was revealed, and the shock continues to reverberate.

The blow did not come from Charlotte residents. It was delivered in a devastating 2014 Harvard University study that ranked Charlotte at the dead bottom, No. 50 out of 50 cities in America, for intergenerational social mobility. Charlotte ranked lower than Detroit, New Orleans, Philadelphia, Baltimore, and Cleveland.[8]

By some metrics, Charlotte was booming. So, Charlotte's business and civic leaders were shocked, *shocked* to read in the Harvard study that lower income people in Charlotte are largely doomed to remain poor, as are their children. How was it possible that one of the fastest growing cities in the country, America's No. 2 ranked financial center, a city undergoing unprecedented development and known for a great "lifestyle," could be the worst place in the nation for lower-income young people to do better in life than their parents?

This shocking finding threw Charlotte's brand managers into a quandary. It produced a frenzy of initiatives in diversity, equity, and inclusion and an explosion in "opportunity" rhetoric among city officials. The Harvard study's author, Raj Chetty, was invited to partner with Charlotte in addressing the unfortunate ranking. Yet, in Charlotte's brand-driven culture, the issue was defined in the convoluted terms of PR. The cruel reality was bemoaned for damaging the city's brand. No one considered whether the city's brand might be what was causing the cruel reality.

As reported locally, "Charlotte's 50 out of 50 ranking spurred the city and county to mobilize." But a top official involved noted, "The city might not have worked hard had it not been last."[9]

Yet, eight years after the Harvard study, Charlotte's public radio station news reported that if any significant change had occurred in Charlotte to increase social mobility, it was not readily apparent. Nor have city officials claimed that changes in social mobility have occurred.[10]

"On the heels of the study, known locally as the Chetty study," the journalists reported,

> Charlotte spent an estimated $400 million trying to impact areas it deemed critical to giving children a better chance to escape poverty. . . . But now, eight years later, it's hard to tell whether we've made progress on those efforts.

In fact, a follow-up study by Chetty did show some modest improvement for Charlotte's rank relative to other cities. However, a study published in 2025 measuring cities with "the most people in financial distress" placed Charlotte at the bottom in the number six rank out of 100 cities measured. In two of the metrics, Charlotte ranked dead last.[11]

A disappointed participant in those efforts pointed out that the world-class development frenzy had left a huge sector of the city without even grocery stores or doctors' offices.

The emphasis of the initiative responding to the Chetty study eventually shifted from enacting change to developing a "dashboard" to statistically verify conditions and measure changes. More study would be needed. Tellingly, in the 2020 report, the first recommendation listed "to be further explored" related to neighborhoods, a keystone of Sense of Place in a city. In city-planning lingo, the report declared:

> Emphasis should also be placed on supporting current place-conscious efforts in historically under-resourced communities, and better understanding how to improve opportunity at the neighborhood level in a sustainable and scalable fashion.[12]

What was not acknowledged was the ugly fact that Charlotte's world-class crusade is inimical to stable, secure, "place-conscious" neighborhoods. From the destruction of Brooklyn with urban renewal money to the current pattern of displacement through privately funded demolition and redevelopment, the market value of land and buildings reigns supreme over Place.

The inherent tendency of single-minded commercial gain to undermine neighborhoods and social mobility was explained by Jane Jacobs in her landmark book on cities. Jacobs closely collaborated with famed Chicago-based community organizer Saul Alinsky, whose life's work was showing residents how to improve their communities on their own. This frequently required residents to defend their neighborhoods against destructive commercial interests or willful neglect by public officials.

Jacobs studied how poor neighborhoods that lacked political power could gradually improve, which supported residents in improving their lives individually. This is the promise of America, she reminded readers. But, she explained,

> Unslumming depend[s] on the fact that a metropolitan economy, *if it is working well*, (emphasis added) is constantly transforming many poor people into middle-class people, many illiterates into skilled (or even educated) people, many greenhorns into competent citizens.[13]

The Harvard study revealed that Charlotte's "metropolitan economy" is not working well for everyone, even as the city is celebrated for its growth, airport traffic, sports stadiums, and the aggregate capital it attracts. Writing in the 1960s, Jacobs recognized that new economic forces and approaches to city planning stood in the way of the traditional process of "unslumming."

"Successful unslumming," Jacobs wrote, "means that enough people must have an attachment to the slum that they wish to stay, and it also means that it must be practical for them to stay." She added, however, that "unslumming today is frequently halted by the ultimate discouragement— destruction."

Well before the term "gentrification" entered the language, Jacobs noted how poor areas, especially those showing signs of self-improvement, became tempting targets "to clear for a higher-income population."

Today, the middle class, and not only the poor, are being displaced, but the arguments justifying their displacement remain the same. Jacobs explained that when speculators target an area and commercial property owners look to cash out, the few voices of opposition are often ignored:

> The only people who object to destruction . . . are those who have businesses there or who live there. . . . In every city, such protests are discounted as the howls of people of narrow vision standing in the way of progress.

Thus, a city without Sense of Place has no qualms smashing an entire community to pieces and doing next to nothing as affordable housing disappears, in the belief it is all for the good. The voices of protesting residents are dismissed. Any voices calling attention to an area's history or value, or speaking up about what an area means to current residents, are quelled by the city's professional planners, who paint the entire program as positive and predestined.

What would Charlotte be today if Brooklyn had been allowed to improve itself and remain a vital part of the center city, possibly becoming a Harlem of the Carolinas? What would the city be today if homes, buildings, and businesses, including those located on the Square, had been preserved? If Charlotte's real history were not fictionalized through the installation of the "four pillars" and monuments to bank consolidations?

The answers to these questions are difficult to imagine, especially since the wrecking ball did not stop in Brooklyn. Instead, the demolition and redevelopment has moved like a blitzkrieg across many more areas—poor and middle income, industrial and retail, farmland and textile village—as an apparently unstoppable force.

Charlotte's Secret

Far from belying its powerful ambition, Charlotte's bland and malleable countenance is, in fact, the outward expression of the character trait that supercharges Charlotte.

Jane Jacobs and others have described how a city loses character and Sense of Place at the hands of opportunistic developers and well-meaning planners. But it was journalist and author W. J. Cash who probed deeply into Charlotte's *core character* for the secret to Charlotte's hyper-aggressiveness.

Wilbur Cash perceived a close link between Charlotte's heedless elimination of communities, buildings, landmarks, and places of local meaning and Charlotte's undistinguished, "supremely commonplace" appearance. Behind disregard to Place and undistinguished architecture is what W. J. Cash called an "extravagant" ambition responsible for Charlotte's extraordinary rise in wealth and status.[14]

The core set of traits reveals itself, he wrote, in a *type of person* who "overshadows and overruns the scene." That type of person is known by the name of a character in Sinclair Lewis's 1922 satirical novel, named for that character, that earned Lewis the Nobel Prize for literature. The character's name entered the language. His name is Babbitt, George Babbitt.

It took the industrialization of the South after the Civil War for this personality type to come into full flower, but it was present among the earliest White settlers of the Charlotte area. Cash associated this type with Scotch-Irish heritage. As described by Cash, the earliest White settlers of Charlotte "looked upon industry and the getting of goods as pious exercises peculiarly pleasing to Heaven."

Sinclair Lewis opened the novel describing the bland city of Zenith, where Babbitt resided. Zenith is characterized, Lewis wrote, by office towers of "steel and cement" that "aspired." So intense was this aspirational fervor, which views mammon as manna, that Cash wrote, "Without exception, every Southern town which has risen to eminence in the new order has been more or less under its sway. And in Charlotte, where it reached its apogee, it naturally worked most perfectly."

In Charlotte, when the Civil War ended, according to Cash,

The gentry not merely received the Yankee go-getters with open arms, but themselves, and to a man, turned Babbitt without a qualm or a pang and without an iota of change in their proper character—took to Rotary with all the loving gusto with which a duckling takes to water, with all their ancient zest for acquisition and all their historic confidence that they were laying up treasures in heaven.

Social critic H. L. Mencken described Lewis's Babbitt character, and the real-world type on whom he was based, as "a sound businessman, a faithful Booster, an assiduous Elk, a trustworthy Presbyterian, a good husband. . . . [These are] the Leading Citizens, the speakers at banquets, the profiteers, the corruptors of politics, the supporters of evangelical Christianity."[15]

In the Babbitt character, English philosopher C. E. M. Joad saw the same trait that W. J. Cash detected in Charlotte society, a dogmatic belief that earthly commerce is a mystical mandate, producing extreme self-righteousness, or as Cash phrased it, a sense of being "handpicked for Grace."

Joad saw the fullest expression of Babbittry in the works of Bruce Barton, the most famous advertising promoter in American history and the creator of the American icon, Betty Crocker. In a best-selling book, Barton retold the Gospel, portraying Jesus as an up-and-coming, glad-handing entrepreneur. He "picked up twelve men from the bottom ranks of business and forged them into an organization that conquered the world."[16]

Though W. J. Cash's commentary on Charlotte's religious-economic zealotry was biting, he acknowledged its incredible practicality and effectiveness:

> This is the final secret of the town's unbending adherence to its ideals, and the key to its militancy. . . . Yesterday and today, it has made and makes uniformly for the prosperity and security of those who rule in Charlotte. What is more, it promises to keep on making for them indefinitely.[17]

Cash's use of the term "militancy" was not hyperbole. He meant that the furious economic activity taking place in Charlotte was driven by the same martial spirit that inspired the Confederacy, which was now aching for economic requital. He wrote: "Softly, do you not hear behind [the aggressive enterprise and skyscraper construction] the gallop of Jeb Stuart's cavalrymen?"

The drive of the South to regain its former status and wipe away the shame of the defeat of the Confederacy was acknowledged by Charlotte's leading booster and banker, Hugh McColl. In the PBS documentary about the implosion of Bank of America in 2008, McColl says:

> After the Civil War, most of the capital in the South was wiped out. What I saw as part of my goal in life was to see that we had our own banks in the South that could finance Southern industry and Southern businesses and Southern individuals. And I set out to do that, and candidly, have been fairly successful at it.[18]

The militant Calvinism and Civil War grudge also accounted, Cash argued, for Charlotte's acclaimed lack of protest or disruption from the poor or minorities who don't share in the bounty.

Cash attributed the seeming docility of Charlotte's disadvantaged and working classes not to overt repression, but the internalized belief among them that if they are not personally experiencing upward mobility, it's only their own fault and they should feel shame, not anger, at their circumstances.

> Do the peons in the mills begin to rise and protest that to work for five dollars a week — as they do work these last bitter days — is too much for human flesh and blood? Then what better answer than the Presbyterian answer that it is all God's will, ordained from the first day, and so to be endured quietly lest complaining draw down fire from Heaven? What better answer than the Scotch-Irish answer that, if the peon is exceedingly ragged of behind and lean of belly, it is because he is shiftless and unthrifty, because he and his fathers have succumbed to sin and sloth?[19]

In his masterpiece, *The Mind of the South*, Cash noted how Charlotte's commercial ideology began to make its mark on the urban landscape as early as 1914, as the first skyscrapers were built. Cash argued that these skyscrapers had almost nothing to do with real estate or economic need, as they did in Northern cities, but were purely for symbolic expression, like the cathedrals in medieval Europe. Charlotte, he wrote, "had little more use for them than a hog has for a morning coat."

> Look close at this scene as it stands in 1914. There is an atmosphere here, an air, shining from every word and deed. And the key to this atmosphere . . . is that familiar word without which it would be impossible to tell the story of the Old South, that familiar word, "extravagant."[20]

Cash acknowledged that the famed Scotch-Irish spirit for money-making, the "Protestant ethic" that Max Weber identified as the "spirit of capitalism," manifested itself in many other places in America. But, he said, "Scotch-Irish of Charlotte are no ordinary Scotch-Irish but the very peak and cap sheaf of their kind."

Following the end of the Civil War,

> Gigantism . . . set in immediately and has continued through all the years since, with the result that Charlotte today is a sort of holy town, a Lhasa of Calvinism. . . . Its God is not merely a Presbyterian; he is such a Presbyterian as it would be impossible to match anywhere else in the South.[21]

The Calvinist ethic and economic opportunism joined hands in Charlotte to such a degree, Cash observed, that the city made *church-going* one of its most highlighted features in *commercial* proposals and invitations to businesses to come to Charlotte. Cash wrote, the "Chamber of Commerce can reserve its proudest boasting, not for the biggest cotton-mill . . . but for the slogan: '*After Edinburgh, the Greatest Church-going Town in the World.*'"[22]

This has not changed despite the influx of hundreds of thousands from other parts of the country. Business boosters, not church officials or clergy, brag that Charlotte is ranked No. 8 in the country in churches per capita, with about one church for every one-thousand residents. Charlotte is also ranked near the highest among big cities for "religiously active" residents, at 83 percent. As one booster report stated, "everyone goes to church" in Charlotte, and there are 736 "religious venues" within the city limits.[23]

Charlotte is famously the birthplace of evangelist Billy Graham and the site of the Billy Graham Library. It was also the site of a 2,300-acre religious theme park built by Jimmy and Tammy Bakker.

Charlotte is currently home to one of the nation's ten largest megachurches. This megachurch, Elevation, is Charlotte's most popular "religious venue." It proclaims the theology of "prosperity," which holds that God bestows riches as a "blessing" upon those who believe fervently and financially support the church. Elevation Church has nine locations in the Charlotte area, attracting over 27,000 souls each week. The pastor lives in a 16,000-square-foot home with seven bathrooms.

In Charlotte, Cash observed, "Theology and the hog literally make one flesh. To question Babbittry is to question God, and to question God is to question Babbittry."

---

[1] *US News*, May 16, 2023, https://realestate.usnews.com/places/rankings/best-places-to-live (The ranking uses several factors, with the highest value placed on "crime" rates. The next highest factors are "Education" which measures college admissions of high schoolers only and "Well Being", which Charlotte ranked 5th in the state.)

[2] https://www.charlottesgotalot.com

[3] "Close View of a Calvinist Lhasa" by W. J. Cash, *The American Mercury*, Edited by H. L. Mencken, April 1933

[4] "Letter from the South" by James Baldwin, *Partisan Review*, Winter, 1959

[5] 'Play Displays a Growing City's Cultural Tensions" by Kevin Sack, *The New York Times*, March 22, 1996

[6] "Charlotte" by Tony Earley, *Harper's Magazine*, March 1992

[7] "Where the Wrestling Came From: Harper's Story Puts Us in a Bad Light" by Dannye Romine, *The Charlotte Observer*, Mar 1, 1992, p. 5B

[8] "Where is the Land of Opportunity? The Geography of Intergenerational Mobility in the United State" (https://scholar.harvard.edu/files/hendren/files/mobility_geo.pdf)

[9] https://www.wfae.org/race-equity/2022-03-01/updated-chetty-study-data-paints-a-surprising-picture-of-economic-mobility-in-mecklenburg-county

[10] https://www.wfae.org/race-equity/2022-03-01/charlotte-struggles-to-measure-progress-8-years-after-study-ranked-it-50-out-of-50-for-economic-mobility

[11] The report is published by *Wallethub,* a personal finance company that conducts consumer finance research and aids consumers in achieving financial security. See "Cities with the Most People in Financial Distress" by Adam McCann, Financial Writer, *WalletHub,* Feb 19, 2025 (https://wallethub.com/edu/cities-with-the-most-people-in-financial-distress/133346) For a local report on the *Wallethub* research, see "Charlotte Ranks among Cities with Most Residents in Financial Distress" by Symone Graham, Staff Writer, *Charlotte Business Journal,* Feb 24, 2025

[12] *Charlotte Opportunity Initiative, 2020 REPORT* (https://opportunityinsights.org/wp-content/uploads/2020/11/OI-CharlotteReport.pdf)

[13] *The Death and Life of Great American Cities* by Jane Jacobs, Knopf Doubleday Publishing Group, Kindle Edition, original copyright 1961

[14] "Close View of a Calvinist Lhasa" by W. J. Cash

[15] "Portrait of an American Citizen" by H. L. Mencken, *The Smart Set,* Vol. 69, No. 2, October 1922, pp. 138-140.

[16] *The Babbitt Warren* by C.E.M. Joad, 1926

[17] "Close View of a Calvinist Lhasa" by W. J. Cash

[18] *PBS Frontline,* "Breaking the Bank", June. 16, 2009, full transcript at https://www.pbs.org/wgbh/pages/frontline/breakingthebank/etc/script.html

[19] "Close View of a Calvinist Lhasa" by W. J. Cash

[20] *The Mind of the South* by W. J. Cash, Alfred A. Knopf, 1941, Vintage Books Edition, 1991, p. 219

[21] "Close View of a Calvinist Lhasa" by W. J. Cash

[22] "Close View of a Calvinist Lhasa" by W. J. Cash

[23] "These 15 U.S. Cities Have the Most Churches" by Jason Rossi, *Culture CheatSheet,* August 2, 2018, https://www.cheatsheet.com/culture/cities-with-the-most-churches.html/

VI. Searching In The Parks

It would be hard to identify any feature of a major city more important to Sense of Place than public parks. Parks are among the most visible public resources provided directly to citizens, along with public schools, museums, and libraries. They make indelible marks on children and young parents, attaching them to Place and making it feel like Home. Parks are free and open to all: rich and poor, ambitious and indolent. They accumulate and reflect local history. They are essentially noncommercial spaces: free of billboards, advertising, and marketing messages. People come to parks to balance or even escape the pressures of work and getting-and-spending.

Charlotte, according to data comparing it with other cities, has a problem with parks. The Trust for Public Lands ranks park systems in the 100 largest cities of America. This study places Charlotte in the bottom 10 percent. It is not a regional trend. Nearby Raleigh is ranked in the top one-third. It is not a function of a city's size. Chicago is ranked in the top five cities, as is Minneapolis.[1]

More than 60 percent of Charlotte residents do not have a close-by park, accessible by walking. The Charlotte Park system's ranking would be even lower except for some large-acreage parks recently constructed in remote areas. Total acreage is one criterion for overall ranking. Charlotte's allocation of land for parks is less than half the national average, and the city lags far behind the national average in per capita expenditures on parks.

A closer look reveals more extensive problems than the study's snapshot data indicate and shows little promise of significant change in the near-term. A recent report by the Charlotte area park officials showed poor conditions in over seventy parks and recreational facilities that would require as much as $100 million to remedy. Yet the budget for 2021 allocated only $5 million for these needs.[2]

Charlotte's most notable public park is Freedom Park, a one-hundred-acre park located in an older residential area near the center city. Couples get married in Freedom Park. Charlotte's relatively mild, though distinct, seasons are publicly marked there. The explosion of Japanese cherry tree blossoms in March heralds spring. The woods on the edges of the park proclaim autumn with brilliant coloring. When it snows, which is rare and brief in Charlotte, photographers rush to Freedom Park to get shots of children on sleds and building snowmen.

If the Transportation Center "uptown," where bus riders were herded away from the Square, is a Non-Place in Charlotte, Freedom Park is the essence of Place, one physical location known and affectionately remembered by almost everyone in the city.

City parks are significant urban markers of Place, and Freedom Park is the most iconic park in Charlotte. For these reasons, I present some of the untold history of Charlotte's Freedom Park—and my personal experience with the park—in my story about Place in Charlotte.

It is an almost unbelievable tale of how this beloved and iconic park was nearly lost by the people of Charlotte. In two different eras it was almost turned into a commercial theme park and, later, narrowly escaped being made into a national tourist attraction. How the park escaped these commercial attacks and remained a special Place for all Charlotte residents reveals also how Sense of Place can be defended and regenerated in any city.

Parks and Theme Parks

From the podium at the County government center, the project developer told government officials and a rowdy crowd of Charlotte residents in the audience that Charlotte's newest—and most distinctive—tourist attraction would build upon Charlotte's "brand" as a bastion of liberty and freedom. More to the point, he predicted it would bring more tourists to Charlotte each year than visit Pearl Harbor! The turn of the new millennium, which would take place the following year, would be greeted with the thunderous tolling of freedom in Charlotte.

The extraordinary new attraction was to be an exact replica of the revered Liberty Bell in Philadelphia—but far larger, weighing seven times more. Charlotte's bell, which at the time of this presentation was still being forged in Holland, would be the largest operable bell in the world situated at ground level—15,000 pounds, seven feet high and seven feet wide at its base. The promoter, a retired advertising executive, told the audience that when a 300-pound hammer struck the enormous bronze instrument, the liberating sound would be heard for miles. He reiterated that the Freedom Bell was an appropriate symbol for Charlotte as the home of the Mecklenburg Declaration of Independence, signed more than a year before the July 4, 1776, document in Philadelphia.

The promoter omitted that exact replicas of the Liberty Bell were long ago provided by the US Treasury Department to state houses in all fifty states.[3] He left out that the name "Liberty Bell" for the original bell in Philadelphia was coined *after* national independence, *by abolitionists*, referring to liberty for enslaved people, when North Carolina was a slave state. Forty percent of the Charlotte area population was enslaved at the outset of the Civil War. He also did not acknowledge that all credible historians regard the Mecklenburg Declaration of Independence document as a self-promotional myth.[4]

To the local officials who had earlier endorsed the bell project, though, this was all beside the point. They well understood that the "Meck Dec" enhances Charlotte's brand, as would the new Freedom Bell. In the epistemology of boosterism, truth is what sells.

But what was even more significant to the County Commissioners than yet another image-booster for Charlotte, is that the developer had received personal funding for the project from John Belk, former mayor, heir to the Belk family fortune, and the head of Charlotte-based Belk Inc., the largest privately owned department store chain in America. The bell's construction and site development were to be funded by the Belk Foundation, and there would be an inscription honoring Mr. Belk.

In Charlotte, whether to accept the magnanimity of someone of such great status—and in a gesture fusing patriotism with Charlotte boosterism—was not a matter for debate by mere elected officials. Only public displays of religious piety would be accorded more respect. The plan was quickly and heartily approved. The developer told the officials the project was "motherhood and apple pie." He said he couldn't even imagine opposition.

Charlotte residents first found out about the project after government approval, in a front-page newspaper article headlined, "Bells' Backers Hear the Sound of Tourists." The article heralded the coming of the "American Freedom Bell" to Charlotte, supposedly along with a million new, paying tourists.[5]

The one problem—and why there was a rowdy public meeting—was that this patriotic attraction, intended to bring millions in tourism revenue, was to be placed in Charlotte's most iconic and beloved public place, Freedom Park.

The developer and local politicians saw no problem with using the most popular public park in the city for a large tourism project. The director of parks said he thought the tourist attraction would "fit right in" with the park's "theme."[6]

Residents were shocked to hear of their park characterized as a theme park, a "fitting" place for commercial attractions—like an amusement park adding a new rollercoaster. Charlotte has a 400-acre amusement park, called Carowinds, which features an enormous roller coaster and attractions based on cartoon and movie characters. Residents had no thought that the Freedom Bell could be connected to Carowinds in any way. Yet, as in so many other seemingly disparate events in Charlotte, the same financial players and the same promoters, with the same myopic vision and the same obsession with money and growth, are the instigators and shapers. Nothing escapes the common "theme" of commerce.

As it so happened, the closest business associate of the funder of the Freedom Bell was, in fact, the creator and developer of Carowinds. To be shown in the next segment of this story, a far larger plan had been hatched just a few decades earlier, at the time Carowinds was first developed and opened, to make Freedom Park into a kind of sister attraction. That earlier scheme to convert Freedom Park into an amusement park, seven years in the making and involving tens of millions in proposed funding from local and federal taxes, was also stopped by citizen action, but the values and vision that gave it birth did not die. The Freedom Bell was but one of the progenies.

Freedom Park opened in the late 1940s for public recreation. It featured baseball fields, basketball and tennis courts, roller skating rinks, a pond for fishing and strolling around, picnic tables, and a landscaped amphitheater for occasional local events. At its opening, as with all other public facilities in Charlotte at the time, only White residents were allowed to use it. By the 1960s, Jim Crow was officially overthrown. Freedom Park was used and loved by everyone. If there were any "theme," for the park, it had to do with family, exercise, green spaces, and local gatherings. Freedom Park was about *home*, the antithesis of tourism.

The land for Freedom Park was not purchased with tax money but donated to the city by the Mecklenburg County Lions Club. Development costs were also mostly paid by private donors. A campaign was held to raise personal donations of $40 each from thousands of city residents to memorialize Charlotte's 10,000 residents who served during the World War, covering the $400,000 cost (in dollar values of the time) of park construction.[7] The name "Freedom" was selected after a public contest among citizens for suggested names.[8]

Six decades later, the Freedom Bell project moved forward. The ground at the proposed site was tested to see if it was stable enough to hold a massive concrete base to support the seven-ton bell and a structure to display it "at ground level" and uphold the weight of the anticipated tourists. The project would necessarily lead to much more concrete being added to other areas of the park. The plan called for tourists to have access to all available parking spaces, supplemented by buses from remote parking areas.

Freedom Park is located in a mature neighborhood of single-family homes with narrow streets. The residents would be hearing the bell's thunderous F-sharp reverberation in their living rooms. The intrusive sound, the increased traffic, the concocted ploy of "freedom" as a tourism hook—none of that caused a ripple of debate when the project sailed through government review.

What stopped the plans and put the entire project into question was a rare, well-organized protest of Charlotte residents. The residents pointed out that this was a public park, designed for local recreation and dedicated to local veterans of a world war. Yet, according to this plan, the park would become a national tourism attraction, driven by crassly commercial motives. The residents raised a basic question, a matter of public policy apparently not even considered by Charlotte officials or the park director, who saw a "theme"; by the former mayor, who was footing the bill; or by the project developer, who saw only "apple pie." How would the project affect the park and its *intended* use as a public resource for Charlotte residents, they asked?

Implicit in the leaders' routine approval was a core value, an unexamined belief, so embedded in Charlotte that it made approving the scheme virtually automatic. That belief is that public use of a park is a distant priority behind any opportunity to build the city's "brand" and bring in new dollars. Parks, and everything else, exist in service to Charlotte's development. It was never doubted that Mr. Belk's generosity had a dual purpose. What is good for business and good for Charlotte has always been seen as one and the same.

The logic of the tourism scheme was pecuniary, rooted in Charlotte's famous Calvinist heritage that, as W. J. Cash explained, views the "getting of goods as pious exercises peculiarly pleasing to Heaven." Nonpaying leisure, it follows, or any noncommercial activity other than church-going, is somewhat suspect. Poverty is defined not as lack of money but lack of enterprise. Parks, it could be logically argued, cater to and even encourage lack of enterprise.

To Charlotte's leaders, the phony Freedom Bell was real and important because it could be profitable. Within that logic, people strolling around the park's pond having quiet conversations, or a family picnic, or kids playing tag or catch, did not even show up on the ledger when measured against the economic benefit and boost to Charlotte's brand the bell would supposedly provide.

As a resident of the neighborhood near the park, I worked with my childhood friend and neighbor, William Convey, Jr., to organize that rowdy public forum where the developer laid out his grand vision of using Freedom Park to bring "more than a million" tourists. Growing up in that same neighborhood, I could walk from my backyard right into the park. I played Little League on the park's baseball diamond. I learned to play tennis on its courts and to roller skate on its rink. I spent much of my time as a child exploring every inch of the woods at the perimeter of the parkland with my friends. Later, like many Charlotte teens, I took dates to stroll around the park's pond holding hands and feed the ducks. To me and all others in Charlotte who loved and appreciated the park, the Freedom Bell was a home invasion.

So pervasive and unexamined is Charlotte's focus on growth and development that when the Freedom Bell scheme was announced, few residents fully grasped that Charlotte's leaders viewed that urban treasure as a promotional and development opportunity. Few could fathom that city leaders regarded the "passive" use of parks, in contrast to their exploitation as a major tourism attraction, as waste, lost opportunity, or even leading to moral decay. That reality only dawned on many at the meeting where residents spoke up for the park as a place of greenery, reflection, relaxation, and family gatherings. The developer, in a remark that provided a glimpse of the values and logic behind the scheme, retorted that the residents' view did not describe a park but rather a *cemetery*.[9]

The call for citizen revolt was sounded first in a letter to the editor entitled "Bell from Hell."[10] Robust grassroots organizing followed that soon gained the notice of those who had passively accepted the bell scheme as somehow normal and unstoppable.

As more facts were gathered, the absurd and destructive nature of the scheme became apparent and public outrage grew.

The leader of a nonpolitical neighborhood association and the *Charlotte Observer* editorial page, normally a backer of all things commercial, eventually chimed in to oppose placing the bell in the park. Finally, after that rowdy public meeting, involving placards and protest petitions, the County Commission reversed its decision to approve the bell.

In a city where history is infamously ignored or rewritten, the American Freedom Bell was relegated to a status of "historical" monument. It was installed at the Charlotte Museum of History, miles from Freedom Park and which many residents did not know existed. After repudiation as a tourism project, the developer recalculated his rhetoric away from tourism to exalt the bell's "historical" relevance. He described it as a "bridge" connecting modern Charlotte to the 1775 signing of a declaration of independence from Great Britain, omitting that historians regard that mythic document as an early product of boosterism, not unlike the bell itself.[11]

The bell was first officially rung at the museum on January 1, 2000. Predictably, as a dubious Charlotte historical monument, the Freedom Bell was a flop. In 2011, after years of financial struggle, the history museum that housed the bell closed its doors, though it was later able to reopen. However, visitors to the entire museum before closing were, on average, just sixty-one per day, a far cry from the promoter's prediction of about 3,000 daily coming into Freedom Park just to see and ring the bell.

There is a Facebook page for the bell. The bell is also highlighted on the museum's webpage. Its enormous size, the generosity of Mr. Belk, and the bell's claimed symbolism are noted, along with Charlotte's role in the Revolutionary War, including the dubious claims about locals declaring independence from England a year before 1776.

A local magazine's report on the temporary closing of Charlotte's history museum examined why the museum's financial support had collapsed. The report noted that the museum featured the "American Freedom Bell," but hinted that the museum's troubles were linked to a flawed approach to history—one shaped more by boosterism than Charlotte's authentic heritage. No there there.

> "Unlike the Liberty Bell in Philadelphia," the article explained, "which had a supporting role in real events, the 'American Freedom Bell', a gift from the Belk Foundation in 1999, is meant only to 'symbolize the patriotic heritage of the people of Charlotte.' Pretty? Sure. But something was missing."[12]

"A Landmark for North Carolina, Unique in the Southeast"

The failed scheme to use Freedom Park for the Freedom Bell tourist attraction might be dismissed as an isolated lapse in judgment brought on by the overblown vision of a persuasive ad man.

In fact, the bell fiasco was a direct descendant of an earlier and far more ambitious commercial scheme just a few decades before. Business leaders had attempted a much larger project aimed at deriving private profits from the public space most revered by Charlotte residents. Many of the residents who fought the bell were young and did not even know about the earlier scheme. They could not see the pattern.

Just as the bell's origins and its promoters' grandiose intentions have been erased from public memory, this earlier scheme has also vanished from official history. However, I had also been a leader on the front lines of that earlier battle and, when the bell scheme was announced, I knew full well what could become of Freedom Park.

The earlier scheme, a project called the Sugar Creek Canal, was the topic of almost daily news stories and government expenditures from 1968 to 1975. City officials considered resurrecting the project in the early 1980s. The Sugar Creek Canal would have used the entire length of the park and required cutting down surrounding woods, that great wilderness for me and my childhood friends, for parking lots. The plan called for building new street access into the park and introducing carnival-style amusements on the park grounds. Much of the surrounding neighborhood would have been transformed into apartments and businesses. A treasured nature center for children would have been moved away to accommodate tourism traffic.

Whereas the bell's initial costs were under a million dollars in today's currency, the canal project's start-up costs alone were projected to approach $100 million. And, whereas the bell scheme, from today's perspective, appears fake and silly, the earlier project, upon reflection, was blindly destructive, like the urban renewal that was also underway at the same time.

Commercial schemes in Charlotte, even if they involve displacing people and destroying beloved Places, are *presumed* valid if they can promise certain benefits. The benefits—increased tax base, new corporate headquarters, new development of any kind, population growth, or more tourism—must be measurable in dollars and cents.

The evidence for any of these benefits can be as flimsy as blue-sky projections presented with conviction and assumed authority. Charlotte had gone through a contentious episode involving fake projections just prior to the proposal of the canal project. Promoters made grossly inflated promises about one of Charlotte's largest publicly funded projects at the time, a facility called a "civic" center but intended for commercial use as a venue for business conventions. The promoters and city council promised that approval of the new facility would quickly generate $50 million in revenue, producing $1.5 million in new tax revenue (in dollars of the time). Five years after it was approved and with construction underway, it had generated only 16 percent of the promised private development funds or commitments for funds and only 5 percent of the promised annual tax revenue.[13]

Stopping such tax funded schemes—regardless of their absurdity or deceptiveness—requires not just challenging the alleged benefits and claims but, at a more fundamental level, upholding moral justification to stand in the way of Charlotte's "growth." There is almost never institutional support for such positions. Citizens who express disapproval of development schemes must be prepared to endure the local version of being "canceled." Citizen opposition to any project is smeared as "anti-growth," which equates to being considered "anti-Charlotte." For individuals, being so labelled can end careers. It is certain death to political ambitions.

Projected financial gains are thought-stopping in Charlotte, like a cult mantra. Promises of financial returns wipe away glaring realities, preventing leaders and the media from seeing the shortcomings of projects that would otherwise be easily recognized as absurd, inauthentic, and tawdry, like a phony Liberty Bell with fatuous comparisons to the Pearl Harbor memorial. City planners typically show no mercy in response to expressions of sorrow for loss of Home. Nonmonetary considerations carry no moral weight relative to promises of dollar gains for the city.

So compelling are such commercial schemes in Charlotte, they must be understood as expressions of an enduring and prevailing *ideology*, not as just greed or corruption. Adherence to the ideology will cause otherwise honest men and women to deny facts, keep secrets, betray constituents, and blatantly lie, if that is what is required to push through commercial schemes.

Freedom Park, created right after the Second World War, is a relic from an earlier time when noncommercial values still thrived with less need of defense or justification. Charlotte residents of the late 1960s and early 1970s, the time of the Sugar Creek Canal project, were likely still holding on to that older culture in which Place, history, and noncommercial values were still honored. For them, Freedom Park seemed sacrosanct. They did not anticipate that the park would soon be in need of protection, certainly not from their own city leaders. They were slow to realize how the city was changing and what was in store for them.

The neighborhoods most affected by the canal scheme were ones where most residents were White and most properties were owned by White people—people who had largely ignored the massive destruction of Black neighborhoods and properties that had begun just a few years earlier. They never dreamed the motives and beliefs behind urban renewal would ever affect them.

The canal project was, in fact, directly tied to urban renewal. The idea for it emerged just as African American homes, churches, and businesses were being bulldozed and plans were unfolding on seizing and repurposing the property, redesigning the "downtown" and rebranding Charlotte as "world class."

Some of that bulldozed land was located at the upper end of the newly conceived canal. It proposed that this land would be converted into a relatively large park. The park would feature a waterfall and an aquatic area where "gondolas" that would traverse the canal could turn around. The proposed park would utilize some of what had been the only park in Charlotte for African Americans, called Pearl Street Park. Now that the Black community that had used Pearl Street Park was gone, the new park, it was claimed, would spur even greater commercial development in the area. A few lone voices, all African American, called for affordable housing to be built on the property and provided to the people who had been displaced. City officials never seriously considered it.

At the other end of the canal was Freedom Park. One-third of the total length of the canal would run right through Freedom Park. According to the mayor at the time, John Belk, who later funded the Freedom Bell, the commercialization of Freedom Park was needed to create a new "landmark for North Carolina." An editor of the *Charlotte Observer* saw even greater potential, writing that the canal could "give Charlotte a unique position in the Southeast."[14]

At first, the canal was proudly touted, just as the now-derided Charlotte Civic Center had been, as a powerful stimulus for commercial development, the Holy Grail of local politics. Promoters claimed the canal would generate over $300 million (in today's dollars) of new development in Charlotte.

Sugar Creek Canal was said to be inspired by the *Paseo del Rio*, or River Walk, in San Antonio, Texas. The River Walk, a thriving commercial development and tourist attraction, dated to the Great Depression and was funded in part by the federal Works Progress Administration (WPA). Following a disastrous flash flood in the city that killed more than 50 people, the construction of a dam and a bypass channel tamed a bend in the San Antionio River that passed through the city. Architect Robert Hugman proposed that this bend in the river could be made safer with additional flood control measures and surrounded by commercial development. In 1939, the WPA funded the construction of walkways and bridges and planting of trees to beautify the area. The project alleviated the threat of floods, created much needed jobs in a time of mass unemployment, and revitalized a stagnant and crime-ridden part of the city.

Even with the Depression-era federal support, the River Walk might not have succeeded if San Antonio had not hosted the 1968 World's Fair. The World's Fair brought an infusion of even more funding to develop the River Walk and increased popular recognition of San Antonio. That fortuitous event was largely due to the political influence of then-US President and Texan Lyndon Johnson. The project grew into a major commercial center and tourist attraction with shops, restaurants, bars, hotels, breweries, and offices along its expanding route in the center of the city. The River Walk is authentic in the sense that it emerged from San Antonio's distinct geology and was developed as a result of historical events that shaped the city over several decades.

One Problem: No River in Charlotte

Charlotte hoped to copy the success of the River Walk, but from the start, this project had a major problem. There is no river in Charlotte! The water for the proposed "canal" was to be a no-toriously polluted creek, known as Sugar Creek. Not unlike the later plan to draw tourists to Charlotte to see a faux Liberty Bell, the proposed canal had no basis in tradition, environmental need or local history. Sugar Creek is named for a tribe of Native Americans who once lived in the area along the creek, but the canal plan had no relation to these people or their history.

Additionally, Charlotte could not gain federal funding by claiming the area for the proposed canal needed revitalization. It was not "blighted." It could not appeal to a job-producing program like the WPA, which had helped build the River Walk, or even claim a major flood issue that threatened life or property. Sugar Creek occasionally flooded and caused major property damage, but not in the area where the canal was planned. Incredibly, it was later admitted the canal might *exacerbate* flooding up- and downstream.

None of those factors were initially seen as major drawbacks, however. From the late 1960s, when the canal first appeared in the local news, the city found ever more ways to justify the project as a flood control measure, a boost to land values and the tax base, a parks and recreation program, and even as a beneficial outgrowth of urban renewal. The project was intended to spur development of a public park, corporate offices, and luxury condos in the now deserted acreage at the north end of the proposed canal, where a large African American community had been wiped off the map.

Secret Life of Tax-Funded Commercial Schemes

The chief promoter of Charlotte's Sugar Creek Canal was an otherwise inconsequential city council member, Jerry Tuttle, the owner of a small insurance agency. As with other grand schemes in Charlotte, including the largest and most disruptive of all, urban renewal,[15] the true faces and forces behind them are never known. Put in their places are often implausible and personally inconsequential characters, said to have a personal vision or some great interest in the plan. Tuttle was one such character.

The plan was initially reported as an original idea of Tuttle's after he visited San Antonio and saw the River Walk. He then relentlessly carried the torch for the scheme over the next four years or so, traveling back and forth to Texas and to Washington, DC, talking up what was presented as his "pet project" to the media. He played the role of a persistent, oddball visionary, only wanting to improve Charlotte.

In this manner, the massive project and its disruptive impact were trivialized, for how significant could the program be if someone as ordinary as this councilman could be its originator and chief promoter? The project was depicted as futuristic and idealistic, and therefore innocuous. It was never conceived as actually leading to bulldozers in neighborhoods. News stories appeared almost weekly, yet few citizens took any of it seriously.

The stories did not question whether such a scheme was advisable or ethical, especially when weighed against many other civic and human needs. Instead, stories focused on questions of whether the project was feasible theoretically, from an engineering perspective, and whether millions in federal funds might be obtained to support the project, potentially making it almost free for the city of Charlotte itself. When engineering feasibility was reported positively, the project was presented as *compelling*. Failure to move forward would squander the opportunity. Optimistic reporting regularly announced that federal funding was just around the corner. Federal money never arrived.

In 1974, the project suddenly became a top priority for the city council. Though no earmarked federal funds came in for the project, Charlotte was, however, to receive over $30 million (in today's money) during the first year of the new federal program called Revenue Sharing. This money was partial replacement funding for some of the millions slashed from various social programs under the Nixon administration, reallocated in block grants for use at the local level. Amazingly, the council voted to assign almost half of all that money to the canal, now chiefly promoted by Mayor John Belk, the city's richest and most influential person at that time. Tuttle's work was done.

For their roles in the canal project, Tuttle and Belk are in themselves of no real historical significance or interest, but they do shed light on a tactic through which commercial interests are able to influence public affairs while concealing their involvement, in Charlotte and probably other cities.

As noted earlier in this chapter, the canal scheme was hatched at the very same time a huge, *actual* amusement park, called Carowinds, was also announced for development. This commercial theme park was owned and operated by John Belk's closest business associate, Pat Hall, a person commonly characterized as "secretive" and a "wheeler-dealer." Hall was reportedly one of Charlotte's richest individuals. His home in the city's wealthiest area, Myers Park, looked like a Southern plantation, with a front lawn the size of four football fields. Hall had gained much of his wealth brokering transactions involving large tracts of land for industrial and warehouse use on the outskirts of Charlotte. The most notable and largest was a project on the north edge of Charlotte for production of Phillip Morris cigarettes.

The cigarette plant was over 3.5 million square feet in size, covering 500 acres. When Phillip Morris ceased production, the enormous facility sat vacant for nearly five years. Major tax breaks were extended for a lithium battery manufacturing company to use the building, but that enterprise soon went bankrupt. In 2019, the gigantic building was demolished, requiring more than a year for removal. It is now part of a 2,000-acre industrial site awaiting new tenants and more development. In 2023, the maker of a hyper-caffeinated canned drink announced plans to build a production factory on the site.[16]

A 1972 editorial in the *Charlotte News* linked Hall's soon-to-open Carowinds with the proposed canal, noting both would enhance Charlotte's "vacation potential." At that time, tourists visiting Charlotte were mostly limited to fans of stock car racing, but the editorial suggested that this would change with the "completion of the Sugar Creek Canal or some sort of downtown amusement park."[17]

Carowinds, Hall's 400-acre theme park, opened in 1973. It was insolvent within two years. Unable to meet debt obligations, it was taken over by a national company in the same year that the canal plan was almost finalized by city officials, just before it was stopped by a grassroots campaign of local citizens.

Exactly how or why the canal project became the top priority for the Charlotte government over other needs for which there were active citizen advocates is not known. Regarding any direct or even indirect connections between Carowinds and the Sugar Creek Canal—promoted at the very same time by Charlotte's two closely associated oligarchs—there is no public record.

In understanding how such tax-funded schemes are politically managed in Charlotte, and likely so in other cities, it is useful to understand that the force behind the canal, which was able to gain control of most federal funds coming to Charlotte, was certainly not Jerry Tuttle or even the city council and probably not even John Belk.

It follows that whoever was actually behind the scheme knew very well the plan would never gain public funds and support if the *actual* backers were visible. They also knew that if the full facts and total costs were disclosed, the project would be doomed. The distraction of a George Babbitt-type front man like Jerry Tuttle was necessary, along with invented economic projections and concealment of costs and impact. In its financial projections, for example, the city never included right-of-way acquisition; parking, street widening, and improvement costs; or the legal costs of eminent domain land takeovers. The projected direct costs to the public were almost certainly understated. This sort of public deception, misrepresentation and coverup by otherwise honest people was seen as for a higher cause.

Friends in High Places

Between 1970 and 1974, the canal scheme continued to gain inexplicable momentum. It was endorsed by the Charlotte-area congressperson Charles R. Jonas. Wally Hickel, the former governor of Alaska and US Secretary of the Interior, backed the scheme. Mitt Romney's father, George Romney, former governor of Michigan, then serving as US Secretary of Housing and Urban Development, added support. Mayor John Belk, now the canal's public champion, met personally with President Richard Nixon and reported that Nixon himself favored the project.

During this time, the project began to take on more detail, but no public hearing was yet held where residents could ask questions. News articles referred to the project as a "boat canal," describing amphibious "gondola" crafts. These water crafts would power up and down the creek filled with tourists, after the creek had been dammed, deepened, and made into a concrete channel. No news article probed a detailed accounting or disclosed the specifics of the plan and its impact.

Outside Agitator

As the well-oiled Charlotte machine of spin, front men, and media compliance moved the canal scheme forward, a new phenomenon for Charlotte was taking shape: grassroots opposition that was professionally organized. I was the instigator and agitator (not an "outside agitator," as I am a Charlotte native, though I was labeled as such anyway) behind the protests. I was working at that time as a professional community organizer, trained and inspired by Chicago's famed organizer, Saul Alinsky.

Once they were provided a forum to voice their opinions, citizens expressed not only opposition to the canal scheme but also long-simmering aspirations for improvements to their own neighborhoods. Citizens voiced demands for investment in neglected areas, especially those in the less affluent north and west of the city.

Residents held an evening rally billed as a Tea Party, where Mayor Belk was depicted as a haughty king and the council members as effete and compliant British aristocrats. The group demanded the city council hold a hearing to answer direct questions. They called for the local newspaper investigate the costs and impact of the canal. The meeting was led by people who Charlotte' leaders had never before had to answer to—a roofer and a truck driver from the blue-collar neighborhood of North Charlotte.[18]

This group was joined by another newly organized community group called Friends of Freedom Park who directly addressed the negative effects and misuse of Freedom Park. This group gathered signatures for petitions in the park and surrounding neighborhoods.

The emerging opposition took issue with facts that had been concealed or trivialized. Researching the project, for example, revealed a fact almost never referenced noted by the media during all the hype and coverage: that the largest single landowner along the canal was the Rouse Company, a national enterprise with over $350 million in revenue (today's dollars).

The Rouse Company was likely part of the group pulling the levers from behind the curtain. Rouse owned a large shopping mall and other properties along the route. It had a history of developing festival marketplaces (open-air or warehouse spaces with shopping stalls) and enclosed malls. Rouse is also regarded as the pioneer of food courts. Rouse was the owner of a large mall in San Antonio, ten miles from the River Walk. Rouse developed the entire town of Columbia, Maryland—a totally planned city operated as a private company and controlled by a board composed mostly of Rouse-connected people. To bolster the canal program, Rouse announced that it would donate some land near its Charlotte mall along the route of the canal.

It is worth noting Rouse's post-canal history and its later transactions with John Belk, a public promoter of the canal. Rouse was eventually absorbed by Brookfield Properties, which was vastly expanding its investments in malls and other commercial and residential properties all over the world. Brookfield currently owns one of Charlotte's largest malls, Carolina Place, which opened in 1991. The land for Carolina Place was owned by John Belk. This land was the originally planned site for the SouthPark Mall, which opened in 1970, but the Belk family and their partners, the Ivey family, later decided to locate the mall closer to town. Belk department store is an anchor in both the SouthPark and Carolina Place malls.[19]

Incidentally, Brookfield is the owner of Zuccotti Park, where the Occupy Wall Street protest occurred in 2011, in the aftermath of the financial collapse of 2008. An *Associated Press* story at the time revealed that Zuccotti Park, where thousands of protestors congregated and camped, was not a public park as many assumed, but was actually private land owned by Brookfield. The space was originally named Liberty Park, but in 2006, it was renamed for Brookfield's board chairman, John Zuccotti.

New York City has 500 such privately owned parks, under a plan that gives developers zoning concessions if they include small open areas in their projects. Yet, these parks or plazas are not truly public, just "publicly accessible" — and property owners often come into conflict with city planners over what limitations may be placed on their use. According to Gregory Smithsimon, a sociology professor at Brooklyn College, "Developers come up with new ways of making the plazas inaccessible." For instance, "If there's one little ledge to lean on, they put spikes on it."[20]

As the *Associated Press* report explained, there is no expectation that privatized parks accommodate a wide range of public activities, including protests. Jerold Kayden, a Harvard professor who has written about privatized public places, explains that these places were available for "eating a sandwich, taking a nap" but "weren't thought of as places to accommodate, you know, debates." During the Occupy Wall Street protests, Brookfield claimed its rules as a private property owner were being violated by the protestors. Thus, private ownership of public spaces has implications not just for recreation, but for political speech. Private owners may restrict public demonstrations and expressions of political dissent.

Like New York City, Charlotte has several essentially private parks in the center city. They are on public land, gained during urban renewal, but privately financed, designed, and developed. As noted in the chapter on Charlotte's downtown, an existing public park on the Square was recently demolished and privately redeveloped. Its name was changed from honoring Thomas Polk, the reputed founder of Charlotte, to instead honoring the former CEO of the Bank of America.

The Sugar Creek Canal was essentially to be a very large private park, intended for commercial activity and as a site for festival markets, with the added expectation that this destination would promote more private development around it. The one-third of the canal route that traversed Freedom Park would make the public park part of this larger private commercial scheme. At the other end of the canal route, a new public park was planned not for local residents but to stimulate more commercial development in that area.

Redefining "Parks"

The citizen opposition to the canal began to coalesce in late 1974 and 1975. Citizens argued that the canal was a boondoggle and that funds spent on it would be diverted from real and immediate needs. As the grassroots opposition grew louder and its message became more difficult to ignore or dispute, the city shifted its messaging, reframing the plan not as a development, but as an investment in parks and recreation, requiring a new concept of "park."

A recently elected female council member came forth—taking the same role as councilmember Jerry Tuttle had earlier—as new canal champion. In a news article entitled, "Canal Plans Change Course," she stated, "It's a park and recreation facility and that is how it should be looked upon." Yet only three months earlier, the newspaper had reported that "planners [of the canal] . . . hope to see nightclubs and restaurants and shops and more." The city director of public works said, "we're going to see mini-central city development." Neighborhood-based opponents received a letter from the Office of Revenue Sharing stating unequivocally that the city's use of revenue sharing funds fell "under the category of Economic Development," not recreation.

Part of the change in the alleged purpose of the project pertained to the upper end of the proposed canal. This part of the planned canal was adjacent to now city-owned urban land seized through urban renewal, formerly an African American neighborhood known locally as Blue Heaven. A twenty-two-acre parcel of that land was considered for a park that would tie in with the Sugar Creek Canal. Others wanted that area developed commercially, citing the sacred stand-by goal to increase the tax base, though it was later discovered that the commercial potential of the area had been overstated.

The idea of using the land for a new public park, though no residents lived nearby any longer, was quickly endorsed, not by the Park and Recreation Department but by a committee of the Charlotte Chamber of Commerce. In a report, the business group stated that "setting aside such open space creates prime sites along its fringes for highest quality development."[21] This new kind of park was intended to be an *economic stimulus*. City Council member, Jerry Tuttle, soon to be renowned for promoting the canal, was the main advocate for using this property for a park named after the obliterated African American neighborhood it replaced, Blue Heaven.

Almost "Heaven"

It would be difficult to overstate the irony of how the redevelopment of the former Blue Heaven neighborhood played out. At one point the plan was to develop a remarkable city park that was framed almost as a restitution for the terrible treatment of the Blue Heaven community. Conjuring lofty values of artistic beauty and urban tranquility in the bare, ruined landscape, a new park, it was said, would be a kind of heaven in Charlotte—Blue Heaven.

To realize that vision and to give the original commercially-motivated park plan a more public-oriented purpose, a local artist and designer, Jack Pentes, presented the city

Council a blueprint of a park modeled on Tivoli Gardens, the famed urban green space in Copenhagen, Denmark. He told the Council,

> "You can have a Blue Heaven all over again . . . this is an opportunity to replace ugliness with beauty, to give our people . . . in the central city something they've never had . . . there is hardly a place in the city today where an elderly man can sit down or where others can stop for 'spiritual food.'"[22]

Pentes's grand vision was presented after discussions of the proposed Blue Heaven Park had already devolved to a crass choice between a non-tax paying park and tax-paying, job-creating business. That framing of the choice, which inevitably tilts toward commerce over beauty and recreation, had prompted a long time and acerbic columnist for the *Charlotte Observer*, Kays Gary, to write that he was not surprised.

> "I don't believe the City of Charlotte has ever bought a square foot of land for park purposes . . . practically all has been given . . . The truth is that Charlotte power is business, first and last. That's the bond and blood and altar." He quoted a candidate for the state legislature as saying of the city council, "I believe they would sell Central Park for real estate development if they were on the New York Council."[23]

But the Blue Heaven Park plan, though no longer imagined as Tivoli Gardens, did not die. As a *commercial stimulus* for the still vacant urban renewal area, it maintained a pulse that was sustained by the far larger commercial scheme, Sugar Creek Canal. In 1970, the park plan shrank to just seven acres and underwent a name change. The newly proposed park would use some of the land of an existing but unused parkland that formerly served the demolished African American community. The park would take over that park's old name, Pearl Street Park.

Opened in the 1940s when Charlotte operated as an apartheid city under Jim Crow, the original Pearl Street Park was the *only* city park specifically for use by African Americans. It was largely unused after the nearby communities it served were destroyed by urban renewal.

In 2021, more than fifty years after the first public debates on a park at the upper end of the now defunct canal, the city re-opened Pearl Street Park, claiming the name honored the "first" (actually, the only) African American park.

The irony of giving the park its original name after removing from the area the people it was originally built for was ignored by the planners. The irony only intensified when Atrium, Charlotte's gigantic hospital system, developed most of the former Blue Heaven area. The new medical and educational complex is now called the Pearl Innovation District or "the Pearl."

How Place Is Lost, While No One Is Looking

The history of the Pearl Street Park offers a bitter civics lesson, the kind never taught in schools. This history teaches how Place can be taken away, right out from under people's feet, while they are looking the other direction. It helps to explain why the Trust for Public Lands ranks Charlotte in the bottom 10% of cities for parks.

The canal scheme showed how the public faces of projects are seldom the actual forces behind large development schemes. The business interests that stand to benefit most from these projects keep a low profile.

An even greater lesson is that public arguments over these projects about "increasing the property tax base," draw attention away from the details of the schemes and toward abstract questions of "policy." They are also often disingenuous. As it turned out, Charlotte's massive medical institution, Atrium, became the largest single developer of the land the Blue Heaven neighborhood was displaced from by urban renewal. Atrium pays no property tax. It is a nonprofit.

Even before Atrium took over, during the most intense years of debate, the 1970s, in which city parks were diminished for their great sin of not producing tax revenue, one large "development" was approved for the Blue Heaven area. It is a publicly owned, 180-unit apartment complex for the elderly. It is exempt from paying property tax.

How did a non-taxable public housing project get approval just when a public park for the same area was being derided as an uneconomical use of tax-generating urban renewal land? One clue was offered in a recent historical review entitled "The Vanishing Blue Heaven Park."[24] That research suggested one individual in particular got that nontaxable, $21 million (today's dollars) project approved. He was none other than Mayor Belk's closest business colleague, Pat Hall, the "flamboyant" developer of the giant amusement park that went bankrupt and the enormous cigarette factory that was later demolished. The article noted that Hall's obituary included a quote stating that he "always liked to keep things private."

Somehow, Hall, owner of one of Charlotte's largest and most ostentatious homes in the city, was chosen to look after housing needs for the elderly, disabled, and poor in Charlotte. In that benevolent role, the article reported, Hall said the Blue Heaven site was "recommended" to him by an architect who had worked for Hall's public housing agency and also just happened to be on the commission overseeing urban renewal land.

On the site where Charlotte's version of Tivoli Gardens, a local "heaven," had once been imagined, nine years later, a little park for the elderly was built to serve the senior public housing tower. It was given the name that the Tivoli dream park was also to have used, Blue Heaven Park. It was adjacent to the eleven-acre park that opened in 2021 using the name of the old park, Pearl Street Park, built under Jim Crow for use by African Americans who used to live nearby. The new park has pickle ball courts.

Reflecting Charlotte's new working definition of parks as *economic stimulators*, which was how the earlier, larger Blue Heaven Park was originally conceived, a county commissioner at the park's opening said, "The location of the park will make it a prime spot in Charlotte's 'innovation district' surrounding a future medical school. And there's so much more to come."[25]

The news reporter at that opening also interviewed an elderly man who once lived in Blue Heaven and came to see what became of his old playground and place where he used to gather with friends. "It was really sad for somebody to take your whole community," he said. "We didn't have anything left—nothing to bring your kids and grandkids to. They took everything, and this park is the only thing we have left."

This man was among those who were first to lose Place, his home, in Charlotte to hidden forces striving for recognition, status, and glory as the "New South" and, later, "world class." All Charlotte residents nearly lost Freedom Park, twice, and residents around the park nearly lost their community as they knew it. But the park and the neighborhood were saved with protests and petition and independent research, impossible for the residents of Blue Heaven in its days of destruction. The massive canal scheme was abandoned. The creek was eventually incorporated into a larger system of noncommercial greenways. The little, semiprivate park adjacent to the apartments for the elderly that had once used the now forgotten name, Blue Heaven, was later renamed Baxter Street Park.

History Redacted

As an aspect of Sense of Place, earlier events in a city shape future ones. Past events are mythologized to build a local culture that forms Sense of Place and attaches people to Place. Conversely, the redaction of history erodes and prevents the development of a local culture and its contribution to Sense of Place.

The Freedom Bell episode offers special value in understanding Charlotte's disregard for real history and how that disregard contributes to its constricted appreciation of public parks at icons of Place. But the history of the Freedom Bell and the understanding it offers, even as the bell sits in Charlotte's "history" museum, is redacted, not available. That it was to be the city's premier tourist attraction, using Freedom Park in its "theme," is nowhere to be found in the official Charlotte story.

So, too, has the entire story of the Sugar Creek Canal been redacted from Charlotte's official history. The greatest threat to Freedom Park, occurring less than twenty years after its construction, is a story untold in Charlotte. The redaction of the canal story erases the story of the largest and most effective movement of Charlotte citizens on a purely local issue. Protesters included a coalition of independent neighborhood groups, a senior citizens organization, and a local labor union, among others.

There is a *Wikipedia* page for Freedom Park. As of 2025, it tells about the creation of the park in 1948 and then skips right up to 2005, when a new park shelter building was constructed. There is nothing about past schemes to redevelop the park or how the park fits into city life. But even that reference to the shelter does not tell the full story.

The same residents who battled the bell also fought off park department plans to replace the old park shelter with a massive new facility. The original proposal that the residents stopped was another example of Charlotte's "gigantism." The plan included cutting many mature trees and building more parking lots, an observation tower, administrative offices, and kitchen facilities for large catered events. The outcome of the struggle was a modest building, scaled to the park's existing design and using the old shelter's footprint—without additional parking, with no observation tower, and with kitchen facilities only for smaller events. The entire campaign to push back on the scale of the shelter project is omitted from the *Wikipedia* entry.

Also not mentioned in the entry is the episode in which the park department planned to sell naming rights of Freedom Park to a Toyota car dealership. The plan involved placing signage at the entrances referring to the park as "sponsored by" the car dealer. The car business also planned to sponsor several events at the park each year involving rock music radio stations.[26]

Before those battles over the "shelter" and naming rights, the residents mounted another successful campaign to prevent many of the cherished Japanese cherry trees—the trees that herald spring in Charlotte—from being cut down. That story, a victory for Place and a lesson in how Place is protected, is told in a later chapter as one of Charlotte's "fireflies" of Soul that flash brilliantly but briefly.

---

[1] https://www.tpl.org/parkscore

[2] "Charlotte Parks Rank among Worst in U.S., According to Survey," *WBTV News*, May. 28, 2021

[3] In 1950, the Christopher Paccard Foundry in Charleston, SC was selected by the U.S. Department of the Treasury to cast fifty-five full-size Liberty Bell replicas—one for each state plus U.S. territories, to place on the capitol grounds of each state.

[4] *NCPedia* describes the *Meck Dec*, "The document emerged at a time when North Carolina was the sleeping and backward 'Rip Van Winkle State' and thus appealed to pride by establishing that the state was not only progressive but also in the vanguard of the independence movement.... a product of legend and patriotic sentiment, (it) most certainly never existed." (https://www.ncpedia.org/mecklenburg-declaration)

[5] *Charlotte Observer*, Jan. 6, 1999, 8-A

[6] *Charlotte Observer*, Jan. 6, 1999, 8-A

[7] *Charlotte Observer*, Fri, Jul 27, 1945, page 10, and *Charlotte News*, May 10, 1948

[8] The April 5, 1945, edition of the *Charlotte Labor Journal*, noted that the name "Freedom Park" was chosen through a contest in which over 400 residents submitted possible names for the new facility that was dedicated to the veterans of World War II. The news story also noted that coinciding with the end of the contest, and the choice of "Freedom" as the park's name, an essay competition was to be held in the schools on "Why is Freedom Park the most fitting tribute to our heroic men and women?" The contest was to be held only in the white schools, the story reported. Freedom Park was a segregated facility when it opened.

[9] *Charlotte Observer*, Feb. 17, 1999, page 4-C

[10] "Bell from Hell Endangers Freedom Park's Appeal" by Bill Convey, *Charlotte Observer*, Jan 19, 1999

[11] *Charlotte Observer*, January 1, 2000

[12] https://www.charlottemagazine.com/saving-history/

[13] *Charlotte Observer*, Jun 14, 1974

[14] *Charlotte Observer* editorial page, Jan. 16, 1971

[15] To this day, the entire Urban renewal program that dispossessed African American communities, drove out smaller and independently owned retail stores from the center city and redistributed the land to governmental agencies and large developers, is implausibly depicted in Charlotte as having been carried out by one person, a former mayor of Charlotte, Stan Brookshire, part owner of a small company that made industrial belts.

[16] "A Pair of Beverage Companies to Invest $740 Million, Bring 400 Jobs to Charlotte Area," by Catherine Muccigrosso and Hannah Lang, *Charlotte Observer*, July 28, 2023

[17] *Charlotte News*, May 29, 1972

[18] *Charlotte Observer*, Dec. 10, 1974

[19] It was reported in November 2023 that the 90-acre Carolina Mall, owned and managed by Brookfield Properties, had defaulted on a $149 million debt. The article noted the mall would have difficulty refinancing in a market of high interest rates. See "What's Next for Carolina Place Mall after It Defaulted on a $149 Million Loan?" by Catherine Muccigrosso, *Charlotte Observer*, November 01, 2023

[20] https://www.cleveland.com/business/2011/10/owner_of_occupy_wall_street_pr.html

[21] "Blue Heaven Park Wins Endorsement of Chamber Unit" by Stan Brennan, *Charlotte Observer*, Mar 9, 1968

[22] "Designer Pleads for Beauty" by Paul Clancy, *Charlotte Observer*, Jan 21, 1969

[23] Kays Gary Column, *Charlotte Observer*, Mar 06, 1968

[24] "The Vanishing Blue Heaven Park," *Sarah Stevenson Tuesday Forum*, August 28, 2021 (https://www.tuesdayforumcharlotte.org/2021/08/28/the-vanishing-blue-heaven-park/)

[25] *Charlotte Observer*, Dec 15, 2021

[26] "Car Dealer Wants to Buy Naming Rights in Park" by Carrie Levine, *Charlotte Observer*, Feb. 07, 2006

VII. Searching
In The Arts

According to the National Endowment for the Arts (NEA), engaging with art can "foster a sense of identity and belonging. It can promote and signal cultural vitality and communal values such as a tolerance of diversity and an openness to questions." The NEA claims the arts promote "ties that bind."[1] In short, the arts powerfully support a city's Sense of Place. Absence or loss of art, in turn, diminishes Place.

In a search for the Soul of a city, examining the state of the arts is particularly relevant. According to a 2023 report, the arts in Charlotte are "on the verge of financial crisis, or even collapse." The report predicts:

> Without a dependable, ongoing revenue stream, the Charlotte-Mecklenburg arts and culture sector could suffer major losses, with organizations of all sizes failing and artists leaving both the field and/ or the Charlotte-Mecklenburg area for opportunities elsewhere.[2]

The report was produced by the city government and the Foundation for the Carolinas, an organization funded by the city's wealthiest and most influential people. Funding for Charlotte's arts organizations had previously been allocated by the Arts & Science Council, but that organization, with close ties to banking, began to falter in the wake of the 2008 financial crisis. Eventually, the city government had to set up an "infusion fund" of emergency tax money to keep the major arts institutions afloat temporarily. The city gave the Foundation for the Carolinas the task of managing and allocating the emergency "infusion" funds. Thus, the role of allocating funding to arts organizations passed from the elite Arts & Science Council to the even-more-elite Foundation for the Carolinas.

The "crisis" discussed in the 2023 report pertains to larger arts organizations, such as the symphony, opera, and several museums, but it hints at a deeper and more longstanding problem that goes beyond funding these major arts institutions. In January 2023, the city's main journal of current events featured an article entitled "Charlotte Has an Arts Problem," acknowledging:

> The symphony, ballet, and art museums have loyal supporters but struggle to make a consistent impression among the public. . . . Actor's Theatre of Charlotte, the only professional adult theatre company in a metropolitan area of more than 2.7 million people, closed last year for lack of ticket sales and venue space. The city has a single theater dedicated to foreign and art film. Opera Carolina is a footnote, and, aside from a few local authors, we have no literary culture to speak of.[3]

Lucifer as Charlotte Art Director

An unpublished fable, written nearly a hundred years ago and attributed to Lincoln Steffens, the famed investigative journalist, may provide clues to Charlotte's arts crisis.

In his extensive investigations of city politics at the start of the twentieth century, Steffens gained fame by uncovering this discomforting fact:

> In all cities, the better classes—the business men—are the sources of corruption, but they are so rarely pursued and caught that we do not fully realize whence the trouble comes.

Steffens was bitterly attacked for this observation, but his meticulous investigations yielded proof of political corruption, including documentation of payoffs and first-person confessions. He indisputably proved the connections of honored people in high places to corrupt "machines" and "bosses." Steffens took the same unflinching approach to the arts, while respecting Bernard Shaw's admonition, *"If you want to tell people the truth, you'd better make them laugh or they'll kill you."* Steffens composed a wry fable to tell a basic truth.

Many millennia ago, according to this fable, a lieutenant to Lucifer, the arch-demon whose mission is to make human life burdensome and painful, reported alarming new developments on earth. Humans, he announced ominously, were learning to move their bodies rhythmically and joyfully with partners or in groups; they had begun to imagine and recite inspiring and exciting tales, giving meaning to the places they lived; they were creating images of nature with bold colors; they were composing lofty and rhyming words to depict beauty and truth; they invented instruments to make a harmony of sounds that lifted away pain, sparked laughter, and stirred movement. Humans discovered they could accompany the instruments with their own melodic voices, which gave them and the listeners great pleasure.

These inventive activities were spreading happiness and joy among the people. Anyone could participate. It cost nothing. It brought people together and reduced conflicts. The activities were relieving the scourge of work and other suffering that Lucifer sought to increase. They were diverting the humans from the fearsome knowledge of their mortality. Worst of all, the activities were being taught to the children, who were imagining ways to create a better future.

What can the mighty forces of evil do to stop all this, he urgently asked his demon master?

Perplexing the messenger, Lucifer showed no concern and told him he did not need to stop it. Instead, he said, he would prevent people from realizing the activities were innate to humanity and everyone could enjoy them for free. He would get them to believe they are costly and only for those with rare talents or tastes or special education and who could afford a high cost. He would ruin it for all future generations.

How can this be done, the devil's assistant asked in awe?

Lucifer replied that he would get the humans to call all these free and native talents and activities ART.

The fable may be fairly interpreted to refer to *earthly* forces with the capacity (equal to Lucifer's?) to persuade, manipulate, and dominate masses of people. The people using these forces would necessarily also have a motive for suppressing full and free artistic expression among ordinary people. These would be the same people Steffens had studied his entire career as an investigative journalist: those with extraordinary political and economic influence, including power over the media.

This fable describes the arts, much as Thoreau viewed connection with nature, as an existential exercise in *personal freedom*, supporting originality, individuality, joy, and expansion of human potential. The transformative power of artistic expression is innate, available to all, and virtually free. But, just as Thoreau perceived regarding human's connection to nature, the fable recognizes that forces exist that view such freedom as a threat, as diversions from the labor, purchasing, and productivity that are the source of their wealth and power.

The inquiry into Charlotte's arts "crisis" that follows puts a modern interpretation to this old fable. It reveals actors who never directly oppose art—indeed, they are acclaimed as patrons of the arts—but who define and control the arts in the city so they never become significant and *independent* forces. Rather, these actors ensure that the arts dutifully serve growth, enhancement of status, and capital accumulation or remain in enclaves where their spirit does not spread widely. In this manner, even as elites piously endorse major art programs, funding controls and other limitations are maintained. The arts stay low in priority, not just in funding but in how they fit into city life, essentially fulfilling Lucifer's fabled mission of shrewd and covert sabotage.

Given the city's quest for world-class status, the arts funding crisis disconcerted many leaders, just as the report that Charlotte was "worst in America for upward social mobility" had. Shouldn't Charlotte's national status and global reach *naturally* produce greater support for the arts?

Lack of economic opportunity and the absence of the spirit of the arts are both soul-stifling conditions for a city. Yet, the management and outcome of the upward mobility crisis does not portend well for the fate of the arts. Follow-up news analyses showed that, despite millions spent on "diversity, equity and inclusion," social mobility data did not appreciably improve.[4]

What prompted action was the published data putting Charlotte in a bad light. Revelations of the desperate position of lower-wage working people in Charlotte were framed primarily as a stain on Charlotte's *brand*. The possibility that the brand itself was a contributing source, even a cause, of economic entrapment, was never imagined. No structural reforms occurred or recommended.

Charlotte's response to the collapse of funding for the arts bears remarkable similarity. But where links between the city's hyper-commercial values and the fate of lower income residents might seem complex or vague, the relationship of those values to the arts is all too clear.

Art as Babbittry

To the inhibitions on artistic expression that Lucifer instilled in humanity in the fable, Charlotte's crisis sheds light on one more limitation on the arts in this city: *art must contribute to the Charlotte's growth and status, in the same ways conventions, tourism, new corporate headquarters, and continued growth of the iconic banks do.* This boosterism factor is present in other cities, but likely not to the degree it is in Charlotte.

Charlotte's insistence that art must contribute to growth and status is consistent with Hugh McColl's "common purpose" for Charlotte, "to make money, build nice things, make it happen."[27] The problem is that most art does not necessarily *make money*. It does not necessarily *build*. It displays, inspires, reveals, and provokes. Sometimes it deconstructs. Art is notoriously unfocused, unpredictable, and unprofitable. Many things might happen from art, but what those are cannot be known in advance. That's kind of the point of art.

McColl did not just shape the center city according to his vision. He is also the city's leading arts patron. A large old church downtown that has been converted into a well-equipped space for art shows and artist studios bears his name as its chief financial sponsor. More important, McColl is the inventor and architect of the corporate funding model for the arts in Charlotte, which subsequently failed as collateral damage of the collapse of his bank.

The requirement that art must express the interests and values of business is also consistent with the "pillars" of Charlotte, proclaimed in the giant monuments on the Square: *Commerce, Industry, Transportation,* and *The Future* (the pillar that originally was to be designated *Religion*). Art is absent, even from the style of the monuments themselves.[6]

The first paragraph of the 2023 report to guide Charlotte in rescuing the arts from its crisis defines the arts as a "creative ecosystem." But in this document, "eco" is best understood as standing for "economic." That is made clear in the description of would happen to Charlotte if the "ecosystem" died or migrated, which the report claims is imminent:

> The Charlotte-Mecklenburg area would lose many other opportunities such as talent attraction and retention . . . workforce development, tourism, and more. . . . [Arts] assets contribute to the city's vision to be a leader in arts and culture tourism, driving the community's economic development goals and contributing to continued development and growth.

The report does also reference the role of the arts in fostering inclusion and social cohesion. It also mentions the need to bring art to "corridors of opportunity," that is, to poor areas where even grocery stores, much less officially funded art, are absent. But statements made by top city officials focused on how the arts could support Charlotte's tourism industry.

Charlotte's mayor pro tem, Julie Eiselt, who headed the rescue fund committee, spelled it out in language that could have come from Lucifer in Steffen's fable. As reported in *Charlotte Magazine*:

> The city wanted some guarantee that the funds would support focus areas it had identified, especially economic development. City council members view the arts as a potential draw for visitors and an opportunity to bolster the pandemic-battered hospitality industry. "Our job," Eiselt says, "is to help get heads in beds. The Panthers [NFL] and Hornets [NBA] bring in millions of visitors and dollars. The arts have the potential to do the same thing . . . It's got to be treated like a sophisticated industry."[7]

Patrons and Peons

Before continuing the search for Soul in Charlotte's arts scene, we must look backward at how the arts crisis came to be.

Under the Charlotte model, which endured for decades, art was a very private affair, with little tax money involved. Funding was quietly managed by a tiny group of wealthy individuals through the Arts and Science Council (ASC). The peons of Charlotte, i.e., everyone else, had little or no involvement. Millions were raised and distributed to artists and institutions that the ASC deemed worthy. The public's contribution was mostly limited to paying taxes that funded performance facilities. Artists and art institutions became ASC wards.

Measured in the short-term, Charlotte's approach to art seemed to work well, prompting no self-examination. Charlotte's corporate and wealthy donors supported art that made Charlotte look good. Sponsorship of the arts, in turn, boosted the images of the business donors. Four institutions that have counterparts in most major cities were the standard bearers: the symphony, ballet, opera, and the city's main art museum, the Mint Museum. Financial support for the arts increased each year, garnering the national recognition Charlotte sought as a financial center and a place of refined and sophisticated taste.

Part of the physical structure of the Mint Museum is a reconstruction of an old US mint building that was located in downtown Charlotte in the nineteenth century. This mint made coins from gold mined in the Charlotte region. The mint was seized by the Confederacy when the Civil War began, and for a short while, Charlotte continued to mint currency for the slave states.

In the mid-1930s, decommissioned and facing demolition, the old mint building was privately purchased, taken down, and reconstructed in the city's wealthiest, most cloistered neighborhood as North Carolina's first fine art museum. Official Charlotte history promotes the mint's historical links to gold mining, now enshrined in statuary on the Square as the foundation of Charlotte's banking industry. Ironically, the preservation and relocation of the Mint building to its elite location was carried out by a federal job creation program, the Civil Works Administration, a New Deal agency that provided government-sponsored work to over four million unemployed Americans. The entire Mint Museum restoration project was completed at a cost of only about one million dollars (in today's currency).[8]

Despite its location in a prestigious neighborhood and the storied history of its building, the museum opened without a notable art collection of its own or funding to develop one, something unprecedented in the world of major urban art museums.[9]

Over time, leaders of the ASC basked in high status, acclaimed for executing a prudent, conservative, and efficient financial model for supporting the arts in Charlotte. The fund-raising program uncannily mirrored the growing status of Charlotte's fast-growing banks, Bank of America (earlier named NCNB, and then NationsBank) and First Union (later Wachovia and then Wells Fargo), which were also the city's major art patrons. Wealthy underwriters of the arts were like directors of a prestigious corporation. Favored arts groups played the roles of skilled artisans proudly serving the great company and its leaders. The refined works they produced made bank executives appear as modern Medicis.

The benevolence and world-class taste of Charlotte's art-patron-bankers is immortalized within the enormous lobby of the new headquarters of Bank of America, constructed in 1992, the tallest building in North Carolina. It is sometimes called "Taj Mc-Coll," recognizing the bank's CEO Hugh McColl's honorific roles as both financial wizard and leading arts patron. The massive granite and marble lobby has the feel of a medieval cathedral.

Upon passing through the immense front entrance, visitors instinctively lower their voices to whispers.

Towering over visitors and employees in the cavernous lobby of the skyscraper are three imposing frescoes, each measuring twenty-three feet in height. Ben Long, the North Carolina-based artist who designed and installed the frescos, also painted a commissioned portrait of CEO Hugh McColl.

What Long's frescos depict is unclear. They are said to be based on an esoteric school of Buddhist philosophy. Whatever they mean, they appear epic, dramatic, and biblical. One of the three panels depicts the construction of the landmark bank building, consecrating it in monumental scale and meaning. The workers' shovels are made of gold and held aloft like the spears of crusaders. These were Long's first secular frescos and the largest of all his pieces. Most of his work is religious in content and often placed in churches.

Private Funding and Artists

The success of Charlotte's corporate model of private funding, closely held management, and art-as-boosterism was tightly tethered to the fortunes of the banks. In 2009, the banks collapsed into insolvency, salvaged only by federal tax money. Simultaneously, Charlotte's arts funding model began a steep decline. ASC's fundraising dropped 34 percent in just one year after the banking catastrophe. The dependency of every major art institution on the failing ASC put the arts community at grave risk.

The 2023 city report on the distressed state of the arts in Charlotte attributes these troubles to the banking crisis (not the actions of the bank leaders) and the COVID-19 pandemic. But many artists and grassroots art organizations had been voicing warnings and complaints about Charlotte's approach to the arts and its private-equity values for years. Objections focused mostly on how money was allocated, affecting the ability of emerging artists to continue in their careers and the survival of artist-run organizations.

In a 2006 meeting with the president of ASC, a group of artists representing hundreds of local, independent artists from various fields asked a number of pointed questions. How did smaller artists fit into the ASC's plans for facilitating Charlotte's transformation into a "world-class" city? Were ASC leaders aware of developments in the arts at the street level? What criteria were used to allocate funds?

This group of artists noted that out of the $13 million in grants given out in 2006, only eighteen actual artists received grants, for a total of less than 0.25% of the grant money. The group pointed out that the ASC's fifty-seven-member board did not include even one professional artist or any individuals with formal arts education. How did the board members inform themselves about the art world of Charlotte, they asked?

The artists also probed the largely unexamined finances and operations of the prestigious and very private ASC. The top eight staff members at ASC made a total of $900,000 in 2005, they claimed. Meanwhile the average salary for a full-time artist working for a large affiliate arts organization (such as the symphony) was $32,000, with artists working for smaller organizations making much less.

The artists raised the delicate issue that the ASC president/CEO's annual compensation, with salary and perks totaling almost $400,000 (today's dollars), was almost $100,000 more than the money awarded all thirty-one recipients of the Community Cultural Connection Grant combined. They compared the salary of the ASC's vice-president of grants to the entire amount granted to "art initiatives" in the north part of the county. The VP got more.[10]

Voluntary or Else

Artists also voiced criticisms and warnings related to how the ASC *actually* got its money. When its sources—enlightened and generous banks and other corporations—suddenly declined, people asked how could such loyal, benevolent companies quickly and simultaneously turn their backs on the arts in Charlotte? Given that the allocations were tiny relative to the banks' vast assets, and in light of the enormous backing the banks received from the federal government, how could funding to Charlotte's arts get slashed?

The inquiries brought to light some information that was rarely spoken of and never critiqued in the media. The great majority of the corporate money was not coming out of company coffers, which would affect profits, but the pockets of the employees. The banks, the chamber of commerce, and all other major companies in the Charlotte area were using "workplace giving" to fund the Arts and Science Council.

The plan, described in a 2001 *New York Times* article as "based partly on the payroll-deduction," was ranked the best in the country for per-capita giving. The article compared this program for funding symphonies and opera companies to the United Way's fundraising, which is also based on employee payroll deductions, for services for children, victims of natural disasters, and the needy and elderly.

Ironically, Charlotte's United Way charity program became embroiled in its own payroll deduction controversy when it was revealed that it paid its president $1.2 million in salary, expenses, perks and pension contributions, the 4th highest in America for local United Way executives. Perks included season tickets for NFL Carolina Panthers games and a country club membership.[11] The pay was higher than Atlanta's counterpart who raised twice as much in contributions.[12]

In plainer terms, the Arts and Science Council funding system was an annual corporate shakedown of employees, who were brought into meetings called by management and asked by their superiors to pledge portions of their weekly pay. Failure to cough up could be a career setback. Going along was all but mandatory.

The *New York Times* article profusely praised Charlotte's "workplace giving" scheme. Charlotte's leaders saw this article as redeeming the city from the disgrace it endured just five years earlier in the same paper when church leaders and some politicians attacked the city's arts program over a performance of *Angels in America*, the award-winning play about the AIDS epidemic in the gay community. Back then, the *Times* called Charlotte a "Bible Belt town," to the horror of Charlotte's brand managers.

The laudatory 2001 story also included that hated term, but in a new context, one that remarked on Charlotte's transformation into "a center of the New South." Charlotte was described as a place where passengers "can fly directly to Europe," with a "cultural life considerably richer than many other comparable cities."[13]

The "driving force" behind the transformation, as the *Times* reported it, was bank executive Hugh McColl. McColl said the workplace giving scheme was planned without even the need for a public meeting, but by "consensus" of a small group of businesspeople he had contacted, and now it has catapulted funding for arts to new levels. Companies moving to Charlotte learn to participate, he said, if they want to be part of "Charlotte's business culture."

The article reported that in 2000, 70 percent of the corporate funding to Charlotte's arts came from employees in contributions automatically taken from their paychecks. The average annual contribution was about $350 (in today's dollars), but some gave much more. The article noted that "schoolteachers and construction workers [are] among the most faithful."

Critics pointed out the obvious. The funding program took money from people who could possibly not afford it and were unlikely to attend a symphony or opera performance and transferred it to organizations patronized largely by the city's wealthiest citizens. These critics saw the scheme as taking from many and giving to a few. Ironically, the *New York Times* article that glowingly described the plan was entitled "Spreading the Wealth."

Since it could be career suicide to openly challenge the program, resentment had no expression. This may partly account for the plan's dramatic collapse a few years later, resulting in the emergency tax fund for the arts.

The consequences of the forced program may also have spilled over into politics. Before the "infusion fund" was hurriedly established, the city tried to enact a tax-based version of mandatory giving to pay for arts organizations. A referendum was called for enacting a sales tax, the most regressive form of taxation. Voters in the city that the *New York Times* had described as a New South haven soundly rejected it. Seventy-eight percent of the voting precincts opposed the arts tax, with minority support for it coming mostly from downtown and affluent areas.

In the 2023 report on the arts crisis, the city and the elite Foundation for the Carolinas laid some of the blame for the private arts funding deficit on the employees no longer supporting "workplace giving." But there was no commentary on what "workplace giving" was, how it functioned, or why it collapsed. "The model that funded the Charlotte-Mecklenburg arts and culture sector for many years, *which included robust workplace giving*, no longer provides sufficient funding," it reported (italics added).

The report attributes the decline in workplace giving to the mysterious workings of the global economy, even making a prediction of an imminent economic downturn, sealing off any discussion of reviving workplace giving. "This trend [declining "workplace giving"] is expected to continue due to what many economists believe to be an impending recession."

One prominent art patron, also an artist himself, dared to lay out some nasty truths about "arts" funding in Charlotte in a featured editorial in the *Charlotte Observer*. He argued that "workplace giving" to the ASC disconnected the people of Charlotte from the arts community, achieving the very opposite mission of the arts. Money was siphoned to a private "broker," the ASC, without regard to the preferences of employee donors. Believing the arts were being fully funded by the ASC, which bathed in esteem and its own self-promotions, many local art patrons did not contribute directly to their favored arts groups. Thus, the centralized corporate model disconnected artists and art organizations from their own patrons. Arts organizations became helplessly dependent on the ASC.

Perhaps worst of all, the funds gained from compulsory workplace giving, officially called "voluntary," were credited to the company or its executives, not the individuals who complied with requests to donate. This created resentment, even hostility—*directed towards the arts*—which should have bound Charlotte together and lifted spirits.[14] Lucifer of the fable would have smiled.

Claiming Romare

With this background and with some insight into the requirements for boosterism imposed on ART in Charlotte, it should be no surprise that Charlotte, North Carolina, is not well known for art or artists. Few in any field of art come to mind as Charlotte-based, or even Charlotte-inspired. There is a Wiki page listing seventy-two writers from Charlotte. It is unlikely the names will be recognized by many people. I am included in the list.[15]

There is one major exception. Charlotte is home to artist Romare Bearden. A greenspace park was built and named for him in the center city. He is acclaimed as a native son.

Since his national notoriety stretches back to 1945, one might think Charlotte has celebrated its "son" for many years and that he might have been an inspirational pillar of the art world in Charlotte. But, of course, this could not be. Bearden was African American.

Romare Bearden was born in the home of his grandparents who were property and business owners in Charlotte. His father was also born in Charlotte. The family home, in Charlotte's Third Ward, was demolished and the entire area razed during urban renewal begun in the 1960s.

Racial oppression drove Bearden's parents from Charlotte when he was a small child. Romare Bearden's father was harassed and almost arrested by police in Charlotte when Romare was a little boy. Romare was much lighter complexioned than his father, causing the police to suspect he did not belong to his father or that his father was guilty of an interracial relationship. Romare's parents quickly departed for New York City, where he grew up. He did occasionally return to visit and stay with his grandparents before the family home and neighborhood were demolished by the city.

Bearden's art career began on his return from military service during World War II. There was a feature article in the *Charlotte Observer* as early as 1952 on an exhibition of Bearden's work in New York that noted his Charlotte birth.[16] Then, nothing was reported locally for about fifteen years, despite his growing international fame.

A longer biographical piece appeared in Charlotte in 1967, entitled "Charlotte Native Is in New York Art World Spotlight." A few years later the *Observer's* literary editor, Harriet Doar, who also penned the 1967 piece, included a paragraph in her column about the release of the new book, *The Art of Romare Bearden: Painting of Black America, 1931 to 1970.* She noted the North Carolina Museum of Art in Raleigh had just acquired its first Bearden piece—a collage, the medium Bearden is known for. She wondered why Charlotte did not have any of his work on display.[17]

The news report of the Bearden artwork purchase by the North Carolina museum noted that by that time Bearden's work had already been displayed in one-man exhibitions at the Corcoran Gallery in New York and Carnegie Institute in Pittsburgh. It also reported that his work was owned by the Metropolitan Museum of Art and the Whitney Museum of American Art.

By the early 1970s, Bearden was so well-known that the Museum of Modern Art produced a retrospective of his work. The show traveled to California and led to Bearden creating a large mural for the city of Berkeley for its city council chamber.

In 1976, the governor of North Carolina bestowed the highest cultural recognition of the state on Bearden, and he was given an honorary doctorate degree from a prestigious college north of Charlotte. He had been elected to the American Academy and Institute of Arts and Letters.

In 1980, an exhibit of Bearden's work was finally held at the Mint Museum of Art. An article in the *Charlotte Observer* announcing the exhibition noted that this was the first time that Bearden, sixty-five years old at the time, had been honored in the city where he was born. The exhibition included nearly sixty works. It was sponsored by Phillip Morris, whose company name and logo were prominent on all promotions. Phillip Morris was at the time developing the gigantic factory near Charlotte, brokered by Mayor Belk's friend, Pat Hall. The factory eventually made 155 billion cigarettes a year, mostly Marlboros.[18]

The Bearden show at the Mint Museum was accompanied by multiple stories in the media that focused as much on the prestige Charlotte was garnering from the show as on Bearden himself. One of the first articles set the tone. It was entitled, "Bearden Exhibit Will Put Mint on Cultural Map." The curator of the exhibit, Jerald Melberg, was quoted as saying that he had been "assured of national coverage" and that "art critics from major newspapers and magazines will be here." The event, the article stated, would bring prestige not just to the Mint Museum but to the city of Charlotte.[19]

In 1985, Bearden returned to Charlotte for an exhibition at Melberg's private gallery. Melberg, who had organized the earlier exhibition at the Mint, became Bearden's representative in the area. Charlotte's wealthiest held parties and dinners in Bearden's honor. From that point forward, Charlotte promoted Bearden as one of its own. Romare Bearden died three years later.

View from the Bottom (Memoir)

A small group of artists and supporters are gathered at the Charlotte Art League building, an old warehouse showroom. The space has been roughly refurbished and maintained by the sweat of volunteers. Tonight, we have gathered to hear a report about how our organization "fits in" to the Historic South End—the new name that consultants have devised for the area where we are located. This is a strange and off-putting theme—insulting, if we are honest—but we recognize the powers behind these fresh-faced presenters: the giant banks; real estate developers; and city planners responsible for permits, zoning, and traffic controls. We listen humbly. Until now, we had never been officially visited by any representatives from Charlotte's high places.

Our group, the Art League, is the anchor on the street that had been partially abandoned and dilapidated and some thought even a bit dangerous when the center was opened. The idea of the group having its own center in this forgotten area was conceived by a small group of women in the early 1990s, led by intrepid local artist Peggy Hutson. A lease was negotiated and an old warehouse and design facility became a nonprofit, artist-run center, dedicated to supporting emerging artists. Volunteers worked for a year—painting, installing lighting, and erecting wall separators to create studios, a small kitchen, and an open area that functioned as a gallery and classroom. The Art League quickly began to transform the area into the city's most vibrant arts district.

Following the League's lead, artists leased nearby spaces for small galleries and studios. In the same block, a funky delicatessen with a small beer garden opened across the street, followed by a non-franchise coffee shop and a burrito place. Food, coffee, and beer—simple and cheap. A distinct vibe developed that, like a work of art, cannot be fully described in words. There was a sense of liberation from the unspoken judgments that could be sensed elsewhere in Charlotte, and people made connections that would not occur anywhere else. Entry to the Art League and all the galleries was free. Snacks and wine were served, also for free, with donations requested.

The once-a-month, Friday Art Crawls attracted thousands of visitors and other artists. Affordable art was sold. Other artists got inspired to make their own art. Visitors represented the faces of Charlotte: all colors, young and old, affluent and barely getting by, button-down and purple hair, speaking different languages. All the divisions and status symbols silently imposed by the business culture were absent. No single corporation, benefactor, or institution dominated. There were no franchises, no monopolies, not even corporate sponsors. Planning and marketing were minimal and straightforward—no hidden messages, no embedded advertising. No one is getting rich or famous, but this arts area is enriching many people from all over the city.

Part of what gives meaning to the freedom and creativity around the Art League is that it is taking place just a short distance from the Square. It is urban, in the heart of things. It has history. The scene is diverse and inclusive without effort. The art created there is real art, initiated and sustained by emerging and established artists and art patrons. The artistic district of the Art League is an authentic Place.

The meeting with the consultants began with their telling us—like we didn't know—that the Art League has made a big contribution to Charlotte. Then, assuming an authority over us that we did not realize they possessed, nor had we consented to, the consultants inform us that the League needs to make major changes. They use oblique language, mostly in the passive voice, and cite agencies with intimidating initials. The consultants tell us that the Art League is viewed as "amateurish." They cite some internal disputes among members, as well as the unpolished appearance of the building. That's not appropriate for area's future, they say.

Major changes are coming to our district, the consultants explain: hundreds of new luxury apartment buildings, street upgrades. The new light-rail line, running on tracks directly behind the League's building, will be a momentous catalyst to new development. We have only seen a tiny beginning of what is coming.

Of course, we know about impending changes, but we still do not grasp the main message. We knew of the critiques of the artist-run League but didn't think they had significance to anyone outside our organization or perhaps to other artists. Financially, the center depends on no outside organizations. We think what we have created will endure based on its self-sufficiency, the spirit of creativity it generates, and because it brings so many people together. Meanwhile, it costs the city nothing at all. This is the dreamy way artists think.

Finally, they present what in the consulting world is called the "takeaway." It seems that for all we have been doing, unfortunately we are located in the *wrong area*. Our street is part of a sector of the city that will soon transform at an almost unimaginable scale, they inform us. Where we are is not a designated arts district.

While we had been relishing the "buzz" our art brought to the previously dormant area, others with grandiose ambitions and who owned, rather than rented, buildings around us had been formulating a vision for the neighborhood. A "branding and design" firm had invented a comprehensive, new identity for the area now to be called "Historic South End." The plan did not include spaces for little galleries and nonprofit art centers. It was for enterprises paying much higher rents.

In a news story by the local public radio station, the owner of the design firm confirmed what we at the Art League immediately thought when we first heard the name Historic South End—that it was a joke:

> That was tongue-in-cheek, because the truth is about Charlotte in general and South End in particular, there's very little that's historic. Charlotte's always been about boosterism—about inflating reality—so we thought it was a tongue-in-cheek nod to that history of Charlotte.[20]

Of course, cynical joke aside, the area does have history. Those who are from Charlotte or have been residents over the last decades know that not so long ago, in the area near our Art League building, there had been a major grocery store, movie theater, furniture store, popular barber shop, men's clothing store, and many other businesses. On land now occupied by a huge Lowe's home improvement center, there had been a small, independent laundry, owned and operated by my own parents. The businesses served the middle class and blue-collar sectors of what was known for about a hundred years as Dilworth and Wilmore. Dilworth is one of Charlotte's oldest neighborhoods. It includes, in one area, large and stately homes from the 1920s. Nearer to the League are small residences built for workers at the nearby textile mill and warehouse and distribution facilities for industrial operations.

This history is not the kind that fits the brand. It will need to be erased, like downtown was, and as events unfolded, it was determined that the Art League must disappear too. The nearly twenty-year era of a funky, friendly, and free arts district will vanish and be redacted from the official narrative.

Unsurprisingly, as the public radio news story recounted, the invented new name, originally meant as parody, didn't take off immediately. More "history" was needed. The brand manager, with fellow developers, promoted the lore of Charlotte's trolley cars, abandoned long ago and the tracks paved over for auto traffic. An old trolley car was purchased and placed in a large garage area as an attraction. For a brief time, a trolley ran on the tracks with the newly built modern light rail. Meanwhile, the brand manager convinced a client from California to open a brewery nearby and name it "South End Brewery." As the brand manager explained, "No one knew, really, what South End was as a district, but if this cool restaurant came out of it, well, people would know it then, right?"

South End boomed but soon the trolley and its garage were removed. The brewery closed. The Art League lost its lease and had to move out. For $2.7 million, a real estate investment company specializing in gentrification[21] purchased the buildings that housed the Art League and the burrito property. Most of the galleries met the same fate. The beer garden and coffee shop were demolished and replaced by an enormous, multistory office complex. One of the last icons of the neighborhood to go was Price's Fried Chicken, the city's most popular take-out chicken place. Simple, cheap food—which had added to the art scene's sense of freedom—went away with the galleries and studios.

As the consultants described these impending changes, we at the Art League did not envision these events, not at the scale and speed that they were occurring, and only now, as they say in the consulting world, are we "getting the memo." In the brief question period, I make a further inquiry about "arts districts." How is it possible, I ask, that this district—with the most art galleries, a self-funding, artist-run center offering affordable studio space, a gallery with juried shows, and art education, and where large numbers of Charlotte residents come each month to enjoy and support the artists—is not an "arts district"? What else could it be called?

They repeat what they said earlier about a new identity, Historic South End, with new apartments, high end retail, offices, and national franchise coffee shops and restaurants on the way very soon. Without the PowerPoint and laser pointer, they now speak more bluntly, a bit annoyed that I had not grasped the "takeaway."

In the convoluted logic of marketing, the area with the most artists is to be cleansed of art because artists are not part of the plan. A century-old neighborhood is to be demolished, given a make-believe new name that no one had ever heard of, and then declared "historic."

This transition period—during which the area is still part of Dilworth and Wilmore, and the Art League, small galleries, burritos and cheap beer define it—confuses the branding of "Historic South End." Driving out artists, pricing out galleries, demolishing actual historic buildings, all under the auspices of governmental planners and consultants, tarnishes the exciting story of revitalization. Revitalization means bringing life to what was lifeless. It implies a certain entrepreneurial spontaneity, not a product of brand managers and consultants. Our very lively era, with our pioneering center in old Dilworth and Wilmore and its vibrant art scene, doesn't fit the narrative.

Partly in confusion, and part obstinacy, I push on. If what is here now must be displaced because this is not an official arts district, then what *is* Charlotte's *official arts district* where artists wouldn't be displaced?

They refer to the section of downtown, a block below the "financial district," the city's most expensive real estate, where the prestigious new "uptown" Mint and Bechtler art museums are now located next to each other. Both museums are recipients of millions from the Arts and Science Council, corporate donations, a special tax on car rentals, in addition to private endowments. Across the street from the two art museums is the Gantt Museum. Dedicated to African American history and culture, the Gantt

Museum is housed in a four-story, 46,000-square-foot building, constructed at a cost of more than $18 million. It is named for Charlotte's first African American Mayor, Harvey Gantt, a close associate of bank CEO Hugh McColl and department store magnate John Belk, and one of the earliest and strongest promoters of the "world-class" dream quest. These institutions visually proclaim—mostly to out-of-town visitors—Charlotte's cultural sophistication and embrace of "diversity."

Art as Showcase

We all knew of the two prestigious museums, but few of us thought of their location as an "arts district." No artists could afford rent in the area. There were no public places to chat or argue. It is an intimidating, business-like neighborhood with the feel of a corporate office park. Nevertheless, we learn, this area is Charlotte's showcase "arts district."

As the plan evolved, we learned the district would be named the Wachovia Cultural Campus in honor of the Wachovia Bank, which planned to build a forty-four-story headquarters to anchor the "cultural campus." Wachovia went belly-up in 2008. The building was subsequently occupied by the offices of Duke Energy—Charlotte's giant utility company, the largest in America—and called the Duke Energy Building. Briefly, the "arts district" was called Wells Fargo Cultural Campus, after Wells Fargo took over Wachovia in a taxpayer bailout. But at this point, Wells Fargo was not in a position to use the new building. Later, the anchor building was blandly renamed 550 South Tryon, for its street address.

Today, Wells Fargo is reclaiming the tower and moving many of its employees from its three other uptown buildings into it.

Two enormous Wells Fargo signs—fifty-four feet high, 3,760 square feet in area—were installed on the building, one on each side of the tower. Bank officials said the giant signage is part of a "nearly $500 million commitment to enhance employee's experiences while working at the building."[22] Another aspect of the plan to "enhance employees' experiences" is a new requirement for employees to come to uptown to work at the corporate offices on more days each week rather than working remotely from home.

The massive signs reportedly broke an unofficial agreement with rival Bank of America not to dominate Charlotte's skyline with bank logos. Another large bank, called Truist, had already made its giant logo prominent atop the cityscape. No citizens directly opposed the Wells Fargo signage atop the "arts district," as some had when the Truist logo appeared in the sky. One local news organization asked various people for an opinion. The article on local reactions was entitled, "It's Giving 'Tacky': Mixed Opinions Erupt over Wells Fargo Skyline Sign Before It Even Goes Up." Besides calling the signs tacky, people quoted in the article wryly noted that each sign was larger than most Charlotte apartments or remarked that the money spent on the signs could be used for better pay for workers. But others acknowledged in their interviews that Charlotte is, after all, a bank town, and the signs merely confirm this.[23]

Though Wells Fargo is reoccupying its predecessor Wachovia's tower, during the time the bank was indisposed due to the mortgage crisis, financial backing of the culture campus was taken over by the foundation of Leon Levine, founder of the 8,000-store Family Dollar chain. It is not called Family Dollar Store Campus, however. In 2003, the Levine family sold that business for $9.5 billion. The district is now called the Levine Center for the Arts. Development costs exceeded $150 million.

The Mint was unique when it was founded in the 1930s for having no art collection of its own. On the other hand, the Bechtler, Charlotte's second most prestigious art institution and located in the Levine Center for the Arts, is unusual in that it was established as a *private and permanent* collection that cannot be exchanged for collections of other major galleries.

The Bechtler collection, characterized as "Midcentury European," was assembled by the Bechtler family, Swiss manufacturers of industrial filtration systems. Andreas Bechtler, a son of the company founder who lived in Charlotte and worked for the family business, inherited part of the collection. He proposed to donate the collection if the city would build a museum to house it, named after the Bechtler family benefactors.

Walking by the Levine Center for the Arts may not excite the art vibe experienced in the humble Art League area. But passersby know it's an area for art when they encounter the "Fire Bird" in front of the Bechtler Museum, a favorite of tourists and conventioneers. Officially entitled *Le Grand Oiseau de Feu sur l'Arche*, the statue stands nearly eighteen feet in height and weighs almost 1,500 pounds. Designed by a French-born artist, it was purchased by Andreas Bechtler and permanently installed in front of the museum in 2009, after it had been exhibited in various other cities for almost twenty years. The Charlotte art landmark features 7,500 small pieces of mirrors reflecting the skyscrapers, traffic, and museums nearby.

The statue depicts a mythical bird with stretched-out wings, perched atop a wide arch foundation. However, many Charlotte residents and visitors mistook the sculpture's design and meaning, and few understood its French title, translated as *Large Firebird on an Arch*. They saw a birdlike creature with long bowed legs in bell-bottom pants, reminiscent of the pose of John Travolta in the '70s film, *Saturday Night Fever*, dancing to Bee Gees songs. This icon of the "arts district" was soon fondly nicknamed *Disco Chicken*.[24]

Artists Starving (For Attention)

Institutional funding for the arts is in crisis, and ART in Charlotte is additionally burdened by boosterism. But a search for Soul also finds photographers, poets, painters, sculptors, writers, dance groups, musicians, filmmakers, theater companies, and independent art galleries that endure or even flourish in Charlotte. The vast majority do not receive official arts funding. But they do their part to foster communal values and "ties that bind," which the NEA says art, by its nature, enhances.

However, local, independent artists, the lifeblood of art in any city, proverbially starve from a great need being unnourished in Charlotte. This is the need for *recognition and respect*. Perhaps the most dispiriting of all responses to art and artists is to ignore them or regard them as irrelevant and unworthy even of notice, unless they serve the city's narrow commercial goals. This is Charlotte's equivalent of the requirement in some countries that art must adhere to a particular political ideology.

When arts funding collapsed, Charlotte's community of independent artists was suddenly discovered and prominently noted in the city report on the arts. The report disclosed, "Charlotte underperforms in employment in occupations of arts education, museums, theater, independent artists." The report also noted that compared to three other peer cities, Charlotte is at the bottom in employment for independent artists and performers.

This would be an important realization, if all meaningful artistic activity could be categorized as belonging to an "industry," which is the sense one might get from the city official overseeing the arts funding crisis. But art does not lend itself to this commercial definition, and artists themselves do not measure their work or their value strictly or even mostly according to commercial balance sheets. The Charlotte report on the state of the arts described the current situation of most artists to "self-fund" their work as "unsustainable." Yet, financial insecurity and "self-funding" have always been the status quo for independent artists in Charlotte and most cities.

Charlotte had commissioned a study specifically of independent artists, entitled, "Business Realities of the Charlotte-Mecklenburg Creative Community." Despite the commercial-sounding title, the study did reveal *noneconomic* factors—public attitudes, recognition of local artists, level of public interest—which artists themselves explained can be even more important than dollars and cents.

Of the more than 600 artists interviewed and whose data were collected, almost half expressed *dissatisfaction* in Charlotte. Reasons included "lack of presence of or support from the artistic community and lack of recognition of local talent, in addition to lack of sustainable work opportunities."

Also, among those *most satisfied*, the main source of satisfaction, the report noted, was "feeling supported by the community of other artists," though these respondent's satisfaction "did not tend to extend to a feeling that the Charlotte-Mecklenburg community overall was supportive of the arts."[25]

The report quoted one artist, voicing a sentiment shared by others, as saying:

> I love Charlotte. I love creating here, but my work is often seen as more valuable by organizations and businesses that hire me outside of Charlotte.

Art as Commodity

In general, artists in Charlotte cope with, and even expect, financial insecurity, as artists typically have everywhere in the world. Most artists are led by their imaginations and desire to create rather than because they anticipate financial remuneration. Charlotte's native son, Romare Bearden, went out of his way to never reveal his earnings. He is quoted as saying, "You should never go into art to make money. That comes—if it comes—as an accident and has nothing to do with the quality of art."[26]

The need of artists for recognition and respect, a need that comes before, for many, the need for financial return, is intrinsic to the nature of art itself. Separate from profit-loss measurements, which mercilessly govern business, ART is subject to public, personal, and professional "criticism" regarding formal quality, authenticity of message, and its effect on the viewer's sensibilities. An artistic production can be declared a creative triumph even if it is a financial failure. A failed business is generally granted no such redemption.

This esthetic valuation of art puts art outside the bounds of the commercial market, where Charlotte's report seeks to locate it and which leads officials toward commercial remedies. Art not only does not fulfill a market demand; it may actually offend or inflame. To view artists as producers of market-based commodities that fulfill consumer demands, add to the city's financial wealth, and enhance business and government leaders' reputations is to replace the spirit and freedom of the arts with ART, as Lucifer of the fable sought.

Art in a Bottle

Charlotte artists do face one economic factor that developed recently and existentially threatens their "sustainability." Their most basic logistical requirement—a place to work or perform—is becoming unavailable in Charlotte's hyperinflated real estate market. Due to lack of affordable space, the number of art galleries has declined in Charlotte, despite the city's booming population growth. Lack of galleries diminishes the public presence of art. Lack of studio space thwarts the development of even an underground art scene. Art must migrate. It was the rising value of real estate that wiped out the "arts district" occupied by the Art League. NoDa, another area, was also renamed, gentrified, and cleansed of most of its arts scene.

Attempting to address the threat of lack of studio space, which really could "starve" artists out of the city, the city's report highlights the arts center named for Hugh McColl as offering some artists "affordable" studio space. Rent for a twelve-by-twelve space at the McColl Center is about $500 a month, roughly double the rate per square foot of an average apartment in Charlotte, yet still more affordable than arts spaces in general.[27]

Following reports that independent artists were "underemployed" and many are leaving the city, subsidized rent at dedicated locations under the government or art patron management has become the main strategy to support independent artists in Charlotte. Artists no longer seek out and create artistic spaces. No space is affordable now. Instead, they are directed to pre-planned structures designated by the city government or corporate leaders for art and artists.

Directly across the street from the McColl Center is a recently opened and much larger subsidized studio space facility owned and managed by the county government. It formerly housed an office complex for law enforcement, social service, and licensing departments.

Called Visual and Performing Arts (VAPA), the facility also includes exhibition, performance, and teaching areas. It was originally the old downtown's popular Sears department store, later acquired through urban renewal and made into a county office complex. Studio rents at VAPA are lower than at McColl's, around $200 a month.

A trip inside VAPA is an immersion experience. In a labyrinth of hallways and three floors, including the basement, accessed through locked doors and elevators, the building houses as many as 400 artists and arts groups, all together in one building. There is a waiting list of more applicants. The Sherriff's Department continues to occupy office space at the center of the building, so the creative environment is interrupted by the sight of armed law enforcement officers going about their business.

Art fields represented in VAPA include drama, comedy, literature, photography, sculpture, wood working, murals, fine art painting, chorus, portraiture, and fabric artistry. Because of the facility's previous use as government offices, most of the studios are fully enclosed, separated by walls from floor to ceiling. The building is mostly windowless. There is a private parking area enclosed by a high chain-link fence, with one entrance and one exit.

By making space available at a low cost, VAPA helpfully addresses the restrictive real estate situation facing independent artists and smaller arts organizations. But the city's report acknowledged that lack of funding is not at the core of the crisis, at least with regards to independent artists. "Funding support is out there," the report observed, "But Charlotte has a ways to go regarding truly valuing working artists and creatives in the way they deserve to be *seen, valued, and supported*" (italics added).

With regards to artists being *seen, valued, and supported*, one shortcoming of VAPA is its antiseptic uptown location. Few artists or patrons would otherwise come uptown, which lost its connection to the rest of the city decades ago. As soon as someone steps outside, the center's art buzz vanishes instantly amid the traffic and towers. Pedestrians are rarely seen. There are no cheap beer, coffee, or burrito places nearby where artists and patrons can hang out. Enormous construction projects are underway in the area.

VAPA has been open for two years, yet few Charlotte residents know it exists. There has been minimal coverage in the *Charlotte Observer*. Artists report that many people still come to VAPA seeking county social services, which were moved two years ago. A sign in the front of the building directs citizens to where the various services are now located.[28]

Also notable is the sheer scale of nearly 400 artists and arts organizations concentrated in one standalone building. VAPA can only partly be treated as *additional* support for artists. According to its founders, VAPA came into existence as a response to the demolition of another art facility, Spirit Square, a treasured center of creativity in Charlotte. A former church, Spirit Square was used as a space for plays and exhibitions as well as artist studios. Most of the facility was recently demolished and all tenants were forced to move out. What is left of the building will become part of vast new complex of retail and office spaces. The public library was also recently demolished, along with the city's innovative Museum of the New South, eventually to be relocated to a giant new complex. Completion of the complex is years away. Some groups that had met at these facilities took refuge in VAPA.

Others now in VAPA were made artistically homeless by the closing of another nonprofit and subsidized art center, the Midwood International and Cultural Center. A historic grade school converted to a community center and subsidized by the county school system, it was home to community organizers, the League of Women Voters, art studios, music teachers, and photographers. The center also held the International House, which provided volunteer-taught foreign language classes and other programs that served newly arrived and undocumented immigrants. The Midwood Cultural Arts Center is being demolished for new luxury apartments.

Colonizing ART

These concentrated and subsidized art centers are somewhat analogous to the provision of affordable housing in the form of "projects" where the poor were concentrated, a form of cultural segregation. Art as a "colony" within the city, in government operated "centers" would be a modern adaptation of Lucifer's plan of restricting ART in the fable.

One more element to VAPA inescapably conjures the specter of colonization. The concentrated facility of hundreds of artists not only addresses the intolerable real estate cost factor, but also historical and institutional discrimination and exclusion of minority-identified artists and arts groups.

The city's report on the state of the arts acknowledged that, though White people are now a minority of the Charlotte's total population, three-fourths of art grants had gone to White-led and predominantly White arts groups and artists. According to report:

> Only nine of the 38 organizations that received ASC Operating Support Grants funding from 1991-2020 were African, Latinx, Asian, Arab and Native American-serving

organizations. This paradigm must shift for cultural equity to become a reality.

VAPA is a response to this history of unfairness and imbalance, but it remains under the supervision of the institutions that perpetrated the earlier discrimination. It was instigated and is currently overseen by the traditional White and moneyed arts establishment of Charlotte. Founding patrons include two large architectural firms, the county government, the ballet company, the McColl Center, and an organization representing the largest corporations in uptown. Current sponsors include the elite ASC, the city's Infusion Fund, the city government, and the ultra-elite Foundation for the Carolinas.

On the other hand, of VAPA's twelve founding members and current board, the majority represent groups that the city's report identified as excluded and underrepresented.

Concentrating artists within government-designed districts and creating corporate-style "culture campuses" is surely more nurturing for Charlotte's soul than the earlier pattern of sequestering art in elite neighborhoods. For independent artists, it is an advance over the fate of removal, redaction, and "revitalization" meted out to our Art League.[29] It may also save Charlotte from large-scale migration of artists to nearby small towns or other cities, which the city predicts would occur if no remedial action is taken.

VAPA is a visible break from the long-standing pattern of exclusion and the containment of ART as a private domain of the elites, dating back to the conversion of the mint building into an art gallery ensconced in Charlotte's wealthiest neighborhood. It marks the end of racial and ethnic exclusion in art funding, a vestige of Jim Crow.

The question remains as to whether the great talents and energies of VAPA's eclectic tenants will spread into other parts of the city. The role of art is to nurture the Soul of the city, and, according to the NEA, "to foster a sense of identity and belonging, tolerance of diversity, openness to questions, and ties that bind." Will VAPA limit the influence of the arts? Or support the arts in their mission of fostering connection?

[1] "How Arts Work," *National Endowment for the Arts*, https://www.arts.gov/sites/default/files/How-Art-Works_0.pdf

[2] https://www.charlottenc.gov/files/sharedassets/city/v/1/streets-and-neighborhoods/documents/arts/state-of-culture-report_web.pdf

3 "Charlotte Has an Arts Problem" by Allison Braden, *Charlotte Magazine*, January 19, 2023

[4] https://www.wfae.org/race-equity/2022-03-01/charlotte-struggles-to-measure-progress-8-years-after-study-ranked-it-50-out-of-50-for-economic-mobility

[5] "Charlotte's Power Elite Confront a New Order" by Ken Gepfert, *The Wall Street Journal*, Nov. 4, 1998

[6] On first seeing the giant statues on The Square, it is hard not be reminded of the old Soviet style art and architecture, in which art was used as a form of propaganda. Called "socialist realism," its purpose was to limit perspective and emotional expression, the opposite of real art. Soviet art promoted the claims and goals of the Communist Party, Charlotte's of the Chamber of Commerce. (https://en.wikipedia.org/wiki/Socialist_realism#:~:text=Socialist%20realism%20was%20the%20predominant,the%20Soviet%20Union%20in%201991)

[7] "The Queen's Gambit: Behind Charlotte's Arts Sector Shake-Up" by Allison Braden, *Charlotte Magazine*, March 7, 2022

[8] "Mint Museum—Charlotte, NC" https://livingnewdeal.org/sites/mint-museum-charlotte-nc/

[9] "Charlotte Has an Arts Problem" by Allison Braden, *Charlotte Magazine*, January 19, 2023

[10] References to this meeting are based on notes for the meeting that were published and circulated by attendees and on direct interviews.

[11] "United Way Perks for Gloria Pace King included Panthers Season Tickets, Country Club" by Lisa Miller and Julie Rose, *WFAE*, January 28, 2009

[12] "They Gave at the Office" by Frank Maley, *Business North Carolina*, Oct. 27, 2011

[13] "Spreading the Wealth; As a Booster of the Arts, One City Proves a Model" by Stephen Kinzer, *New York Times*, Nov. 12, 2001

[14] "The Cultural Life Task Force Missed an Opportunity" by John H. Clark, *Charlotte Observer*, July 6, 2004.

[15] https://en.wikipedia.org/wiki/Category:Writers_from_Charlotte,_North_Carolina

[16] *Charlotte Observer*, Aug 3, 1952

[17] *Charlotte Observer*, column by Harriet Doar, Sept. 6, 1970

[18] "Home of Future $740M NC Drink Manufacturing Site Has Storied, Troubled History" by Catherine Muccigrosso, *Charlotte Observer*, July 13, 2021

[19] "Bearden Exhibit will Put Mint on Cultural Map" by Ellen Scarborough, *Charlotte Observer*, March 16, 1980

[20] "The Surprising Story of Charlotte's South End" *WFAE*, June 10, 2013 (https://www.wfae.org/local-news/2013-06-10/the-surprising-story-of-charlottes-south-end)

[21] The firm is Asana Partners, a private equity company based in Charlotte with offices around the nation and in Europe. See "Art Gallery Moving to a New Home in Another Trendy Area" by Ely Portillo, *Charlotte Observer*, Dec 16, 2017. A Google search of "Asana Partners and gentrification" affirms the characterization.

[22] "Wells Fargo Proposes Major Change to Charlotte's Skyline" by Matthew Ablon, *WCNC*, September 27, 2023

[23] "It's Giving 'Tacky;' Mixed Opinions Erupt over Wells Fargo Sign before It even Goes Up" by Alexandria Sands, *Axios Charlotte*, Oct 2, 2023

[24] *Roadside America* describes the Charlotte art district icon: "French-American artist Niki de Saint Phalle. She died years before it was purchased and moved to the front of Charlotte's Bechtler Museum of Modern Art—and perhaps that's for the best, since locals have embraced her work not as a serious piece of sculpture, but as 'Disco Chicken.' Standing 18 feet tall, covered from top to bottom in shards of shiny glass, it does indeed suggest a barnyard fowl wrapped in a coating of mirrored disco ball, with 1970s Soul Train flared pants and a strutting John Travolta pose straight out of *Saturday Night Fever*." (https://www.roadsideamerica.com/story/28428). *Trip Savvy*, the vacation-planning website similarly notes the "affectionate" nickname and describes it along with "the *Il Grande Disco* and the four statues in the middle of Uptown." (https://www.tripsavvy.com/firebird-sculpture-charlote-583845)

[25] https://www.charlotteiscreative.com/wp-content/uploads/2022/08/REPORT-Business-Realities-Charlotte-Mecklenburg-Creatives-August-2022.pdf

[26] *The Charlotte Observer*, October 5, 1980

[27] The studio spaces at the McColl Center are advertised as a "prestigious address." Spaces of 9x9 or 12x12 are advertised from $135 to $400 per month. See https://mccollcenter.org/press-news/a-prestigious-address. In January 2024, the McColl Center advertised a 154 sq. ft. (about 12x12) studio for $485.10

p. mo. (https://mccollcenter.org/artists/thestudios). The average apartment is described as 941 sq. ft. and costing $1653 per mo. (https://www.rentcafe.com/average-rent-market-trends/us/nc/charlotte/)

[28] A search of *Charlotte Observer* articles from 2021 to present turns up only 13 references to VAPA, including routine announcements of events and features on groups or artists. Author interviews with several of Charlotte's leading fine artists revealed they were unaware of VAPA's existence or had not visited it.

[29] The Charlotte Art League struggled for survival after losing its center in "Historic South End." The organization gained a new location in an industrial park near the light rail train line, in expectation of diverse new development of the area. It gained $30,000 from the city "infusion" fund. (https://www.charlottenc.gov/CS-Prep/City-News/Arts-and-Culture-Advisory-Board-Awards-More-Than-719K-to-Artists-and-Creative-Groups). After moving to the new area, it was forced to move to another nearby building, and then it was verbally notified of eviction due to an unpaid rent balance of $200,000. Its director and entire board resigned. Today, it is in a smaller space with new leadership and some of its debt forgiven. It continues to offer affordable studio space to as many as 50 artists. The continued operation of the Art League is testimony to the resilience and tenacity of independent artists. See "Charlotte Art League Avoids Eviction, will Stay in NoDa Home" by Nick de la Canal, *WFAE*, May 19, 2024 (https://www.wfae.org/arts-culture/2024-05-19/charlotte-art-league-avoids-eviction-will-stay-in-noda-home)

VIII. SEARCHING IN THE NEIGHBORHOODS

There would seem no greater locus of a city's Soul and social character than its neighborhoods. Whatever else may occur in a city, the most important measure of the quality of daily life is where we reside, where we lay our heads at night, right?

Or so it seems in myth, memory, and imagination. Yet, are there any television series currently set in neighborhoods or that are about neighborhood life? What novels address neighborhood drama and interactions? How much of our social network is embedded in our neighborhood? What about work connections or family relationships? Are neighborhoods today where we "live," or—in the terminology used in some African American communities, long faced with discrimination and absentee landlords—where we "stay"?

In a thought-provoking piece in *Wilson Quarterly*, author Tom Vanderbilt dared to raise the obvious question, "In an era of global cities and digital communities, do we even need neighborhoods?"[1] This is part of the larger question addressed at the start of this book, is Sense of Place now just obsolete sentimentalism?

In every city, job mobility, absentee-investor ownership, and technological change, as well as rising home prices and rent, are at odds with the ideal of stable, nurturing neighborhoods. But Vanderbilt's question is especially pertinent to Charlotte. Its mission to be "world class," to erase old identities and continuously reinvent itself, inherently conflicts with neighborhoods—the bastions, at least ideally, of constancy and shelter from commercial intrusion.

Unlike measures of park acreage per capita or levels of support for arts, there are few quantitative metrics that could be used to evaluate neighborhood life or assess Charlotte's neighborhoods as expression of social character. Levels of home ownership are often cited as indicators of "home." Charlotte's owner-occupied rate is about 20 percent lower than the national averages.[2]

We can learn more by examining the history of Charlotte's neighborhoods. In the 1970s, I was an instigator to a neighborhood activism movement and witness to the movement's birth. Neighborhood organizations began to challenge the values of Charlotte's power structures. This led to a reshaping of city government. Charlotte's neighborhood uprising—like the battle to save Freedom Park, which was part of this movement—has been left out of Charlotte's official history. Yet this movement was a significant event in the history of Charlotte's neighborhoods and offers insights in our search for Soul in Charlotte.

Neighborhood Paradox

Tom Vanderbilt's inquiry into the history and current state of American neighborhoods reveals an apparent paradox: the concept of neighborhoods tends to take on more importance precisely when neighborhoods as places where residents are connected by social ties come under threat.

In all cities today, neighborhood life is diminished by work-driven transience, commercial development, prohibitive home pricing, and digital social networks. Yet virtually every city in America now claims to be a "city of neighborhoods." In an Orwellian feat of PR, city boosters highlight what the cities' own commercial goals and actions tend to degrade.

Charlotte's official PR website, charlottesgotalot.com, reflects the national trend toward hyping neighborhoods like tourist attractions:

> Lush parks and greenways, cozy diners, world-class museums, lively breweries and quirky boutiques—Charlotte's neighborhoods draw their distinct characters from these hallmarks. Discover the city's beautiful boroughs for yourself.[3]

"City of Neighborhoods" was appropriated as a marketing tool from Chicago, which really does have a mosaic of neighborhoods. These neighborhoods have meaningful histories, and they are integral to Chicago's system of governance. The conversion of what is real to something abstract for marketing purposes recalls the definition of "lifestyle," which, as will be seen, solves the paradox.

Many Charlotte neighborhoods are under constant pressure from rezoning, road building, gentrification, and redevelopment. A member of my family lives in a pleasant, stable, and affordable suburb, a neighborhood near a large mall, with modestly sized homes built in the 1970s. A developer spent nearly a year canvasing homes, making tempting buyout offers, with a plan to acquire the whole neighborhood of single-family homes in order to demolish them and redevelop the area with upscale homes, offices, apartments, and condos. City planners support this type of neighborhood takeover as "infill," providing greater density to accommodate growth and boost the tax base. This is a modern, privately funded form of urban renewal, now displacing middle-income families.

Those in the neighborhood who wanted to take the financial offer were outraged that others (like my family member) blocked the plan by refusing to sell. Those who wanted to stay likewise resented the eager sellers. The neighborhood's Soul was badly torn.

The "boroughs" —a term *never* actually used in Charlotte— that Charlotte's official website recommends visitors "discover" include dense concentrations of newly constructed apartments and recently rebranded and gentrified areas. The website also promotes a vast, upper-income suburb at the far edge of the city limits that could be "discovered" only after a long drive and easily seen only through a windshield. There is little to walk to in the community. A nearby large business district must be driven to and is intersected by a six-lane roadway.

The list of "boroughs" does include some smaller and older areas near the center city that are walkable, have history, and feature mixed housing styles. They are near public parks, though these parks may not be "lush." Perhaps one of these neighborhoods has a museum, though it may not be "world-class." These areas are small and among the most expensive places to live per square foot. Many are also losing whatever "distinct character" they might have. Older homes are being replaced with McMansions, and "quirky boutiques" are being displaced by franchises.

The paradox Tom Vanderbilt identified, that neighborhoods came to be celebrated "assets" of cities only as they came under threat, occurred in two main phases: an era of commercial and industrial expansion in the early twentieth century, and a later era of suburbanization and White flight that began in the 1960s.

In the first phase, some of Charlotte's oldest residential areas disappeared or shrank under early commercial and industrial expansion. Those early city neighborhoods in Charlotte and elsewhere were integral parts of the central business district, or they grew around a mill or factory.

Their disappearance or reductions by roads, loss of public transit, industrial expansion, rezonings, and plant closings set off the first phase in the ennoblement of the "neighborhood." Today, in Charlotte and other cities, the remains of those old areas are celebrated and preserved. Large parts exist today only in photos, or in simulated styles, having vanished long ago.

The threats to Charlotte's historical African American neighborhoods were more extreme. Most housing was absentee-owned, with abominably substandard conditions. All of these neighborhoods suffered from neglect, lack of facilities such as parks, and lack of city services such as code enforcement. All were geographically restricted by legalized discrimination. The largest African American community was eliminated entirely by urban renewal. Well before White communities began to "defend" their residential areas in Charlotte, African Americans experienced their neighborhoods as enclaves of security and identity, real Places with meaningful histories, *under threat*.

W. J. Cash mockingly described Charlotte in 1933 as the city was well into this first phase of decline of older residential areas and the new "neighborhoods" had begun to grow. He witnessed what he termed, "so called skyscrapers, a girdle of factory villages and subdivisions, of warehouses and spur tracks, of chain stores and filling stations, of country clubs and snooty suburbs." In the center city, he described "two or three blocks of moribund old houses set back in shaggy lawns along North Tryon Street" (now home of Bank of America skyscraper) as it descends to the Seaboard depot (later demolished and moved much further out), and African Americans residing "in alleys" (which were later demolished with urban renewal).[4]

According to Vanderbilt, as cities became larger and more diverse, and populations became more mobile, city planners and home builders looked for ways to make new residential areas "feel more local." What emerged were what we think of today as "neighborhoods." Unlike the old communities, which had a mixture of home styles and sizes, and had businesses or factories mixed in or close by, the new neighborhoods varied according to just one factor—level of affordability. Each one was a housing monoculture, with homes of all approximately the same price level.

People can move into one of these developments from the opposite end of the country and still have a sense of familiarity. Most are designed with a school within walking distance. Businesses and major roads are at the outskirts, discouraging cut-through traffic. Some have public parks within walking distance.

Vanderbilt notes that Jane Jacobs saw in these ubiquitous housing developments "a confining sterility." Jacobs described these neighborhoods as "artificial towns" with simulated "village life." Without "means for civilized self-government," she questioned how these new neighborhoods could give meaning to city life.

Despite criticisms, the new style of neighborhoods only multiplied. No new model has replaced them. Newer neighborhoods only differ in their higher density, poorer quality housing, and even greater sameness.

The next and far more powerful phase of neighborhood "threats" came with Fair Housing laws, urban renewal, and inner-city turmoil. This was the era of White flight, when the expression "There *goes* the neighborhood" spread among middle- and lower-middle-income White homeowners.

For Charlotte, perhaps a bit later than some larger cities, this prompted the era of sprawl and creation of exurbs, as many people chose long commutes over urban ties. Textile mill towns whose residents used to pour into Charlotte for shopping and entertainment became "bedroom communities" whose new residents rarely come into the city except to work.[5]

Within the city, urban renewal displaced entire Black neighborhoods, while new antidiscrimination laws, enacted nationally, made it possible for African American families to move to or purchase homes in areas that were formerly forbidden. People's lives and social networks were disrupted as housing and commercial development in the "inner city" was removed in order to build luxury condos, faux brownstones, sports stadiums, government centers, office towers, and museum districts. Some of the poverty that had been geographically concentrated in the center city shifted into the older suburbs.

Boss Jim Crow

At the beginning of the twentieth century, investigative journalist Lincoln Steffens uncovered that major business interests were behind the "political machine," run by corrupt "bosses," in the cities he wrote about. If he had researched midcentury Charlotte, Steffens would have found those same business interests controlling everything, but without the need for a machine.

Had Steffens looked in Charlotte for a "boss," he would have discovered not a Boss Tweed or even a Mayor Daley, but *Jim Crow*. Segregation, often portrayed only as restrictions on public transport or who could order at lunch counters, was, first and foremost, a coordinated system of political control. Segregation oppressed all Black people, but it also functioned to politically disempower White people who were not affluent or well-connected. As Charlotte historian Pamela Grundy wrote in *Legacy: Three Centuries of Black History in Charlotte, North Carolina*, "Without Black allies, working-class Whites lacked the voting strength to challenge elite priorities, and their voting rates declined as well. To solidify their hold over the state, White leaders wove White supremacy into every aspect of daily life, building a system that became known as Jim Crow."[6]

Under Jim Crow laws, Charlotte operated segregated park systems. There was only one park open to people of color. Black children could not use the city swimming pool. There was a separate hospital for Black patients. African Americans could not enter White-patronized restaurants or motels. Some retail businesses had separate entrances for African Americans, and separate bathrooms and water fountains, notoriously not kept as clean. Black people were restricted from most jobs that offered a living wage. Housing was strictly segregated and there were very few homes available for Black people to buy. My own parents' home, purchased in 1948, had a standard clause in the mortgage that the property could only be sold to a person of the "Caucasian race."

Jim Crow, Neighborhood Realtor

Boss Crow was also a major force in real estate. Segregation shaped all Charlotte neighborhoods and created one of Charlotte's most lucrative income sources for some real estate owners. Over 90% of the housing units in Brooklyn, the largest African American community, were owned by absentee landlords, i.e., landlords who did not live in, and rarely visited, the properties they rented out. Black tenants could not move except to the few other segregated areas, and therefore had virtually no bargaining power. Among the absentee Brooklyn property owners (actually living just a couple miles away in the affluent southeast) were some of Charlotte's most prominent White families and business owners.

A 1960 news feature in the *Charlotte Observer* listed some of those names and revealed how these mostly renter communities were the most profitable real estate in Charlotte. The housing units generated more than 50% returns *each year* from rent payments. With little code enforcement, the cost of repairs was very low. Property tax was minimal, as it was based on assessed valuations, not revenue. About $10 million *a year* (in today's dollars) in rent payments were transferred from the poor Brooklyn residents to wealthy Charlotte landlords.[7] Under this apartheid system, properties in other Black neighborhoods would have generated similar money transfers at these extraordinary rates of profit.

By the 1960s, Charlotte was forced to cast off its Old South identity. Jim Crow was officially overthrown. Brooklyn was demolished. The absentee landlords were paid for their properties, which were transferred to the government for use by government agencies or resale to businesses.

It was the destruction of Brooklyn that opened the second phase in which neighborhoods took on a new salience in Charlotte. New and better homes for the forcibly displaced residents were not immediately planned or built. No comprehensive, workable plan existed at all for a new use of the land. Without immediate need or public interest, only one justification could be acceptable in conservative Charlotte for the government to seize 238 acres of private property and remove 2,000 homes and businesses. The reason crassly advanced was that it would be extraordinarily *profitable*, on a scale greater than under Jim Crow. A front-page story in the *Charlotte Observer* entitled, "A New Brooklyn—It'll Pay Dividends," made the case.

> Suppose city officials could look out City Hall windows some morning and see it as Urban Redevelopment officials say it can be ten years from now. . . . [They] would grab each other and dance down the corridors. They would have found a gold mine!

The story further explained that a consultant "foresees a demand for the area for businesses" and that city officials "say they get more inquiries about space and land for these purposes than for any others."

The article offered one illustration of how the tax value of a parcel of Brooklyn land, just taken over by a White-owned business, produced double the taxes—meaning the land's value had already doubled.[8]

When Saul Alinsky Came to Charlotte!

It was during the second phase of the ascendency of "neigh-borhoods," in the early 1970s, that the previously innocuous word "neighborhood" became a loaded political term. Charlotte's neighborhoods rose up and made demands for direct represen-tation, quality of life, and residential stability. From that conflict, Charlotte's neighborhoods would later devolve to become the "beautiful boroughs" hyped by city boosters.

It was at this time when Charlotte residents broke, at least par-tially, the Jim Crow model of political control that "wove White supremacy into every aspect of daily life," as historian Pamela Grundy described it. Though federal laws and court decisions ended the reign of Jim Crow, vestiges of its political system re-mained in Charlotte. The entire African American population was treated as one single element. White residents were manip-ulated with racial fears, while services were neglected outside of the elite area where city leaders lived.

The new neighborhood groups that mobilized at this time were not focused on racial equality, but addressed daily life con-ditions for all residents, other than in elite areas, that Jim Crow had covered up or kept in place. Most remarkably, the neighbor-hood movement involved coordination and cooperation between mostly White and mostly Black associations. This community or-ganizing drive was conducted with guidance from the famed or-ganizing training school of Chicago-based Saul Alinsky and was brought into conservative Charlotte—by me.

I had studied Alinsky's work in college, traveled to Chicago to gain training in his seminars, and was idealistically inspired by the profession he had created, "professional community or-ganizer." Alinsky's Training Institute that I later attended was in a modest suite of offices on Michigan Ave. in the middle of Chi-cago's Loop. There I sat with young community organizers from other cities, social justice activist Catholic priests, Latino farm labor organizers, African American civil rights workers, Quaker peace movement leaders and others to learn how ordinary people can build power through grass roots, democratic and peaceful organizations.

Alinsky gained national prominence from a profile of him and his work in the very popular book in the 1960s by Charles Silberman, *Crisis in Black and White*, and later in a powerful profile in *Harper's*. Saul Alinsky died suddenly of heart failure in 1972 but his organization, Industrial Areas Foundation, continues with community organizations in more than sixty-five cities across the United States and in other countries.

Alinsky's approach is not liberal or conservative. It is about building "people power," the building block of local democracy, using publicity, petitions, voting, boycotts, and other forms of peaceful direct action. Jim Crow, conversely, was about suppressing democracy. What made Alinsky's views "radical" is that he pointed out how existing structures of leadership were related to the problems that affected neighborhoods. Change required building new networks of power. Community organizing was a *disruptive* process of finding and training new leaders and building organizations as new structures of local power. This was achieved through the hard work of addressing neighborhood issues that were *immediate*; not vague, idealistic, or achievable in the distant future; *concrete*, having direct and understandable effects on daily life; and *winnable*, producing actual, measurable change.

This method of focusing on practical, daily-life issues and using the unity of people as leverage was a bulwark against race-baiting, which diverted attention away from those same issues and sought to divide people. The goal was to assemble all the various elements of community, like beads on a necklace, into one new and unifying democratic association.

My work began in North Charlotte—the area now gentrified and renamed NoDa. At that time, North Charlotte was mostly White with some Black residents, all blue collar, with many former workers of the textile mills that were recently closed.

The organizing work began with mundane conditions like rodents in vacant lots. Later, as the newly formed "North Charlotte Action Association" strengthened, it was able to change citywide policies on trash pickup. Eventually, the group had enough influence to prevent the local school, Highland Elementary, from being closed. The school board had frozen funds intended to upgrade the school. Only after protests and petitions by the neighborhood association were funds released. The breakthrough came with a decision to expend over $2 million to upgrade the school. This was likely the most significant victory which enabled the community to hold together.[9]

Over a five-year period, I organized groups in about ten other neighborhood areas, among them Plaza-Midwood, Elizabeth, Hoskins, Ashley Park, Camp Greene and Westerly Hills, forming a multi-neighborhood coalition. This coalition eventually fielded a "neighborhood" slate of candidates, called the Charlotte Neighborhood Council, for seats on the city council. I also assisted with forming a local senior citizen activist group that succeeded in lowering fares for public transit.

I organized neighborhood action groups in the former textile mill areas and older neighborhoods close to town. One reason several of these areas are able to persist today with distinct character is that the neighborhood leaders in that era petitioned to *downgrade* zoning on some streets to prevent home demolitions. On the westside of Charlotte, the groups sought better ambulance services, among many other needs neglected in that area.[10]

Several of the groups fought against road extensions and widening. One group blocked cut-through traffic by parking cars on both sides of the street, bringing traffic to a standstill while residents held placards about neighborhood safety. Initially, the complaining residents were told traffic flow took legal precedence over neighborhood concerns and could not be impeded. The implicit logic was that traffic flow helped commerce; neighborhood safety supported Place. Commerce trumped Place. Residents persisted and won new signage restricting turns into their community during rush hours. Today's ubiquitous speed bumps on neighborhood streets and new cul-de-sacs are partially the legacy of that effort.

It was one of these new groups that saved Freedom Park, Charlotte's equivalent of New York's Central Park, from being turned into a tourist attraction with the Sugar Creek Canal, as discussed in chapter six.

To protest the city's skewed priorities that neglected neighborhoods, a coalition of groups staged a protest on the very visible overhead walkway — later demolished — between government buildings. The protestors handed out bogus dollar bills with the picture of Mayor John Belk printed on them. On another occasion, we deposited bags of leaves at the door of city hall to protest proposed sanitation service cutbacks. Services were reinstated. The neighborhood groups from various districts were frequently at city council meetings confronting the city's leaders.

Neighborhood activism gained institutional structure and spread to more areas when I ended my work under the original grant to the Charlotte Area Fund, which had restricted me to the North Charlotte neighborhood. I organized a seminar of various Charlotte labor, church, and neighborhood leaders and brought Richard Harmon of the Saul Alinsky Training Institute to Charlotte to conduct a two-day seminar. The group raised about $200,000 (in today's dollars) to enable me to work independently for several more years in any neighborhood. The group called itself Charlotte Citizens Action Council. It was led by a prominent physician, Raymond Wheeler; Caroline Miller, the wife of another doctor; and a prominent pastor, Harcourt Waller. Waller was active in opposing the Vietnam War. He led efforts to offer support to Black students and maintain calm in the newly integrated public schools. He was fired from his position as pastor for reasons that were undisclosed but were generally believed to be connected to his activism in Charlotte.[11]

I also worked with several mostly Black associations to oppose expansion of Charlotte's airport. This was the campaign that likely awakened city leaders to the inevitability of changing the structure of city elections to better represent Charlotte's population. Officials viewed the airport expansion as key to growth and bringing national recognition to Charlotte.[12] Neighborhood groups, and a senior citizen association I organized, defeated the airport expansion bond in a referendum by a margin of 53 percent to 47 percent. The city had proposed spending $320 million (in today's dollars) to expand the airport terminal.

The unified *financial* interest for Charlotte to get the enormous facility that exists today was reflected in the newspaper headline on the day after the voters soundly rejected using tax funds to expand the airport: "Five Councilmen Favor 2nd Vote on Airport." The story featured a large photo of a grim-faced Mayor Belk, one of the wealthiest people in Charlotte, and two other council members who reliably represented "downtown" watching the devastating voting results. There was almost no media coverage of the defeat itself or about the opinions of voters, only a public declaration that, one way or another, Charlotte would expand its airport, with funding from local taxes.[13]

Previously, it had been possible to pass bond referendums with the combined votes of affluent White people and a secured block of Black voters, overcoming the unorganized and disaffected lower and middle-income White areas. The upset showed that this model was no longer working.

Neighborhood activism eventually led to a citywide referendum in the late 1970s in which the city's governance was changed to create districts that were each represented by a member of the city council, giving direct political voice to each section of the city.

The referendum was held after a coalition of neighborhood groups organized a petition to put "district representation" on the ballot. Most of the incumbent council members opposed it, as did the mayor and department store magnate, John Belk, and other established business interests. The district plan won by a tiny margin of less than 100 votes.

Challenging Charlotte's Great Divide

Government "like a Business"

Since 1945, Charlotte operated with an "at-large" city council. The system was said to be run like a business, without self-dealing politicians, for the equitable well-being of all. Every citizen could vote for candidates for all seven council seats.

In reality, it was Jim Crow in a business suit. The council was all White, and almost exclusively male. (One woman served a few years during a thirty-year period, and one other woman was appointed to serve out the term of a male councilmember, a bank executive forced to resign over a conflict of interest in city dealings with his own bank's properties.) Nearly all councilmembers, male or female, were connected to major business interests, and all resided in the same wealthy southeast quadrant of the city.[14] The seven councilmembers were assured of their own "district's" support. The rest of the city was unorganized, often dispirited, and never aligned on alternative representatives.

People in the other three quadrants of the city saw the council's actions very differently from how the council depicted itself in its self-promoting narratives, but these parts of the city had no voice. Their disaffection and resentment reflected the issue author Jane Jacobs foresaw as the weakest aspect of the new "neighborhoods"—self-government. She wrote:

> Let us assume (as is often the case) that city neighbors have nothing more fundamental in common with each other than that they share a fragment of geography. Even so, if they fail at managing that fragment decently, the fragment will fail. There exists no . . . all-wise "They" to take over and substitute for localized self-management.[15]

Charlotte's all-White and southeast-skewed city council absurdly claimed to be that all-wise "They." Eventually, one African American man, Fred Alexander, was admitted. His family owned a funeral home. He worked as property manager of a large all-Black rental housing development, owned by one of Charlotte's most powerful White families. His election was depicted as resolving the representation needs of all African Americans in Charlotte. It was still claimed that a city council selected with an at-large election system could represent everyone equitably.

Four years later, another candidate, Joe Withrow, was allowed in to represent the city's west side, where many middle-income and blue-collar White families lived. This "westsider," a real estate developer, was treated as if he represented the residents of that one area, while the other members, who resided in the affluent southeast, were characterized as magnanimously representing the interests of the whole city. The hypocrisy and inconsistencies of the old model were showing stress.

Whites Can't Be Organized

The question of how race was used as a force of control drove the decision of where I would start my organizing efforts. A nonprofit organization, the North Carolina Fund, provided funds for my work. The organization was started under direction of North Carolina governor Terry Sanford as a state-level precursor to the national War on Poverty of President Lyndon Johnson.

Leaders at the North Carolina Fund were acutely aware that racial fear was historically used to discourage White residents from building community improvement organizations. The North Charlotte neighborhood was a very affordable, close-to-town community that many thought the White residents would quickly abandon when more Black residents moved in or even close by, which was already occurring.

White people in North Charlotte lived in fear of blockbusting potentially resulting in loss of their home equity—their life savings, for some—or other unnamed, dire consequences arising from Black families moving into their neighborhoods. Beyond the racial prejudices that were inculcated in all White people in the South, blue-collar and lower-income White residents were also menaced by a belief that those in power—though they always smiled and said they were defending their interests—would mete out economic and social punishment if race-based rules were not followed. Affluent areas were exempt from this fear-baiting and economic insecurity due both to their political power and the high prices of homes, which deterred most people of color from moving to these neighborhoods.

For White residents in lower- or lower-middle-income areas to organize against city policies, and potentially to form alliances with Black residents, flagrantly broke the rules of the social order that governed the city. Southern workers were told that if they considered forming a union, the company would immediately replace them with others who would work for even less pay.[16] Similarly, residents of lower- and middle-income White neighborhoods feared the repercussions they might face for organizing or participating in oppositional politics.

Because of these circumstances, the North Carolina Fund suspected that the perception that Whites in Charlotte could not be organized to advocate for their own interests was likely correct. But the North Carolina Fund wanted to test this out. I got the job to try to organize a community association to improve living conditions and give the residents more power over their lives against the twin forces of manipulation through racial fears and Charlotte's business oligarchy, which for decades were jointly represented by Jim Crow.

Strikes, Riots, Civil Rights... Community Organizing!

The North Charlotte organizing project, which set off the neighborhood movement, was experimental, but was not motivated by merely theoretical concerns. That neighborhood's need for "localized self-management" as Jane Jacobs called it, or just "neighborhood power" as Saul Alinsky saw it, was real and evident. City services and code enforcement were being neglected. In recent years, the local mills had closed. The population was aging. City officials were considering closing the local public school. The homes were quite small, many in the mill village style, and developers and rental-landlords were eyeing the area. At that time, no one could imagine college educated, well-paid White people buying these old houses and gentrifying the area, as began to happen less than two decades later. The community was viewed as obsolete, finished, and ripe for redevelopment—a candidate for a fate close to that dealt to Brooklyn, Charlotte's largest Black community obliterated by urban renewal.

North Charlotte, in my youth, was routinely referenced in demeaning and derisive terms, yet also with a sense of respect. It was considered tough and low-class. The ubiquitous Charlotte version of the smiling, glad-handing George Babbitt did not reside in this neighborhood. The residents of North Charlotte were seen as uncooperative in fulfilling Charlotte's destiny of growth. They often voted in referendums against city bonds for downtown projects or expansion of infrastructure.

Whatever else North Charlotte was, though, it was a real Place, with history and a distinct identity. In a city dominated by commercial values, however, this was regarded not as a strength but a flaw, an obstacle to growth. Also, it was an open question whether the residents would unite to defend against the forces of decline and neglect.

North Charlotte became the focus of a community organizing effort for one other reason. A rare event had just occurred in Charlotte, a tumultuous labor strike by the city's sanitation workers, some of whom lived in or near North Charlotte.

In 1968, the same year that Charlotte's sanitation workers voted to form a union, their counterparts in New York City called a strike. National news showed rotting trash piled up in New York's crowded urban canyons. Governor Nelson Rockefeller imposed state control over New York City's trash service and negotiated a settlement.

That spring, Martin Luther King went to Memphis, Tennessee, to support striking sanitation workers. While in Memphis, King was murdered, triggering violent protests across the country. The efforts of sanitation workers to improve their lives with better pay, more respect, and safer working conditions were viewed with apprehension by many in power. White elites saw civil rights and trade unionism as an explosive mixture that they feared would lead to anarchy.

Jim Pierce, the Southern director of the union that represented Charlotte's sanitation workers, American Federation of State, County and Municipal Employees (AFSCME), was the connection that led to me to organize North Charlotte. Pierce had worked with migrant workers in sugar cane fields in north central Florida and textile workers in cotton mills. He was a personal friend of Martin Luther King, and he had been working in Memphis during the sanitation workers strike that Reverend King came to support. Pierce's life was inspired by a conviction that freedom and opportunity for all working people had to be built on self-determination and a base of power. He saw unions as a vital, supportive institution for enabling African American workers to gain access to civil rights.[17]

The initial strike of city-employed sanitation workers that Pierce led resulted in a pay raise and an "agreement" with city officials—not a contract, as the city was legally prohibited by state law from contracting with a union. North Carolina was considered at the time the most anti-union state in America.

Later, the workers said the city did not abide by the agreement, and several more strikes were called without Pierce's involvement. In the end, the strike and the union were crushed, but it sent shock waves through Charlotte's leadership. A labor union had gained support and was active among city sanitation and water department workers in a city with decades of adamant anti-union policy. Equally notable, the strike had involved cooperation between White and Black workers.

While consulting with the North Carolina Fund, Jim Pierce recommended North Charlotte, where some of the sanitation workers lived, for the neighborhood organizing effort. I came to his attention as candidate for the organizer position through serendipitous connections. After a very positive meeting, he recommended me. The work was to be structured as a special project of the Charlotte Area Fund, the local arm of the Office of Economic Opportunity, the agency responsible for the so-called War on Poverty. The agency's director, Robert Person, also approved me, after a similarly positive interview. I had a small budget to open a field office and great latitude in my actions, reporting directly and only to Robert Person. I was 23 years old.

Invisibility (Memoir)

The North Charlotte I entered as a young community organizer was a shadow of the North Charlotte I knew of by reputation while growing up in Charlotte. The closed and now silent
textile mills took away that area's bravado. The independent
little business district along North Davidson Street had lost its
anchor stores. Within the community, churches and the public
school, Highland Elementary, were the institutional mainstays.
They meshed with extended family ties, a rich local memory of
baseball leagues, labor strikes, workplace camaraderie, technical
skills and a proud work ethic.

Whereas North Charlotte had endured "downtown's" disre-
spect for decades, now without its industrial asset, the residents
and the community were quickly downgraded to the lowest
status meted out by the powers that be: *invisibility*. It is a status potentially more dangerous for the residents than purposeful
discrimination. Mindless neglect characterized North Charlotte's
position relative to those who ran Charlotte. The financial and political interests factored no negative consequences to themselves
for whatever they did or did not do in the area. It was a vacuum,
ripe for an urban renewal-scale removal and profit-taking, without need to invent justifications or claims to any higher purpose.
Opportunity for profit, the North Star of the city's vision and direction, required no explanation.

I rented a space on the ground floor of a mixed use old building at the corner of Davidson and 36th, a block from what was
formerly North Charlotte's version of the Square, at 35th. I acquired an old desk, a manual typewriter, a hand-cranked mim-
eograph machine for printing fliers, and some folding chairs
and worktable, all donated. The Ford Foundation grant that
paid my modest salary covered the rent, utilities and telephone.
This was the "headquarters" for the fledgling North Charlotte

Action Committee (NCAC), Charlotte's first community organization guided by a Saul-Alinsky-trained organizer and the "radical" vision of grassroots democracy in a city dominated by oligarchy and the vestiges of Jim Crow. In that humble little space, I met with residents and held strategy meetings with leaders. Its small size also worked well for meetings with invited city officials. Even with a small group of activists attending, the room felt packed and energized.

Sitting at my desk I looked through a glass door at a few businesses still serving locals, a bakery and a furniture store. But there was one business front also visible from my desk that was patronized by people from all over Charlotte, the only reason they likely knew of North Charlotte at all: the city's one X-rated movie theater, the Astor. Not the theater itself, but the daily visits it received by people who otherwise didn't know or care about the neighborhood were a kind of insult on top of injury felt by local residents and symbolized the sense of invisibility.

Launched in 1970, the North Charlotte Action Committee (NCAC) had many initial successes and gained support in every corner of the community. It had generated an extensive feature article in the *Charlotte Observer* —a first to focus on the residents, their history, aspirations and struggles—as well as coverage of NCAC's "demands" for fair representation and equitable city services. Its reputation for success and spunk had spread around Charlotte. Residents in other neighborhoods contacted me asking about organizing assistance in their areas.

Then, just as it was getting established, NCAC faced its greatest organizing challenge in which failure would likely be lethal for the group and the community's future. Millions (today's dollars) in funds for upgrading and improving its 450-student neighborhood school, Highland Elementary, were being withheld. The money had already been approved in a

1967 bond referendum. The school was critical to the students' needs and the community's cohesion. Yet, reflecting the area's invisible status, the school was now being treated as already extinct. Top school officials gave clear indication that the funds would not be spent at Highland.[18]

The immediate challenge was to gain the promised funds, but the deeper challenge was for the community to break out of invisibility, to be acknowledged as a neighborhood with a future. Not only was North Charlotte rendered invisible by the city's prevailing financial values, recognition was made even more difficult by the city's preoccupation with the federal court-ordered integration of the schools involving busing of thousands of students. Charlotte was in the national spotlight and its quest for a New South identity was in jeopardy. Business leaders were coming forward to prevent Charlotte from being described as a North Carolina version of Birmingham or Little Rock.

NCAC's campaign for Highland Elementary was not contingent upon or related to busing. Improvements were needed for students wherever they lived but Highland was situated to readily serve White and Black children who lived in close proximity without need of extensive busing. It already operated on an integrated basis within the guidelines of the court order. Invisibility, not racial or economic parity, was the obstacle to funding.

North Charlotte had succeeded in getting the attention, sometimes with unconventional methods, of city officials regarding local services and code enforcement. It was, however, still unseen by countywide school officials. The neighborhood had voiced its needs and called on the school system to keep its word to improve Highland. Response was minimal and unpromising.

One day, at this time, I sat at my desk looking out across 36th Street, when a large, shiny Cadillac, a rare sight for the area, parked on the street. I immediately recognized the well-dressed individual getting out of the car, a member of the school board! He was coming to talk, maybe to visit the community and see the needs and value of the school to the neighborhood. His very appearance was a breakthrough against the scourge of invisibility. These were my excited, hopeful thoughts as I viewed him standing next to his car.

But he did not cross the street. I watched him lock his car and walk briskly . . . into the Astor Theater.

Neighborhood Soul—Disappeared

From my six-year immersion in North Charlotte and in many more Charlotte neighborhoods, I gained a unique perspective on how "Soul" manifests and expresses itself in neighborhoods, then and now.

I learned that Sense of Place is not about social status, amenities, or home equity. It exists when and where people are directly engaged in their community to sustain and improve quality of life. It is a *social* value. It cannot be quantified financially. When it is, it is often treated as a cost, a liability. For example, the North Charlotte and Elizabeth neighborhood associations of that era, which I organized, petitioned to *reduce* the number of units allowed per acre. This meant an immediate *reduction* in property values.

This decision would be almost unthinkable today. Likely, any group action to enhance Place at the cost of property value would be viewed negatively and possibly blocked by lawsuits. Home has largely been replaced by "real estate," which is always measured in terms of economic value. Neighborhoods are now defined as "assets" of Charlotte—like ART, parks, and hotels.

Yet, the longing for Place remains, which makes it important to remember this time when political engagement fostered connection to Place and neighborhood spirit prevailed, just as commemorating great achievements and sacrifices is important to preserving the spirit of patriotism.

I therefore felt sorrow and dismay when I discovered that North Charlotte, the neighborhood where the neighborhood movement began, has been "disappeared," like Dunbar in Joseph Heller's novel *Catch 22*.[19]

Sense of Place is damaged, obviously and unspeakably, when a neighborhood is suddenly demolished with every building eradicated, as happened to Brooklyn under urban renewal. Yet, the impact can be almost as destructive when most buildings are left intact, but the lives of the residents, and the identity and memory of the neighborhood are erased as if they never existed. Brooklyn's name was preserved, at least for branding purposes. But for North Charlotte, the first step of disappearance was to eradicate its name, which had stood for nearly a century.

"North Charlotte" was disappeared and replaced with the invented "NoDa," an affectation of SoHo in New York City. SoHo was still known as an arts district at that time, though now it is just a high-end shopping enclave. The historic name "North Charlotte" with its lingering reputation of "low class," unprogressive attitudes, and citizen resistance, was deemed bad for marketing. The name and all the work of its residents to sustain the neighborhood were banished into oblivion. The history of NoDa at the website, NoDa.org, covers the 1970s period when residents mobilized to save the area from industrialization and to maintain and upgrade the neighborhood school. There is not one word on the site, NoDa.org, about the years of organizing efforts or any of its leaders.[20] Predictably, at least from a modern perspective, NoDa has followed the path of Soho. It is no longer an art enclave but its opposite, a pricey, fashionable district.[21]

Currently, a new campaign is underway to superimpose yet another brand name on the neighborhood. NoDa and several adjacent communities, each distinct in its history, are now being melded into one as the "Mill District." This new branding program, like the previous one, rewrites history according to a marketing script. The NoDa brand promoters give the following account of the neighborhood's recent history:

> The mid-century demise of the textile industry frayed the fabric of this tight-knit community, until a pair of artists sparked a revitalization effort in the eighties.[22]

Acknowledging that the North Charlotte neighborhood had been renamed as part of a marketing scheme would tarnish the new "mill" theme, making it appear vacuous. The term North Charlotte is therefore omitted entirely from the history.

The narrative makes the implausible claim that "a pair of artists" saved the area. The contribution of the two referenced artists, Ruth Ava Lyons and J. Paul Sires, is historic and launched the next era for North Charlotte. It does not, however, account for how North Charlotte had remained relatively stable for almost twenty-five years, against the specter of block-busting and mill closures. It does not explain how streets and homes had been upgraded in recent years, a solid percentage of homes remained owned by their occupants, and the local school had been saved from closure. This was part of the legacy of the work of long term residents, and the community organizing years. Acknowledging this era and those residents would muddle the new brand and so, like the neighborhood's historical name, they are eliminated from the story.

The area's own residents, with the assistance of community organizers, had stabilized and upgraded North Charlotte/NoDa during the city's most volatile period, when school busing, housing integration, and block-busting racial fears were making their strongest impact, well before art galleries arrived. This is fully documented in many news stories reporting on the North Charlotte Action Association (formerly Committee) and the records of the city council.

The minutes of the mid-1972 meeting of the Charlotte City Council record one of the neighborhood's great accomplishments, gaining more than $6 million (in today's dollars) of funding for street and other improvements and grants and loans for upgrades to individual homes as part of a mostly federally funded Neighborhood Improvement Plan (NIP).

The city council meeting minutes report that the president of the neighborhood association, Reverend Paul Horne, one of the strongest and most visible neighborhood advocates, was in attendance to approve the program on behalf of the neighborhood. My presence at the meeting is also noted. The city manager reported to the council that the North Charlotte area had "an owner-occupancy which is relatively high; it is approximately 51 percent, with a very active citizen resident groups."

> Reverend Paul Horne, President of North Charlotte Action Association, ... the people of North Charlotte are very much in favor of a NIP program operating in the community... distributed over 500 questionnaires to homeowners and absentee landlords asking for an opinion about NIP. The responses received overwhelmingly favored NIP coming to North Charlotte.

> Reverend Horne stated all-the improvements to North ...the North Charlotte Action Association has fought for in the past year and a half - concentrated housing code enforcement to prevent deterioration; upgrading of the poor street pavement in the community; improvements to the inadequate drainage, which every year damages property and homes. They have maintained from the beginning if the city is committed to supporting strong and decent communities in Charlotte, these improvements are essential... the NCAA has fought for the clearing of overgrown vacant areas, improved services from the public health department, a better community school, health care facilities for their part of town, and improved city services like trash collection... This can happen because the people are already working for the very improvements NIP proposes, and because the people want to be involved in supporting and assisting the operation of the program.[23]

The new campaign to impose a super-brand of Mill District has recently encountered objections based on the uncomfortable fact that these mill-worker neighborhoods had been maintained for many years as White-only under Jim Crow laws. African Americans were generally restricted from mill jobs or were given the most menial and lowest-paid work.[24]

Further, the new historic narrative supporting the Mill District branding does not include the dramatic change much of the area went through in the 1960s. When thousands of Black families were evicted from Brooklyn, many moved into those old mill areas, while White residents fled to the suburbs. This was the era when Charlotte lost much of its White working class.[25] Sense of Place includes shameful as well as admirable history, which often does not serve the narratives of boosters, brand managers, and property developers.

Anatomy of "Disappeared"

How is it possible that more than a decade of neighborhood activism, which led to the restructuring of the city council, is not historically documented and acknowledged in Charlotte?

Charlotte has a Museum of the New South but it has never produced an exhibit on the era, nor have museum staff ever interviewed me about the six years in which I organized multiple neighborhoods.

This question was directly addressed in a 2003 editorial in the *Charlotte Observer* by columnist Mary Newsom entitled "Disappeared?"[26] I had brought Mary Newsom my large scrapbook filled with news clippings *from her own newspaper* that documented much of my work and the issues addressed by the multiple groups. She was shocked that as a long-time Charlotte resident, having lived in the city for nearly twenty-five years at that time, she knew nothing about the groups, the leaders, the actions, the victories, or me. As a professional commentator on city trends, local history, and quality of life issues, she was dismayed that she never knew Charlotte ever had an Alinsky-trained, paid organizer aiding neighborhoods just before she arrived. She had only heard vaguely that "neighborhood activism" had prompted the major change in city governance.

After talking with me and reviewing the extensive documentation I showed her, she raised the question in a published editorial,

> "Would Charlotte's neighborhood movement and district representation even have happened without Fitz-Patrick's paid organizing work? Possibly not."

She then addressed the larger concern I raised with her that "all the people who worked so hard in North Charlotte [were being] lost to civic memory." They were disappeared from Charlotte's official history, portending that anyone else who dared violate the rules of the "Charlotte Way" would similarly vanish.

In her editorial, Newsom acknowledged that in all her work with city officials and others in power in Charlotte, beginning only a few years after my organizing years, she didn't remember anyone mentioning the North Charlotte group, or me. She then offered — and did not disagree with — the reason I advanced as to *why*. "They (the neighborhood leaders and I) were "disappeared" *on purpose*.

In the article she recalled for her readers "what Charlotte was like in the '70s," explaining:

> Political power was consolidated among a few white businessmen . . . [and] the business oligarchy made the important civic decisions. Labor organizing or anything that smacked of it . . . was quickly squelched.

Of the groups that I organized, she wrote:

[They] focused on nuts and bolts issues. . . . They asked politely but if necessary they kicked up a fuss. They had to fuss a lot. But they had successes. . . . The scripted, false-front-polite Charlotte way abhors confrontation and protest politics ... Charlotte's business, government and social establishment want no reminders of a time when working people took on the power structure and won— effectively using organized protest. That's not the Charlotte way.

The Charlotte Way

The "Charlotte Way"—which editorial writer Mary Newsom connected to Charlotte's distaste for confrontational politics—is more often invoked to claim that Charlotte has special values that prevent racial violence. It is more than a euphemism for the "false-front-politeness" that Newsom also identified as characteristic of Charlotte. It is core to Charlotte's social character.

As I learned during my organizing work, the Charlotte Way was as entrenched a part of the local system of control as Jim Crow. People who do not follow the Charlotte Way face real consequences. Newsom's editorial included an example from my time as an organizer of how the Charlotte Way was enforced by the business oligarchy:

> Department store magnate John Belk, one of the city's richest men, was mayor. FitzPatrick describes what it was like when people from the North Charlotte mill neighborhood began to speak up before City Council.

> Tell us your name," Mayor Belk would boom. Then he would ask, "And what church do you go to?" Then, "Ah, yes, I know your minister." Or, "My friend so-and-so goes to your church." Someone less attuned to the South's subtleties of power would hear only pleasantries. But working people might feel an ominous reminder that a powerful businessman, if displeased, could pressure a minister or a boss and make life hard.

Newsom's editorial did not explain what "make life hard" might mean. This reticence, too, is part of the Charlotte Way. The brutal consequences of breaking with the Charlotte Way are seldom spoken of, nor the exact structure of the chains of command that communicate a direct threat or carry out suppression. The system of control has many eyes, ears, and arms.

In a follow-up letter I offered Newsom a less "subtle" example:

> One of the leaders of the groups I was working with . . . was given an ultimatum from his employer: "Do you want to be a politician or an employee of this company?"

> This was for speaking out [as a private citizen and local neighborhood representative] against a Charlotte road project. It turned out his company, in another division, did substantial business with the state Department of Transportation. A word of disapproval was apparently expressed from Charlotte leaders to the DOT which then leveraged this employer [located] in a faraway state, where the Charlotte citizen thought his managers would not even know about his community efforts much less care. He never imagined they would be pressured to prohibit it.

This person, an articulate and dedicated community leader seeking to protect Charlotte as a Place, after consulting and praying together with his wife, resigned from the community organization, never to be heard from again in the public sphere.

If Newsom's editorial fell short in its description of the Charlotte Way, it is that it seemingly placed this system of control, enforced by a business oligarchy, in the past. There is no reason to think that this system does not remain and is just as effective today.

The Visible Hand

If civic struggle and direct political engagement instill Sense of Place, what is the status of neighborhood activism today? And what is the status of Charlotte's old saboteur of activism—Jim Crow, political boss and real estate tycoon?

Today in Charlotte, as in many cities, virtually every neighborhood has an association. With members representing seven districts—the system created due to neighborhood activism—the Charlotte City Council is no longer confronted by "neighborhood" leaders claiming the council only represents "downtown" interests. The city government now aids, trains, and promotes neighborhood associations. The city maintains a directory of neighborhood association leaders and holds annual retreats to train them. The city even employs its own surrogate organizers, called "neighborhood advocates," to "help you achieve your neighborhood goals."[27]

Charlotte's neighborhood leaders graduated from being disparaged as complaining activists to becoming honored insiders. Guided by the boldly Visible Hand of Charlotte's all-consuming commercial culture, neighborhoods with "distinct character" joined "glittering" towers, sports stadiums, the Mint Museum, and the convention center as attractions promoted by boosters.

The ascent of neighborhood associations occurred gradually over about fifteen years, following the era of neighborhood activism that led to the restructuring of the city council. This ascendence can be explained by the pattern pointed out by Tom Vanderbilt discussed at the beginning of this chapter: neighborhoods take on rhetorical and symbolic meaning precisely when their status as real Places is threatened or uncertain. The boasts by cities across the country proclaiming various versions of the slogan "city of neighborhoods"—*beautiful boroughs* is Charlotte's version—emerged as neighborhoods were degraded by urban growth, congestion, digital networks, transience, and skyrocket-ing real estate prices. The current talk about neighborhoods has to do with branding and the replacement of life with lifestyles. In the rhetoric of boosterism, a "neighborhood" is no longer a Place where life is experienced, but a market abstraction— something to purchase, consume, discard, and purchase again in another lo-cation. Neighborhoods are not created by residents but provided to them as an *amenity*.

View from the Inside (Memoir)

About forty of us are seated at tables in the church basement. Most of us don't really know each other, except maybe by name or where we live. There's little socializing. Business begins. We hear the reports of the latest MLS listings of home sales in our area and increased pricing. There are updates on improvements to several properties, including granite counter tops, entire new kitchens with Bosch appliances, the addition of a large master bedroom suite, and new patios with pergolas. For other properties on sale, nothing at all was done, and these are likely to be "tear downs." The meeting includes younger new arrivals and some longtime residents, who are differentiated not just by age but home size. In a reverse of earlier patterns the young are far wealthier than their elders. Though some neighborhood residents are young couples who don't have children yet, these young people already have houses that dwarf older ones where three or more kids were raised.

The great income divide is visible even in the parking lot, as trim Teslas and crouching Beamers sit by bulky old Chevrolets. Increasingly, the smaller houses that once characterized the community no longer "fit in." Most of us had heard rumors that a treasured little shopping center at the edge of the neighborhood, including a beauty salon catering to some of the local older ladies, including my own mother, has just been acquired. Now we hear that there are plans for that entire area to be demolished and replaced with an upscale grocery chain. One person comments that this seems senseless since there are already three other major grocers nearby. This new one will include a Starbucks and a bar where beer and wine by the glass can be purchased and imbibed while strolling aisles. There will be a drive-by window for online orders and a full grocery delivery service. Several people express sorrow about loss of the local businesses, but others remind them that, overall, it is very good for property values.

A police officer standing at the side of the room is introduced and walks to the front. He is armed and wearing a flak jacket. The officer is young, bulked up. He reports the data on neighborhood "crime" in the previous month. As usual, not a single violent incident occurred. The contents of a few cars, left unlocked, were pilfered. The officer sternly advises that all cars be kept locked and cameras installed at front and rear doors.

The officer also notes that undercover agents were in a nearby neighborhood park and confronted several men who appeared to be planning a possible meet-up in the public restroom. A titter of laughter can be heard. No arrests were made. One resident objects to police treating the men as suspects merely for talking in a public parking lot. But another rises quickly to thank the officers for keeping the neighborhood safe. She is given a supportive round of applause. The officer thanks her and the others and urges all residents to call 911 on seeing anyone in the neighborhood who looks like they don't belong. A middle age African American man stands up in the rear to say his son often walks or jogs in the neighborhood. Would the sight of him justify a call to 911? The officer reassures him that as long as someone is not engaging in any crime or about to commit a crime, they have nothing to fear.

The date for the next meeting is announced. Most people leave immediately. There is little to share that was not already on Facebook or NextDoor, but a few chat amiably with the district city councilperson who attended and the police officer.

When Alinsky Came (Back) to Charlotte

One event—that would have seemed unimaginable two decades before—demarcates the transition of neighborhoods in Charlotte from sites of troublesome activism to the "beautiful boroughs" featured on charlottesgotalot.com. The notorious Saul Alinsky organization came back to Charlotte, this time *invited* by none other than Charlotte's newest oligarch, Hugh McColl! As reported in the local newspaper, with McColl's support, about thirty churches planned a return of an Alinsky-affiliated and -trained professional organizer.[28]

Alinksy's methods were no longer feared but were now sought out to direct activism toward enhancing Charlotte's national brand. As in all other aspects of Charlotte branding—renaming "uptown"; inventing "Historic Southend" and "NoDa"—history had to be redacted and rewritten. From 1994, when plans for the McColl-blessed invitation to Alinsky were first reported, all the way through 2010, when the program silently vanished, not a single news organization in Charlotte ever acknowledged that an Alinksy-affiliated organizing program had existed in Charlotte before.

As part of these efforts at branding, the earlier years of the neighborhood movement were erased. The new—spoken of as the first—organizing program was not actually focused on neighborhoods. That might imply broad disaffection. Rather, the organizing mission was to "help"—the organization's name was HELP, Helping Empower Local People—one specific subgroup, *poor people*. Presumably, everyone else was satisfied with the status quo, thanks. The focus on the poor also framed the organizing effort as a politically innocuous form of *charity*. As part of a helping mission, the program would be overseen by Charlotte's least politically controversial institution, the churches. The first news report was headlined, "Pastors Shaping Group to Fight for Poor's Needs." The work of the group would be covered by the newspaper's religion reporter.

Foreshadowing the disastrous 2014 Harvard study that found Charlotte to be the worst city in America for poor residents to improve their station in life, McColl seemed aware that the ugly face of poverty detracted from Charlotte's world-class status and that efforts to address poverty were needed, beyond financing commercial growth.

Reflecting Charlotte's famously Calvinism-inflected culture and view that the root of poor people's problem is not lack of money, but lack of *enterprise,* McColl's publicized view was that he hoped Alinsky's methods might stir the poor to help themselves. Asked about why he supported the "radical" Alinsky coming to Charlotte, McColl said that, in his understanding, Alinksy's approach "starts and ends with self-help."[29] This view ignored that Alinsky's approach included confronting local forces that obstructed self-improvement.

The pastor first publicly interviewed about HELP was from a small church in a very poor area, known for its social service activities and multiracial and income-diverse congregation. An outpost of liberal Christianity, the congregation enjoyed financial and volunteer support from members of some of Charlotte's wealthiest churches. The church was located next to Charlotte's oldest public housing project, built in the 1930s. In the 1980s and 1990s, the area had suffered from the crack cocaine epidemic and gang violence, and the church's current pastor had reportedly undergone a personal transformation in his thinking about how to serve the poor. He was inspired by an essay by religious writer John McNight, "Why Servanthood is Bad."[30] In his first year at the church, he organized a six-week study program of McNight's views, which one church leader summarized:

> Government programs are dangerous because they do for people what people should do for themselves. . . . [Those who want to help should] give money directly to those who need it, not to social workers or other bureaucrats. . . .People have the right to make their own decisions without interference from others, no matter how well-meaning. . . . Social work [is partly to] blame for continuing to oppress African Americans.[31]

HELP called attention to many of the classic conditions of poverty—lack of housing; low wages; crime; and unemployed, idle, despairing youth.[32] Much of HELP's work was, at first, viewed as unobjectionable by Charlotte's business leaders. This did not last. Seeking funds for affordable housing and campaigning for a "living wage" for city-employed workers, HELP soon came into conflict with "downtown" and its chief spokesman—the sales-guy mayor, Pat McCrory, the one who sought to have the drama *Angels in America* altered for a Charlotte performance.[33]

In a scenario almost identical to my own organizing experience about twenty years earlier, in which neighborhood organizations united to oppose and defeat a bond referendum to expand Charlotte's airport, HELP wound up opposing a bond referendum for a downtown arena for professional basketball. The arena bond was voted down, and HELP was given substantial credit for the defeat. In both cases, the bond opposition campaigns were leverage for new priorities. In Charlotte, as in other cities, the fundamental needs of neighborhoods were set aside for the subsidies and "stimulus" of downtown real estate and for more growth and world class status. The only way to get local needs addressed was to deny the city's elite their coveted priorities.

HELP inevitably had to challenge those priorities, as earlier groups I organized did for exactly the same ends. Little had changed in two decades. It was an illusion of some Charlotte leaders, including banker Hugh McColl, that HELP's mission "started and ended with self-help" and was unrelated to the city's and his own mission of growth and status. Only when the needs of the poor collided with the growth and status plans did those needs of the poor become relevant.

As the next part of the story shows, there is one issue, in which the interests of local people that enhance Soul and Place and the priorities of the powerful that diminish it, could not be separated: *how a city educates its children*

---

[1] "What Place Do Neighborhoods Have in Modern Cities?" by Tom Vanderbilt, *Wilson Quarterly*, Fall 2013

[2] Charlotte's owner-occupied rate is 52.7% and the USA's is 64.6% (https://datausa.io/profile/geo/charlotte-nc/?compare=united-states)

[3] https://www.charlottesgotalot.com/neighborhoods

[4] "Close View of a Calvinist Lhasa" by W. J. Cash, *The American Mercury*, Edited by H. L. Mencken, April 1933

[5] A map showing the political leanings of areas of greater Charlotte, using color-coding, shows dark blue in the center, getting lighter moving out from the center, turning to pink and then dark red in outer suburbs and ex-urbs. (https://bestneighborhood.org/conservative-vs-liberal-map-charlotte-nc/)

[6] *Legacy: Three Centuries of Black History in Charlotte, North Carolina* by Pamela Grundy, Nerve Media Productions LLC, 2022)

[7] The reference to this news story is in *Legacy: Three Centuries of Black History in Charlotte, North Carolina* by Pamela Grundy, p. 72-73, Queen City Nerve. Kindle Edition, citing the article, "Brooklyn Homes Give Owners High Returns" by Joe Doster, *Charlotte Observer*, January 11, 1960, p. 1-B

[8] "A New Brooklyn—It'll Pay Dividends" by Joe Doster, *Charlotte Observer*, January 10, 1960

[9] The decision was announced at a meeting attended by representatives of the North Charlotte Action Committee, Rev. Paul Horne, Gilbert Hatley and me. See: See "Highland School Help in Sight" by Warren King, *Charlotte Observer*, January 9, 1971

[10] The situation on the westside of Charlotte only worsened over time. See a mid-1980s account, "Life West of Tryon, for Many It Means 2nd Class Existence," *Charlotte News*, Apr 18, 1983

[11] "Pastor Offers to Advise Men Who Oppose Draft" by Sam R. Covington, *Charlotte Observer*, Feb 08, 1971

[12] "6 Groups Oppose Bond Referendum" by Mark Brock, *The Charlotte News*, April 4, 1975.

[13] "Five Councilmen Favor 2nd Vote on Airport" by Mark Brock, *The Charlotte News*, Wed, Apr 09, 1975

[14] From 1945 into the early '70s, the council was virtually all-male. One woman, Martha Evans, was elected during this time. She was a popular figure in Charlotte and later was elected to the state legislature. She ran for mayor of Charlotte two times during her Council tenure and was expected to win but encountered unnamed opposition. She later claimed her Mayoral candidacy had been opposed by "downtown" interests because, "I was considered a wild-eyed radical and all I was doing was giving the Negroes an equal opportunity, and they [downtown interests] didn't want it." To oppose her, she stated, they recruited and then backed businessperson, Stan Brookshire, who won. Brookshire subsequently led the urban renewal program that wiped out Brooklyn, the largest African American community located downtown. See the oral history interview with Martha Evans at https://docsouth.unc.edu/sohp/html_use/A-0318.html

[15] *The Death and Life of Great American Cities* by Jane Jacobs, (p. 117). Knopf Doubleday Publishing Group. Kindle Edition.

[16] Paraphrasing the more crudely worded message to White workers by business owners at that time, "You keep the unions out, and we'll keep the Blacks out."

[17] Oral History Interview with Jim Pierce, July 16, 1974. Interview E-0012-3. *Southern Oral History Program* Collection #4007. (https://docsouth.unc.edu/sohp/E-0012-3/menu.html)

[18] For documentation of the North Charlotte Action Committee's successful campaign to release funds for upgrading Highland Elementary, see "Come to People, Board Requested" by Kay Reimler, *Charlotte News*, Dec 2, 1970, and "School Board Will Review Projects with Hold Status" by Kay Reimler, *Charlotte News*, Dec. 17, 1970, and "Citizen Action May Win in School Upgrade Attempt" by Kay Reimler, *Charlotte News*, Jan. 6, 1971, and "Board Group OKs School Renovation," *Charlotte News*, Jan. 8, 1971

[19] In the famous satirical novel, the character Dunbar, a bomber pilot and friend of the book's main character, becomes acutely aware of absurdity of war. He becomes critical and insubordinate after the group is ordered to bomb innocent civilians. He speaks openly about the likelihood of everyone in the group getting killed. Military authorities apparently whisk him away secretly, without explanation, and then act as if he had never been part of the group. His friends realize Dunbar was "disappeared."

[20] https://www.noda.org/historyofnoda

[21] SoHo of New York City refers to South of Houston Street. It was previously known as the Cast Iron District due to buildings with cast iron facades. New York urban planner, Chester Rapkin, is credited with inventing the name Soho in 1962. The website, SohoMemory.org succinctly describes the phases that the area went through after it was rebranded, which Charlotte's NoDa followed at a Charlotte-scale: "SoHo used to refer to 'the other side of the tracks,' where poor artists lurked in the shadows in fear of being evicted, where people from uptown went 'slumming.' But now the name SoHo is used as an adjective to describe an aesthetic or a lifestyle that is glamorous and hip." NoDa has priced out the galleries and art studios. It is now known for "lifestyle."

[22] https://www.milldistrictclt.com/noda

[23] Minute Book 57, of the Charlotte City Council, page 159-60, 'The City Council of the City of Charlotte, North Carolina, met in regular session, on Monday, May 15, 1972, at 2:00 o'clock-p.m., in the Council Chamber; City Hall, with-Mayor John-M. Belk presiding.

[24] "NoDa and surrounding areas get a new brand that's a nod to the past" by Katie Peralta Soloff, *Axios Charlotte*, April 21, 2021

[25] When I returned to Charlotte after 18 years living away, I was contacted by a group of college students who were making a study of community organizing in Charlotte. They asked me to direct them to blue collar White neighborhoods in Charlotte. I had to explain that, effectively, there aren't any. They fled the neighborhoods after Jim Crow ended and were terrorized by block-busting realtors. They now live in small towns around the city or in rural areas. Today, I would add that many Black working-class people are losing their homes to gentrification and skyrocketing rent and home pricing and may also be forced to move to those same areas.

[26] "Disappeared? Former Activist Thinks City's Protest Era Is Being Forgotten" by Mary Newsom, *Charlotte Observer*, December 6, 2003

[27] City of Charlotte website page, "Neighborhood Resources" (https://www.charlottenc.gov/Streets-and-Neighborhoods/Get-Involved/Neighborhood-Resources)

[28] "Church-backed Charlotte Group Aims to Fight Poverty at the Root" by Tim Funk, *Charlotte Observer*, Apr 19, 1996

[29] "Church-backed...", *Charlotte Observer*, Apr 19, 1996

[30] https://resources.depaul.edu/abcd-institute/publications/Documents/1995_WhyServanthoodIsBad.pdf

[31] *Small Church With a Big Mission: The History of the First 50 Years of Seigle Avenue Presbyterian Church* by Margaret G. Bigger and Katherine M. Dunlap, A. Borough Books, 1995

[32] "Volunteer Group...", by Tim Funk, *Charlotte Observer*, July 27, 1997

[33] The mayor at that time, Pat McCrory, later served one-term as Governor of North Carolina. Most recently he was the co-chair of the national "No Labels" party, which planned (but failed) to run an alternative candidate to Donald Trump and Joseph Biden for the 2024 presidential election. That role is consistent with Charlotte's political priority of business over partisanship. (https://www.wcnc.com/article/news/politics/north-carolina-politics/north-carolina-recognizes-no-labels-party-pat-mccrory-white-house-2024-campaign-donald-trump-joe-biden-independent-voters-third-party-democrat-gop/275-57848d30-8d0d-44a9-8053-38fda5722660). As Mayor, McCrory was also known for getting the NASCAR Hall of Fame to locate in Charlotte. It is close to the Levine Center for the Arts. (https://en.wikipedia.org/wiki/Pat_McCrory)

IX. Searching In The School System

At the precise time I began my neighborhood organizing in North Charlotte (now "NoDA"), another more direct and disruptive challenge to Jim Crow was occurring. This challenge catapulted Charlotte, North Carolina, into greater national attention than it ever received before or since. But it was not the kind of attention Charlotte boosters so earnestly seek. The new challenge confronted Jim Crow in yet another role, this time as Charlotte's *school administrator*. This tumultuous development was constantly in the local news, and occasionally in the national news, for nearly three decades. Now, few speak of it.

Charlotte's "separate but equal" school system was challenged in court, based on the historic 1954 Supreme Court ruling that ended the legal pretense that racially segregated schools ever were, or ever could be, equal. The race-based, segregated system in Charlotte, as in all Southern cities, was always unconscionably imbalanced and unfair.

A gentle glimpse of that imbalance was offered in an oral history interview with Arthur Griffin, who attended the segregated schools of that era. Much later, he was elected to the School Board in Charlotte. Griffin said the following about his time in elementary school:

> I entered public schools in 1954. That was called Alexander Street Elementary School . . . the colored elementary school at that time for folk that lived in that part of the city. . . . The upper end of First Ward . . . was White. The southern part of First Ward was Black. . . . So as Whites sort of migrated or left the area, they left what's now the First Ward Elementary School. It was an older school, but when we moved [from] Alexander Street to First Ward, we thought it was a brand new school because conditions are so much different with regard to quality of facility going to Alexander Street, since all of the Black kids had to go to one school, we had a double shift, and you would

go to school from 8 to 12, and another shift would come in at 12 o'clock and would go from 12 to 4. And that went on (until First Ward became the school for Black children)—it was like being delivered and going to Heaven.[1]

In 1969, a nearly five-year court battle ended in a federal court order to desegregate. Charlotte appealed all the way to the Supreme Court, which in 1971 upheld the desegregation ruling. Charlotte was ordered to *immediately* end school segregation.[2] Large-scale busing of children from segregated neighborhoods to integrated schools was adopted as the means, along with the closing of some of the formerly all-Black schools.

Despite the disruption, it was apparent to many people, including some of those opposed to busing, that the existing school system was morally, legally, and educationally indefensible. It had been seventeen years since *Brown v Board of Education*. Continuation of the old system, a legacy of slavery, placed Charlotte against the tide of history. This was the very opposite of what Charlotte hoped to achieve in its quest for recognition as "New South" and a "world-class" city.

No Capacity

The busing remedy disrupted one of the anchors of urban neighborhoods, whether Black or White: a neighborhood public school within walking distance of most children. Though opponents often described busing as an onerous new imposition on students and families, it was not unfamiliar. For many students, school buses had been the normal means for getting to and from school every day.

The two challenges to Charlotte's old power structure—neighborhood-based organizing and court-ordered busing to integrate the schools—though occurring simultaneously, were always treated in the media separately. They had common causes, rooted in the city's core values and the legacy of Jim Crow.[3]

Historically, neighborhoods and schools were strictly segregated in Charlotte, by law and social custom. The neighborhood organizing movement revealed the possibility of collaboration across the racial divide, which reduced distrust and laid a foundation for civic and political cooperation based on common goals. Attempting to suppress this movement toward collaboration were fear-mongering real estate companies and some political leaders whose power had historically rested on racial fear and division and personal beliefs in White privileged entitlement.

A similar possibility emerged in the school system to build upon common hopes and needs, while confronting racist fear and those who fomented it.

From my knowledge, training, and experience as a community organizer, it is my view that the widespread recognition of inherent unfairness of school segregation and the necessity of change could have been foundations for a fundamental rethinking of the school system. Such a change would have required an extraordinary and sustained citywide mobilization, based on values of equity of opportunity and support for neighborhoods. This mobilization would have needed to be grassroots, not business-led, and to have engaged church, social, political, and civic organizations, with dedicated leadership focused on the *public school system* and the *value of education* as cornerstones of Charlotte's identity.

As this story has by now made all too apparent, Charlotte had little capacity for such a mobilization. There was no tradition of such grassroots movements in Charlotte. At the time, almost everyone living in Charlotte fell into the polarized racial categories of Black or White. The White community, as earlier discussed, was scattered, unorganized, and controlled by Boss Jim Crow. The Black residents were beginning to mobilize but were still heavily dominated. There were virtually no labor unions. Few churches were engaged with social issues. Both political parties were dominated by the same business elites and their surrogates, who held public office to represent their interests and values. A long history of business oligarchy and Jim Crow had supplanted and suppressed local democratic movements, which do exist in other cities. Leaders who were not business elites were rare. Populism had shallow roots in Charlotte.

Domination by business interests precluded the people of Charlotte from viewing the public schools and education as core elements of local identity or the city's mission. Like other elements of identity, schools and the value of education were secondary and subservient to the higher cause of business expansion. The results were predictable.

Twenty-five years after the court-ordered busing, when the Saul Alinsky organization returned to Charlotte to launch a new community organizing effort in the mid-1990s, thirty churches conducted a survey to determine Charlotte's core problems. They identified two prevailing forces at the root of most inequities and social problems, "racial polarization" and an "obsession with success." In this context, "success" means only economic success, growth, profit, and status. The emphasis on this version of "success" is a value so pervasive that its interplay with Jim Crow, which also pervaded city life, cannot be disentangled.

Schools are essentially noncommercial spaces. But, just as neighborhoods eventually became "amenities" for Charlotte and "assets" for boosterism, over time, the schools made it into the ledger—though not for the mission of education for all, but as elements of tiered status and property value.

The ranking of a local school can be a key determinant of property values and the social status accorded a neighborhood. Intended to ensure that all students had access to an education of equal quality, busing came to be seen as an intolerable cost *to business*, standing in the way of Charlotte's economic destiny.

From End to Beginning

A cursory look at today's schools in Charlotte and the sur-rounding Mecklenburg area reveals racial segregation and in-equity. The situation appears almost as if there had never been a landmark Supreme Court decision outlawing "separate but equal" or a direct federal court order to Charlotte to racially in-tegrate and fairly balance resources and support for all students.

That cursory impression would be generally accurate. A 2018 study of desegregation of schools in the state by the North Caroli-na Justice Center found Charlotte-Mecklenburg schools the most segregated in the state.[4] To reach "racial parity," the report states that Charlotte would now need to reassign 55% of its students, far more than the next most segregated school district in the state. In addition to being racially segregated, the report showed that Charlotte schools were also the most divided by income.

The first publicized attempt at school integration in Charlotte was not under court order but by the brave initiative of just one family. In 1957, a fifteen-year-old female African American stu-dent enrolled in the all-White Harding High School.[5] The nation-ally published photo of her being spit on and jeered at by White students as she walked with dignity into that school on her first day led to writer and intellectual James Baldwin's special inter-est in Charlotte. In his acclaimed 1961, book, *Nobody Knows My Name*, Baldwin wrote:

> I saw the Negro schools in Charlotte. . . . This solved
> the mystery of just what made Negro parents send their
> children out to face mobs. White people do not under-
> stand this. . . . Those Negro parents . . . are not doing this
> out of "ideals" or "convictions" or because they are in
> the grip of a perverse desire to send their children where
> "they are not wanted." They are doing it because they
> want the child to receive the education which will allow

him to defeat, possibly escape, and not impossibly help one day abolish the stifling environment in which they see, daily, so many children perish.

Today, Harding High School, where that lone young woman attempted to get an education—she lasted only a few days before withdrawing due to threats and humiliations—is an almost completely non-White school. Of the 1,234 students enrolled, just twenty-six identify as White.[6] Harding reflects the wider picture of White students abandoning the entire system in which they are now a minority, making up just 24.5 percent. The largest single group is identified as Black, 36.3 percent, followed by 28.6 percent Hispanic/Latino. There is also a sizable group of Asian students.[7]

The official narrative about school integration describes how, after resisting the court orders, Charlotte wisely accepted them, and a vanguard of enlightened business leaders led efforts to "make it work." Ironically, among the most active of these business leaders was the largest owner of Jim Crow-era rental housing for African Americans. Also prominently involved in this effort was an executive assistant to Hugh McColl of Bank of America (in its earlier iteration as NCNB).[8]

This official story emphasizes the great success of that business-led effort, and then tells how it all got ruined by a 1999 decision by a conservative federal judge, who, as a private citizen, had been an active opponent of busing. The judge ended more than twenty-five years of efforts to desegregate.[9]

At this point, the story of school desegregation in Charlotte becomes less clear. There is less news coverage, and there are no heroic business leaders at the forefront. Charlotte drifted, as if carried by natural forces, back to "neighborhood" assignments and "school choice," leading to today's de facto segregated system, which looks much like the old de jure segregation.

A 2016 retrospective article in the *New Yorker* magazine repeats this official story and how the drift eventually led into a cascade of racial and class resegregation:

> When Charlotte-Mecklenburg eliminated race as a factor in student assignment, it . . . created a feedback loop that made the problem worse. Families with the means—most often white families—started to move into whiter neighborhoods, where they knew their kids would go to whiter schools. As a result of the relationship between race and wealth, the social, political, and economic capital became ever more concentrated in a small number of very white neighborhoods.[10]

Other cities likely have similar accounts of how their own school systems are currently segregated, despite antidiscrimination laws, sixty years of civil rights activism, and a general understanding among many people of the harm that racial segregation does to students. Charlotte's story, however, has a special distinction that is relevant to a search for Soul.

The Ultimate Value

It would seem strange only to those who do not know of Charlotte's history of extreme boosterism, dating to the mythical "Meck Dec," that Charlotte is currently able to bathe in self-proclaimed "tolerance" and boast of valiant integration efforts, while at the same time operating the most segregated school system in the state. Adding to the dissonance is that Charlotte held the lowest ranking in America for social mobility for low-income families.

Not only are the schools hyper-segregated, the old pattern of neglect of the non-White schools endured even during the years of concerted desegregation policies. In 1997, a quarter century after the federal court order to offer an equal education to all, and two years before the federal court decision that ended busing as the means of desegregating schools, Charlotte's new Saul Alinsky community organizing program conducted a survey of thirty-six Charlotte schools with an eye to equity and fairness.

As reported in the *Charlotte Observer*, "'Some of the team members were appalled,' said HELP member Chris Baumann. 'They left the schools in tears." The *Observer* story noted that before the community group did the survey, a task force of Charlotte leaders had already verified those "appalling" conditions in a report that called for urgent remedial action.[11]

Reading the report, *Observer* editorial writer, Fannie Flono, wrote that her "mouth dropped." She recounted learning of "brown drinking water, peeling plaster, leaking roofs and filthy bathrooms." She described the findings of the report as "surreal," considering it was from "an area often noted as an exemplary New South city."

The chairman of that task force for the report was quoted, "We knew that the community was not paying the price to care for its children which it would be willing to pay if everyone experienced this."

As would be expected in a system characterized by hypersegregation and unequal resources, Charlotte's schools today perform lower than the state average academically.[12]

History Reviewed

Over time, some reports have begun to call into question the official narrative that Charlotte proactively and successfully desegregated its schools, only to have the program derailed by one conservative federal judge in 1999. These fuller inquiries recall that, before the 1999 court ruling, the school system had already introduced "magnet" schools that began a process of "voluntary" resegregation. Also, inside some of the heavily touted racially balanced schools, academic "tracks" had effectively segregated students within the schools.

These reports document that the heaviest and most disruptive burden of busing fell on the poorest kids. One of the churches that sponsored the later Alinsky-inspired community organizing program was located in the Piedmont Courts public housing project. Church records provided a snapshot of busing:

> [In one year] elementary children in certain apartments went to 1st–4th grades at Winterfield and 5th and 6th grades at Villa Heights. Others attended Elizabeth all six years. A third group rode buses to 1st–4th grades at Lansdowne and walked to First Ward for 5th and 6th. . . . Some who had attended Olde Providence earlier were mis-assigned back there. Fleets of buses would line up in front of the Courts to disburse them all.

> [In a later year, under the "feeder" schools program,] Piedmont Courts was segmented into three feeder areas. . . . One building was divided down the middle, and

children from apartment numbers on opposite sides of the Courts were assigned to the same school. That year, buses were dispatched to Cotswold Elementary, Randolph Junior High and East High School from one section, Elizabeth, Piedmont Junior High, and Myers Park High from another. The remaining children attended Winterfield, Villa Heights, Eastway Junior High and Garinger High. When I was among those who protested, we were told that it was to keep the kids from forming gangs.[13]

Other reports have questioned the level of Charlotte's commitment to dismantling the old Jim Crow system in light of rapid retreat from desegregation starting in the late 1990s. The 2016 *New Yorker* story noted that the school system's vision statement used to read, "The Vision is to ensure that the Charlotte-Mecklenburg School System becomes the premier, urban integrated system in the nation." Today, the word "integrated" is nowhere to be found.

The most insightful and thorough reexaminations venture outside the jargon-loaded and insular profession of education. They contextualize the schools within the larger political and economic forces that shape other aspects of life in Charlotte. In the 2004 book, *Boom for Whom*, local political scientist Stephen S. Smith examined the much-heralded role of what he called Charlotte's "business elite." Local lore tells how these visionaries championed integration and led positive change, trademarking Charlotte as a true New South city.[14]

Smith's analysis of the response of Charlotte business leaders is consistent with their approaches to other issues, which are shaped by the ultimate value in Charlotte, *how it affects business*.

Smith shows that, in the face of negative national attention for Charlotte's early resistance to school integration, business elites launched a campaign to "make it work." One formerly all-Black high school, integrated by busing, was given special public attention for interracial student unity. Tests results showed improvements in academic achievement among the poorer and Black students and no negative effects on others. Though the source of the phrase is unknown, Charlotte began branding itself the "city that made it work."

Smith credits the multi-decade progress in school integration with contributing to the economic boom that occurred in Charlotte over the same time span, from roughly 1980 to 2000. That view hints at a double meaning to "making it work."

On balance and in hindsight, Smith argues the city's elite gained more than the citizens, especially African Americans. For example, he cites data showing the gap in income between Black and White households *increased* during the celebrated years of successful school desegregation, at the same time as the city's overall economy massively expanded.[15] At the end of what was supposedly the twenty-year heyday of integration, the poverty rate for Black people was 340 percent that of Whites.[16]

Further, after the new federal ruling ended legally mandated efforts at integration, and as rapid resegregation occurred, the elites seemingly lost interest. Across the country, resegregation was the trend, accompanied by a litany of new education policies, such as No Child Left Behind, that served as alternatives to integrated, equitable schools. At that point, Charlotte was clear of any risk to its reputation for following the resegregation trend, even in extreme.

From a business perspective, busing for desegregation had been a powerful tool for promoting Charlotte nationally as tolerant and fair-minded. From the same commercial viewpoint, busing eventually became a significant obstacle to attracting major corporations to Charlotte, as one of relocating executives' main concerns was for their children to attend the "best" public schools. Busing complicated these executives' choice of where to purchase a home, as a prestigious neighborhood might be "paired" with a rundown school with lower academic ratings.

At a certain point, *resegregation* became the greater friend of Charlotte's business goals, and this, arguably, accounted for the elites retreat from proactive engagement in education policy.

Smith and others also noted perhaps the most significant factor that is omitted in the heralded story of the "city that made it work": as the school system wrestled with racial ratios and the resistance of affluent areas to "pairing," leaders quietly engineered an enormous state and federal road project to traverse a huge southern sector of the county, leading to the development of one of the largest affluent White sections of Charlotte. The school system accommodated this development by building almost all new schools in predominantly White areas, even though during this period, the percentage of Black students in the system increased relative to Whites.

The road scheme, leading to massive housing development and more White schools, exacerbated geographic segregation and set school segregation in stone when "choice" returned under the new court order. Ironically, the huge tract of land where this new White residential area was developed was the old estate of a former governor of North Carolina, Cameron Morrison. As Stephen Smith recounted in *Boom for Whom*,

> At the turn of the twentieth century, Morrison played a leading role in the disfranchisement of blacks in the state, emerged as one of North Carolina's most influential leaders, and touted his advocacy of white supremacy in a successful campaign for governor of the state in 1920.

The *Wikipedia* treatment of Morrison adds,

> In 1898, Morrison participated in the Wilmington insurrection of 1898, a violent coup d'état by a group of

white supremacists. They expelled opposition black and white political leaders from the city, destroyed the property . . . and killed an estimated 60 to more than 300 people.

The chief proponent of the road and the subsequent housing was Cameron Morrison's son-in-law. The 3,000-acre sector had been his father-in-law's hunting preserve. Another part of that same estate became the site of fellow oligarch and mayor John Belk's anchor department store in the most upscale mall in the city, Southpark.

Tolerance that Pays

When Charlotte business leaders began boasting that Charlotte "made it work," the "it" was not busing to achieve integration. That was mandated. Obeying a court order to correct gross institutional unfairness carried no bragging rights. Nor did it refer to any lofty educational achievement. Busing-related school measurements were too complicated to build a reputation upon. In any event, Charlotte was never academically oriented or distinguished. It had no major university, and no law or medical schools.

Nor did "it" refer to a transformation of values or a racial reckoning for the decades of educational oppression and humiliation under Jim Crow. Charlotte never claimed to have faced down its history of slavery and Jim Crow. There was no truth-and-reconciliation commission.[17] No apologies were issued. No reparations were considered.

"It" was widely understood to mean that Charlotte deserved credit for *tolerating* the integration order and for tolerating integration, even as it was forced upon the city. It complied largely without violence, more or less efficiently, without *official* opposition. Charlotte deserved praise, the "made it work" slogan indicated, for opposition it did *not* engage in and for responses that did not happen. The city managed to gain distinction for what it was *not*. Charlotte was *not* Birmingham, Little Rock, or anywhere in Mississippi.

More than racial balance or how busing would impact neighborhoods or academic achievement, the primary concern of Charlotte's business leaders—and it was *business* leaders who took the lead—was the *national perception* of Charlotte's racial sentiments. Facing a federal court order for immediate school desegregation and with the whole world watching, tolerance was a *commercial*, not a moral, mandate. Business required it.

Charlotte's *actual* racial sentiments were discussed and debated as the city moved from Jim Crow segregation to forced school integration, to national recognition for achieving integration and then back to extreme de facto resegregation. Whatever Charlotte's actual levels of racial fear and prejudice were or are now, the city's leaders kept them from public display by not confronting them. The radical and abrupt change of school integration was tolerated, but so were the social sentiments that had sustained Jim Crow for almost a century and prompted the court order in the first place—the *Charlotte Way*.

The City that Made (Business) Work

When the national currents changed in the '80s and '90s from justice and integration toward business expansion, individualism, entrepreneurship, and "freedom of choice," Charlotte smoothly shifted into hyper-commercial development, led by the same bank officials who earlier championed integration. City leaders focused on attracting new companies, corporate headquarters, and affluent managers. The resegregation of schools and neighborhoods that accompanied this new era was not a concern from the *business* perspective. When resegregation was acknowledged at all, it was cast as an unintended but perhaps inevitable response of the "market," which meant that any effort to reverse the trend was not only not required, it was precluded.

Despite reliable data to the contrary, some even argued that integration had never made any *educational* difference, making Charlotte's tolerance of busing, despite its ineffectiveness, even more noble and praiseworthy. Now, it was argued, sound principles of economics and management could be applied to the public schools. Attempts to improve the schools focused on innovative teacher training, special education for those "culturally deprived," rigorous testing, and greater classroom discipline to help students still lagging in achievement.[18] The legacy of the decades of imposed segregation and inferior resources was treated as having been adequately rectified by the years of busing.

The "best" schools were once again "paired" with the best neighborhoods. Disparity in education came to be treated as the natural order of things, like the widening of disparities in income and wealth that was also occurring at this time. The concerns of the affluent managers relocating to Charlotte regarding the public schools had been addressed. Charlotte resegregated, yet city boosters insured that it retained its notoriety as the "city that made it work."

Necessary Tolerance

Author, educator, and social critic Earl Shorris is among the few who have looked closely at the sentiment of "tolerance" that is expressed in business culture and how this differs from tolerance as a moral position or character attribute. Shorris's analysis is based partly on his years of work in advertising on Madison Avenue. In the groundbreaking book *A Nation of Salesmen: The Tyranny of the Market and the Subversion of Culture*, Shorris explains that *commercial* tolerance is transactional, like negotiated terms, and contingent on market circumstances, which are subject to change:

> Tolerance, which enables the salesman to expand his business [and] sell to people unrelated to him, unlike him, has always been the unspoken aspect of his work. . . . [T]olerance is in his immediate self-interest: He tolerates those who are necessary to him. . . . His attitude is practical, not moral or political.[19]

It is *commercial* tolerance, as Shorris explains it, that enabled Charlotte's business elite to publicly support the federally imposed order to desegregate the schools. The federal mandate singled the city out for its oppressive history of racism, super-seded local authority, reversed a half century of law, and over-turned decades of locally determined school policies. Integra-tion through court-mandated busing was an action that would certainly be otherwise treated as onerous and repellant. In fact, Charlotte militantly resisted it for years in court before the bus-ing order was finally affirmed by the US Supreme Court.

Shorris further explains that *business-based* tolerance is a vir-tue that is never admitted to being transactional, adopted for a time to achieve a commercialized goal. It must always be pre-sented as personal, enduring, and unselfish, unrelated to profit or expediency. The salesman appears to tolerate, Shorris wrote, but personally does have to *be* tolerant. Tolerance is a trick of the trade, not a character trait. Further, business tolerance, like all other things in business, may be *temporary*, lasting only as long as needed to complete a transaction or until success is deemed unlikely or unnecessary.

In the search for Soul in Charlotte, if higher, non-commercial values do not prevail in Charlotte's educational system—normal-ly a cultural touchstone—but, as in other sectors of city life, are superseded by business interests, there remains one more place to look—in Charlotte's churches.

---

[1] *Southern Oral History Program* Collection (#4007), Interview with Arthur Grif-fin, May 7, 1999. Interview K-0168., Arthur Griffin, interviewee, Pamela Grun-dy, interviewer

[2] The court case *Swann v. Charlotte-Mecklenburg Board of Education* was decided on April 20, 1971. The Supreme Court unanimously upheld busing programs to speed racial integration of public schools. The ruling was based on an earli-er decision outlawing "separate but equal" schools dating to 1954. The Swann case had struggled through the courts since 1965 before reaching the Supreme Court in 1971.

[3] When Saul Alinsky's disruptive organization began a campaign, it often taunted the host city's pretensions or failure to live up to its lofty ideals. When

HELP brought the Alinsky organization to Charlotte in the late 1990s, the Alinsky official Arnie Graf jabbed at Charlotte. He told the *Charlotte Observer* that the city has mostly shown capacity to mobilize for sporting events, but not for people's needs. (*Charlotte Observer*, Apr 19, 1996)

[4] "Stymied by Segregation: How Integration Can Transform North Carolina Schools and the Lives of Its Students" by Kris Nordstrom, Policy Analyst, *North Carolina Justice Center* (https://www.ncjustice.org/wp-content/uploads/2018/11/STYMIED-BY-SEGREGATION-Integration-can-Transform-NC-FINAL-web.pdf)

[5] That famous photo can be seen in the *Charlotte Observer*, Sep 5, 1957. It appeared the same day also in newspapers throughout the country and in Canada.

[6] "Charlotte High School at Center of Desegregation Sees Flip in Racial Makeup as Key Players Recount Experiences" by Julian Sadur, *Queen City News*, Feb 16, 2024

[7] https://www.usnews.com/education/k12/north-carolina/districts/charlotte-mecklenburg-schools-102653#:~:text=Students%20at%20Charlotte%2DMecklenburg%20Schools,Hawaiian%20or%20other%20Pacific%20Islander.

[8] C. D. Spangler Jr., a Charlotte billionaire, who served on the school board was the developer and owner of the rental housing. He was also owner of a bank that merged with NCNB, the precursor of Bank of America. The other prominent businessperson to take the lead in Charlotte schools in this era, Joe B. Martin, was an executive at Bank of America and one of the closest associates of CEO Hugh McColl who personally recruited him to get on the School Board.

[9] The federal judge was Robert Potter. A typical account of his ruling, which is treated as the single factor that ended all efforts to desegregate Charlotte's school system and in other cities as well is "Ruling Ends Historic Forced Busing Program" by Richard Lee Colvin, *Los Angeles Times*, Sept. 11, 1999

[10] "The Desegregation and Resegregation of Charlotte's Schools" by Clint Smith, *New Yorker*, October 3, 201

[11] "Inadequate Schools Hurt Student Achievement" by Fannie Flono, *Charlotte Observer*, Aug 20, 1997

[12] 52% of all CMS students scored at or above grade-level proficiency on tests, compared to 53.6% of all North Carolina students, "CMS celebrates small wins but still struggles with student performance," by Alexandria Sands, *Axios Charlotte*, Sep 7, 2023

[13] *Small Church With a Big Mission: The History of the First 50 Years of Seigle Avenue Presbyterian Church* by Margaret G. Bigger and Katherine M. Dunlap, A. Borough Books, 1995

[14] *Boom for Whom?: Education, Desegregation, and Development in Charlotte* by Stephen Samuel Smith, State University of New York Press, 2004

[15] "From 1980 to 2000, the twenty-year period in which Charlotte boomed and became a national economic player, the black/white gap in per capita income *increased* by 3.0 percent", *Boom for Whom?* by Stephen Samuel Smith, p. 50

[16] *Boom for Whom?* by Stephen Samuel Smith, p. 53

[17] "The South African Truth and Reconciliation Commission (TRC) was set up by the Government of National Unity to help deal with what happened under apartheid... [it] gave members of the public a chance to express their regret at failing to prevent human rights violations and to demonstrate their commitment to reconciliation." *Official Truth and Reconciliation Commission Website*: https://www.justice.gov.za/trc/

[18] According to data from the National Center for Education Statistics, 1988 was when the US achieved the highest levels of school integration and the achievement gap between White and Black student was lowest. Reading score differences were reduced 50% from 1971 levels. Test scores rose, for both Black and White students. As resegregation increases, the gap is now growing. ("Choosing a School for My Daughter in a Segregated City" by Nikole Hannah-Jones, *New York Times,* June 9, 2016

[19] *A Nation of Salesmen: The Tyranny of the Market and the Subversion of Culture* by Earl Shorris, W. W. Norton & Company, 1994, Kindle Edition, 2012

X. Searching In Charlotte's Churches

Charlotte is known for a phenomenon that many people find quite peculiar for a city of its size, diversity, and its claim to "world-class" status. Newcomers to Charlotte are often taken aback when asked by a Charlotte resident, on first meeting, *What church do you go to?* Everywhere else they've lived, questions of faith are politely avoided, at least initially, out of respect of privacy or concern for insensitivity. Yet, in Charlotte, as new residents absorb the city culture, they often end up asking others that same invasive question.

What they discover and adopt is key to the social character of Charlotte regarding religious faiths. They learn that the question is not actually a probe of specific religious belief. It is a social signaling regarding civic acceptance and status, in which membership in a church, *any church*, is *integral* and more or less *mandatory*. Actual dogmas and denominations are almost irrelevant, though some faiths are nominally better than others— Presbyterian, of course, being best.

Presbyterianism may be considered the official denomination of Charlotte. The first seven churches established in the area were of that faith. As a *Charlotte Observer* feature, "Presby Power," affirmed, Presbyterians, the descendants of the early Scotch-Irish settlers "helped mold [Charlotte's] personality." The article highlighted influential Presbyterians in Charlotte, including college presidents, bank CEOs, the school board chair, the largest land developer, a former governor, and a US congressman. It described a particular attribute of the "Presby" strain of Christianity, ascribed to the influence of its founder, John Calvin, as "a pervasive kind of work ethic," with "devotion to honor, work and duty."

The president of a Presbyterian college explained, "It's OK with John Calvin if you work hard, be thrifty and do good in the here and now. . . . Calvin respects capitalism." Another college president described the Presbyterian "presumption" that

"God will be the Lord of the Counting House as well as the Church House."[1]

As will be shown, the Presbyterian Calvinism that sanctified "doing good [financially] in the here and now," has evolved into a multi-denominational and secular belief system known variously as "prosperity theology," "charismatic Christianity," "positive thinking," or "The Secret." It is taught in business conferences and self-help seminars as much as from the pulpits of multiple denominations.

The ideology teaches that God, the Universe, or whatever name is given to the Divine Force not only bestows heavenly approval on making money; becoming wealthy is each believer's destiny, intended by Providence. Appropriately, Charlotte's largest Presbyterian Church, the fourth largest in America, is located on Providence Road, which leads through some of Charlotte's most affluent neighborhoods.

In the newer iterations of Calvinism, thriftiness, perseverance, honor, and duty are downplayed in favor of an emphasis on how one thinks, talks, presents oneself, and the importance of keeping company with other believers and "winners." Ideal traits that please heaven and produce prosperity include social conformity, ambition and enterprise, *practical* tolerance, friendliness, and reverence for commercial growth.

Questions, doubts, a dour demeanor, sarcasm, irony, pessimism, or complacency are the new signs of apostasy. Expressing discontent with the general order of society or advocating fundamental social change is heresy. Apostates may no longer face religious sanction, but could still face negative consequences to their careers and social standing. Future political roles can be ruled out.

As part of this evolution, other faiths in Charlotte have been allowed at Charlotte's table of influence and respectability, formerly reserved for Presbyterians. Most have absorbed its tenets regarding enterprise and the godly blessings of wealth. This new ecumenical spirit allows a lessening of old religious prejudices. In particular, old Charlotte's discrimination against "papists" and Jews has greatly subsided, and the formerly lowly Baptists have risen in status.

Overt racial and religious discrimination is discouraged. Among the last holdouts were Charlotte's most prestigious country clubs, Charlotte Country Club and Myers Park. Initiation fees to join these bastions of distinction are $80,000 and $95,000 respectively. As late as the 1990s, neither had even one Black member, and in the case of the Charlotte Country Club, no Jews.[2]

The Faith "Scene"

The *continued* social and economic mandate for churchgoing in Charlotte was reflected in a 2018 *Charlotte Observer* article, entitled, "10 Things You Need to Know to Navigate Charlotte's Faith Scene."

Without acknowledging it, and perhaps even without realizing it, the article affirmed W. J. Cash's searing observation that in Charlotte, *"Theology and the hog literally make one flesh."* The article described church-going in Charlotte in the language of commerce, depicting ancient faiths that offer meaning to life in terms that might just as well be used to describe local breweries. Churches, in this narrative, are among the amenities that add to a great lifestyle. Where else are the expressions of religious faith a "scene"?

The *Observer* article offers a broad overview and reveals significant, if superficial, changes since Cash's days. It notes that Charlotte, which used to have only a tiny Catholic community, is now home to the largest Catholic church in the entire United States, St. Matthew's, with a membership of 10,000 families, twice as large as the biggest Presbyterian church in town. Also amazing to old-timers in Charlotte, this massive congregation is located in the affluent southeast suburb. This is the area that was developed during the school integration crisis and that, politically aided by a major new highway, became the largest enclave of well-to-do White families, especially corporate managers arriving with newly relocated companies.

Catholics in Charlotte used to be poor, working class and aspiring middle class. Many are quite rich now. Under the twenty-year tenure of Peter J. Jugis as bishop of the Diocese of Charlotte, who resigned in 2024 for health reasons, the diocese was among the more politically conservative. The bishop said that he would refuse communion to any politicians who publicly supported abortion rights. He promoted the ancient ritual of the Latin Mass.

There is no concern from Protestant denominations any more about the old tropes of Catholics being bound to Rome, proclivity for alcohol, or large numbers of children. Catholic "parochial" schools are now seen as high status, academically superior, and exclusive. Annual tuition to the Catholic high school: $18,881, less for the faithful.

The newspaper's overview of Charlotte's church "scene" features some of the prominent Black churches and notes that Charlotte is the national headquarters of the African Methodist Episcopal Zion denomination. AME Zion has 1.4 million members. The denomination has historical roots in abolitionism. It played a leading role in the civil rights movement. Clergy of Black churches were the early civil rights leaders in Charlotte, some experiencing violent attacks from racists.

One AME Zion church, located in the center city, is highlighted as hosting community meetings, but there are no longer suspicions from Charlotte leaders of extremism or civil disobedience being fomented in Charlotte's Black churches.

Today, Vi Lyles, an African American woman, is the city's mayor. Like her African American predecessors in that office, she is a political moderate, closely tied to Charlotte's big business interests. She previously worked for the city government in record keeping and accounting. She is a professional administrator.

Harvey Gantt, who served as Charlotte's first Black mayor, is an architect. During his tenure in the early 1980s he championed the mantra of "world-class city."[3] He was followed in office by an attorney. Another African American mayor, Patrick Cannon, was the co-founder of a parking management company in downtown Charlotte. The attorney who was the second African American mayor, Anthony Foxx, became secretary of transportation under Barack Obama. Foxx later became the in-house attorney of the transport company Lyft, where he led efforts to prevent drivers, classified as contractors, from gaining the rights and benefits of employees.

The secular, moderate, and business-oriented profiles of Charlotte's Black mayors reflect that the Black churches are no longer a font of political leadership or social activism. Black churches are now politically mainstream institutions within Charlotte's church "scene."

The article on Charlotte's "faith scene" also describes the fifty-four-acre Jewish facility called Shalom Park, which includes both Reform and Conservative Jewish temples. Shalom Park is referred to as "the center of Jewish life in Charlotte." People of the Jewish faith, numbering about 15,000 today, like churchgoing African Americans and Roman Catholics, are accepted as Charlotte insiders now, based on civic adherence to the common faith of business.

For many years in Charlotte, Jewish people were kept at the margins of power and inclusion, though not nearly as comprehensively as Black citizens. At a time when antisemitic attitudes were still mainstream, one of the better-known Jews in Charlotte was Ellis Berlin, the owner of Berlin's Pawn Shop, located in the old downtown, for more than twenty-five years. Ellis Berlin fought Charlotte's powerful urban renewal program and filed lawsuits to attempt to save his store. He ran as a candidate for city council advocating alternative policies to Charlotte's business elites. He also helped neighborhood groups that were in battles with city hall. Berlin's store was ultimately demolished and his business forced to move away from the center city.[4] Today, there are no prominent Jews, or local people publicly identified with any religion, who directly and openly challenge the Charlotte business establishment on the grounds of morality or social justice.

The most famous Jew in Charlotte until his death in 1981 was the colorful figure Herschel Goldhirsch, known in Charlotte as Harry Golden. Golden was born in Europe and lived and worked in New York City before coming to the South. That he was notable partly just for being Jewish is an indicator of the historically marginal position of Jews in Charlotte. Golden came to Charlotte in the 1940s. He gained fame as an author and publisher and for being a "Southern Jew," which was considered an exotic combination. He was interviewed on national television shows about living in the Bible Belt. He effectively used humor to advocate for civil rights and other liberal causes. In the late 1950s, it was disclosed that he had spent four years in prison for investor fraud when he had run a brokerage house in New York City called the Bucket Shop. The revelation had little impact on the affection he had won in Charlotte. Golden said many Christian clergy in Charlotte, having little contact with Jews, assumed he was an expert in the Old Testament. He said he actually knew very little, but they never seemed to notice.[5]

Today, Charlotte's Jewish leaders are hardly colorful outsiders. Shalom Park hosts many educational and cultural events. Two of the most notable and wealthy families of Charlotte, the

Levines and Blumenthals, hold naming rights over major art institutions and medical facilities in Charlotte for which they are major philanthropists.

The *Observer's* updated overview of Charlotte's religious "scene" also acknowledges the many other denominations that have grown in Charlotte from, Bahai to Mormon, and the multitude of Baptists. Like Baptists elsewhere, Charlotte's Baptist congregations vary widely in beliefs. Of course, the article pays tribute to Billy Graham, friend to US presidents, who was born in Charlotte, and his "library," which is a national tourist attraction in the city.

Lhasa of Calvinism

Charlotte is not famous for great cathedrals as in Europe or even Washington, DC; there are no meditation centers like Houston's famed Rothko Chapel; no new denominations or spiritual movements were originated as in New England or upstate New York. No moral movements were launched such as the Great Awakening in New England, transcendentalism in the Boston area, the civil rights struggle in Atlanta or Birmingham, or the New Age in California. And Charlotte is not the hallowed home to any noteworthy theologians.

Charlotte is, however, where religious practice is *amplified*, like it is with its banks, hospitals, stock car racing, and energy company, to *enormous* scale. Congregations of simple Baptists, humble Catholics, and traditional Calvinists transformed into "worldwide crusades," the nation's largest parish, millionaire-led megachurches and the world's largest religious theme park. It is the pervasiveness, scale, and intensity of religion that led W. J. Cash to call Charlotte the "Lhasa of Calvinism," comparing it to the mysterious holy city of Tibetan Buddhism.

Delving into Charlotte's religious character leads inevitably to where scale and intensity reached the greatest level, the largest and most influential of all of Charlotte's religious institutions. That is the world-famous Heritage USA, founded by disgraced evangelist Jim Bakker.

In the 1980s, more than 6 million devotees *a year* poured into Charlotte North Carolina to visit Bakker's 2,400 acre Heritage USA," Charlotte's greatest site of religious pilgrimage. Six times as many people each year went to Bakker's temple as visited the locally revered Billy Graham Library *in total* since it was consecrated more than 15 years ago.

Broadcasting live from his modern satellite television studios in Charlotte, Bakker reached tens of millions more all over the world, with his "Praise The Lord" (PTL) programs and ministry.

Overshadowing Billy

Official narratives of Charlotte's religious mark on the world herald Charlotte-born Billy Graham, who spiritually counseled US presidents and traveled the world conducting his famous "crusades." Yet, Bakker's core teaching, prosperity theology, is the more powerful movement in Christianity and, arguably, a truer *reflection of Charlotte* than Graham.

The *New York Times'* columnist Ross Douthat referred to "the most influential work of popular theology published this century." It is not any of Billy Graham's thirty-three books, but one by megachurch pastor Joel Osteen, entitled *Your Best Life Now: 7 Steps to Living at Your Full Potential*, a warmed-over version of Bakker's core message about material "blessings" coming to those who believe.[6]

Billy Graham, like artist Romare Bearden, is celebrated by Charlotte boosters as a native son. The main highway to Charlotte's hub airport is named for Graham, as a park in uptown is for Bearden. But also, like Bearden, Graham never lived in Charlotte as an adult or during his career. He was never a member of any Charlotte church. For fifty years, the Billy Graham organization was headquartered in downtown Minneapolis on a 2.3-acre facility with a staff of over 400. It moved into Charlotte only in 2001, after Graham's health was failing and his library was opening. Samaritan's Purse, an international relief agency that is part of the Graham organization, is also not based in Charlotte, but in Boone, N.C., where it is run by his son Franklin, who lives in Boone.[7] Billy Graham retired in 2005, followed by years of illness including cancer and Parkinson. He died in 2018 at age 99.

An inconspicuous low-rise office building, called Graham Park, sits where the family home of Billy Graham was located. The actual 2,400 square foot house, originally on the 300-acre dairy farm, was sold by the Graham family in the 1980s to developers. The house was purchased from those developers by Jim Bakker's PTL Club and moved to the Heritage USA where it became part of Bakker's theme park.[8]

Graham's message of ecumenism among faiths and racial co-existence coincided with prevailing social trends and federal policy. His notoriety was also based on his condemnation of Communism, a theme that resonated with the prevailing political policy of that time. Some of his moral views and messages against homosexuality and the rights and freedoms of women were at odds with social trends and are now less remembered.

By 1990, Jim Bakker had departed from Charlotte in handcuffs, convicted of criminal fraud for deceiving followers and misusing millions in donated funds. As the chosen locale of his booming empire, Charlotte had basked in Bakker's fame and his growing political and religious influence. Upon his conviction, Charlotte quickly began to erase all historical connections. A profile of the city in the *New York Times* in 1991 said Charlotte's "fixation on image" led boosters to emphasize that Bakker's famed facilities were actually never in Charlotte but "just over the border in South Carolina."[9]

Bakker's wife, Tammy, died of cancer in 2007. Jim Bakker continues a televised ministry from Missouri—but their imprint and reflection of "Soul" in Charlotte are present and palpable.

Bakker's Love Child

Despite official disavowals of Bakker and the omission, typical of Charlotte, of the Bakkers in the *Observer's* overview of Charlotte religion, the Bakkers's presence was acknowledged, implicitly. The article named the *number one thing you need to know* about church life in Charlotte:

"We are big into Elevation Church."

Elevation is the No. 1 church in Charlotte. And, for those who remember the style, message, and popularity of Heritage, Elevation Church will not be mistaken for anything but the love child of Bakker's lucrative ministry.

The article explains that Elevation is Charlotte's fastest growing church, with ten locations in Charlotte and more than 20,000 Charlotte-area members. Attendance numbers alone do not reflect the church's full impact. Its "charismatic" pastor, Steven Furtick, has nearly 2.5 million Facebook followers from around the world. Weekly attendance is over 14,000, and another 40,000 watch the services via livestream. Elevation wins international awards for its music, and books by its pastor become bestsellers. Elevation is one of the ten largest mega-churches in America. Like St. Matthew's, the largest Catholic parish in America, Elevation's main facility is in Ballantyne, the southeast suburb that is the cultural and spiritual vortex of Charlotte's new prosperity.

Officially, Elevation Church is Baptist, though it is not connected to the Southern Baptist Convention. People of all denominations attend its services, which are described as exciting and uplifting. The pastor is often said to be "on fire with the Lord." Elevation Church is classified as evangelical, and best known for promoting from the pulpit the blessing of prosperity as the earthly sign of Heavenly Grace.

Sectarian Divide

The dominance of Elevation and its "prosperity" theology can also be measured against the church that represents its theological inverse in Charlotte. Myers Park Baptist is located in the heart of Charlotte's oldest and most prestigious neighborhood. It was founded nearly 80 years ago. Its official mission is:

> to be an inclusive community for spirituality and social justice. . . . We are committed to educating on white privilege, dismantling racism, and denouncing white supremacy in every iteration, until all people, regardless of race, are fully affirmed, welcomed, and included in the social and economic fabric of our society.[10]

In his first sermon following the election of Donald Trump, November 10, 2024, pastor Benjamin Boswell said the nation faced a "Bonhoeffer moment" referring to the courageous stand of German theologian Dietrich Bohhoeffer in the 1930s against Hitler and National Socialism and for which he was executed by the Nazis. Reverend Boswell told the avowedly liberal Myers Park Baptist congregation:

> [The election of Trump] means fascism has swept in with the wind and our nation has elected a man who openly describes himself as a "dictator." But Bonhoeffer is more than a description. The question is not just, "Is this a Bonhoeffer moment?" but "How will we respond to it?" . . . will we stand up, speak the truth, witness against injustice, help all the victims, and jam a spoke in the machinery of empire?[11]

A few weeks later, Pastor Boswell, who had led the congregation for nine years, was asked to resign. The church board voted overwhelmingly against him. The head of the church board at the time, Marcy McClanahan, told *NPR* that the main reason was declining attendance, down to just 150 souls a week, less than half of previous years' attendance, she said. The church claims a membership of over a thousand.[12] Church Deacon Robert Dulin said some people who had left Myers Park Baptist made complaints about Pastor Boswell's focus on social and racial justice.[13]

The forced resignation has disrupted the Myers Park congregation, Charlotte's religious bulwark of the social justice interpretation of Christianity. But, the "prosperity" sect, exemplified by Charlotte's Elevation Church, though dominant, is not without detractors in Charlotte. Publicized controversy arose over Pastor Furtick's parsonage, a 16,000 square foot mansion with seven bathrooms. The "allowance" given to a church pastor for the parsonage, even if not owned by the church itself, is legally exempt from the pastor's income tax. The amount given to Pastor Furtick for his mansion is not disclosed. However, for comparison, a local news investigation revealed that the pastor of a similar megachurch in Texas who is a close associate of Furtick received a "parsonage allowance" of over $20,000 per month. Additionally, when the pastor uses the tax-free "allowance" to pay property taxes and mortgage interest, those costs are personally tax-deductible.[14] Pastor Furtick reportedly has a personal net worth of $60 million. Elevation was one of the first churches in America to install a new technology in its entry area—ATM machines.[15]

The controversy over Furtick's palatial parsonage was sparked by a television news story by Charlotte's award-winning, 16-year veteran investigative journalist, Stuart Watson, in January 2014. Within less than a year, Watson was fired. He publicly attributed the firing to a shift toward less news department budgeting and reduced local investigative work.[16]

The Faith of Babbitt

Beyond its sheer size and wealth, to appreciate the wider relevance of Elevation Church to Charlotte, it is useful to recall W. J. Cash's historical observation of stereotype George Babbitt, whom he said, "overshadows and overruns" [Charlotte], and H. L. Mencken's description of Babbitt, "a faithful Booster... a trustworthy Presbyterian... Leading Citizens...the supporters of evangelical Christianity."

Mencken called the faith of Babbitt "Presbyterian," meaning Calvinism, which Charlotte proclaims as its religious foundation. The backers of the giant statuary on the Square in Charlotte's uptown had originally planned a monument to this Presbyterian tradition as one of Charlotte's four "pillars."

Calvinism is the genesis of Prosperity Theology. In America, Calvinistic beliefs have taken on new titles and styles, while maintaining or exaggerating the empowering and comforting belief that each person can personally "touch the divine" through prayer and positive thinking to obtain *financial* "blessings," which are sacred evidence of being in God's good grace.

A modern interpretation of the meaning and impact of the "prosperity gospel" is offered by *New York Times* religion columnist Ross Douthat in his book, *Bad Religion: How We Became a Nation of Heretics*. He traces its prevalence beginning in the 1980s. Today, he ruefully admits, Christianity for many has become a "marriage of God and Mammon":

> The gospel of wealth has come of age. . . . [B]y explicitly baptizing the pursuit of worldly gain, prosperity theology has helped millions of believers reconcile their religious faith with . . . unbiblical wealth and un-Christian consumer culture.[17]

The Church of Amway

The path to understanding how Elevation, a church congregation that looks and acts like a *business,* is Charlotte's predominant religious institution leads back to a business enterprise that looks and acts like a *church*—Amway.

This is an insight from historian, Dr. Eric G. Weinberg, in *Creating Heaven on Earth: Jim Bakker and the Birth of a Sunbelt Pentecostalism,* a work that cites, among many other sources, the research on Southern cities by historian, Matthew Lassiter, earlier referenced in this story. Weinberg's thesis is supported by an extraordinary cluster of Amway connections to Bakker and by Amway's extensive political and financial influence in Charlotte where Bakker was based.

Amway is the oldest and largest type of enterprise, known as "multi-level marketing." Founded in 1959, Amway has current revenue of over $7 billion and operates in 100 countries. The US Federal Trade Commission unsuccessfully sued to shut Amway down as an illegal pyramid scheme in 1975. Amway's hallmark product is a commodity laundry soap that few people would know the name of. The company is far better known for the aggressive recruiting by its followers to invest in the Amway "business opportunity" with rights to recruit yet others and effective requirements to purchase Amway products as part of the income proposition. The recruiting involves an extraordinary claim that the company has a secret for providing "unlimited" success to participants who hold unquestioning belief in the "system." That system involves an "endless" recruiting chain, that claims the capacity to expand exponentially to "infinity" with money flowing upward from later recruits to earlier ones. Many people describe Amway as a secular type of religion. It is accused of operating a pyramid scheme and engaging in cult persuasion and control methods. Its founders proclaim an extreme version of Dutch Calvinism as their guiding faith and the basis for the business.

Three of Amway's greatest promoters, the "top guns" of a global recruitment system—Dexter Yager, Bill Britt, and Don Storms—were all based in the Charlotte area. Their recruiting network, consisting of millions of people and extending into many countries, siphoned tens of millions of dollars back to these three men *in Charlotte*.

Yager was Amway's undisputed king, the peak of its recruiting machine. His power extended into the heart of Charlotte politics. Yager was the largest donor and most important backer of the first woman ever elected mayor, Sue Myrick, who later was elected to Congress to represent a district that includes most of Mecklenburg County. Yager contributed and raised over $400,000 (in today's dollars) for Myrick's campaign, much of which was collected from Amway recruits under Yager's direction. Myrick was also an Amway distributor herself and gained additional benefits as a paid motivational speaker at Amway events organized by Yager.

While based in Charlotte and working within the Amway organization, Yager pioneered a legally challenged financial scheme that was also adopted by Britt and Storms, among others. Amway recruits were persuaded to purchase "success tools" directly from Yager, creating a separate, internal profit center sourced from direct payments to him by Amway recruits and unrelated to their Amway product purchases or sales.[18]

The main "success tools" were motivational audio tapes produced in Charlotte at a multi-million-dollar enterprise privately owned by Yager, with estimated sales of more than $70 million (today's value). Yager tapes and rallies were part of a vast indoctrination program by Amway that taught the "prosperity" dogma with assumed religious and economic authority.

Each recruit was instructed to listen to tapes repeatedly every day and purchase new tapes weekly, at a cost of about $500 a year (in today's dollars). Production costs to Yager were a tiny fraction of the price charged to the recruits per tape. All were told the tapes were *indispensable* for success in Amway. No data were produced showing those in the "tape a week" program were any more successful than others, though many claimed the program caused them to *lose* even more money.

Yager established a multi-level reward system for his sub-recruiters in which they were authorized to sell his tapes and receive a portion of the profits and to authorize others below them to do the same. It was called by whistle-blowers a "pyramid within a pyramid."

An additional part of the private reward system was selling tickets to Yager-organized Amway events, some drawing as many as 80,000 Amway recruits. The inspirational messages and metaphysical dogmas narrated on the tapes were presented from the stage by Yager himself and famous religious, business, and military figures. US presidents such as Ronald Reagan and George H. W. Bush were paid hundreds of thousands to speak at the events.

According to Yager's tapes and speeches, lack of success in Amway could only be the result of undirected, negative thinking that he called "stinking thinking." Failure to gain wealth is, therefore, a *moral* failure, a type of sin. The events, requiring paid admission, and the monthly tools purchases were said to aid the recruits in learning how to transform their lives by adopting the proper mindset. Many came to believe Amway—and Yager—were their only hope for deliverance from a life of failure or mediocrity.

Charlotte: Amway Mecca

Before Bakker drew millions of the faithful to the sacred shrine of Heritage USA, Charlotte was Mecca for millions of

Amway believers, who traveled to the city at the direction of Dexter Yager. Charlotte's largest conventions were sponsored by Amway. They looked and sounded just like Bakker's religious celebrations for good reason.

Just as Pastor Furtick's prosperity celebrations at Elevation have the feel of Jim Bakker's uplifting and profitable ministry, Bakker's "Praise the Lord" ministry was modeled on Amway's style, dogmas, financial practices, and evangelical messaging.

One thread connecting Yager to Bakker and Furtick is their common dogma linking prosperity to marital bliss and personal fulfillment. Yager always made his supportive and worshipful spouse, "Birdie" Yager, a key part of his public image. Bakker famously presented his uplifting message in partnership with his adoring spouse, the cosmetically famous Tammy Fae. Furtick attributes the power and success of his ministry to his sacred bond with wife, Holly, who cofounded Elevation and is a public celebrity at the church.

Dexter Yager was Bakker's earliest and strongest backer and mentor. When Bakker lost control and was effectively evicted from his theme park and facing criminal charges, Dexter Yager personally provided a home where Bakker could take refuge.[19] To close the theological loop, when Yager passed away in 2019 and Birdie in 2023, funeral services for both were held at . . . Elevation Church.

As recounted in Weinberg's *Creating Heaven on Earth*, Bakker's collaboration with Dexter Yager of Amway began even before he arrived in Charlotte. They met through a Christian business group in Charlotte called Full Gospel Business Men's Fellowship International.

Bakker was "mesmerized by Yager's success," Weinberg wrote, and arranged for Yager to become a board member of the future PTL Club. Weinberg says the following about Bakker's relationship with Yager:

> Over time, Bakker and PTL provided Yager with many recruits and vice versa . . . Bakker was especially interested to learn how to apply Yager's inspirational messages and techniques to his own ministry. In fact, he was so enthralled that he became an Amway sales associate and attended weekly meetings with Yager, Doug Wead and other important members of the Amway organization.[20] These meetings and the connections with Amway and with Yager inspired Bakker to make prosperity theology an even more important part of his ministry and he began to learn from Yager how to market and sell his message. Yager, meanwhile, endorsed PTL and encouraged his distributors to support Bakker's new network.

The "success" that bedazzled Bakker was dramatically demonstrated in the enormous motivational events Yager conducted in Charlotte at its coliseum and convention center. Well before the city became known for its hub airport, banks, or professional sports, Amway devotees all over America and in other countries knew of Charlotte, North Carolina, as an Amway holy place, with Dexter Yager as its high priest. Pilgrims came to Charlotte to bear witness to Amway's promise of prosperity. By car and plane, and eventually tour bus, they arrived at the Amway cathedral: the enormous and lavish home of Dexter Yager, Amway's highest ranking recruiter and Charlotte political kingmaker, the personification of the "success" that Amway promised all followers.

The awesome 15,000 square foot house, the gigantic $350,000 (in 1995 dollars) motorhome, the three Rolls Royces in his 2,400 square foot garage, the seven-seat private jet, Yager's loving wife and children, his ever-positive attitude, and his benevolent desire to help others were living proof of the earthly blessings available to those who *believed,* followed, and invested in Amway.[21]

Clergyman Bakker's promises of "fulfillment and prosperity" aligned seamlessly with *salesman* Yager's promises to provide a "way of life" (Amway, American-Way). Both required that followers pay for entry and then continue paying to learn of and unlock their own secret power. Fervent belief and continuous consumption of inspirational instruction were the magic ingredients for gaining promised rewards. Both drew millions of followers — to *Charlotte.* Virtually all the investors in each lost money. Both Bakker and Amway stand accused of operating Ponzi schemes.[22]

Ponzi as Pastor and Business Coach

Among regulators, consumer advocates, and some attorneys, it is well known that Charlotte has a storied history and infamous reputation as a center of multi-level marketing and pyramid schemes. This notoriety is founded upon but extends far beyond Amway's deep local involvement.

In 2006, Charlotte gained notice in the *Wall Street Journal* for being home to a Ponzi scheme called 12dailyPro. The fraud was operated from an apartment in Charlotte by a thirty-four-year-old Charlotte resident. The court-appointed receiver estimated that approximately 175,000 individuals were involved.[23] One Charlotte victim told the *Charlotte Observer* that he was facing a $20,000 loss. Others invested from hundreds to as much as $6,000, according to victim accounts.

The scheme made the absurd promise to produce 12 percent returns *every day* for 12 days. Investors were supposed to "surf" internet ads each day for a few minutes in order to "qualify" for the profits. Strangely, though tens of millions were lost by hundreds of thousands, the fraud was never criminally prosecuted. The North Carolina Attorney General never brought a case. It was ultimately shut down by federal regulators at the SEC in a civil case for not "disclosing" that the "returns" came from new investors, in a "robbing Peter to pay Paul" transfer.[24]

When the first local news story appeared about the absurd claims of 12dailyPro, the company had a convention scheduled in Charlotte just a week later with an expected attendance of 500 hopeful "investors."[25]

In 2008, the headquarters of the multi-level marketing company ACN relocated to Charlotte. ACN is most famous for being publicly endorsed and promoted by Donald Trump, who was reportedly paid more than $10 million in endorsement speaking fees.[26] The Trump family was sued based on charges that Trump knowingly made false claims that ACN was a lucrative income opportunity.[27] ACN was prosecuted by the State of Montana for deception based on data showing that the average ACN participant in Montana suffered a net loss of more than $700. ACN does not disclose "average" income when soliciting consumers in the US to invest. Past Canadian disclosures showed an average income of less than $10 a week, *before expenses are deducted*.

In 2010, it was reported in a local investigative news report that prominent Charlotte figures, including a popular newscaster and the wife of Bank of America CEO Ken Lewis, were recruiting for the pyramid scheme Fortune High Tech Marketing.[28] This multi-level marketing scam was shut down by the Federal Trade Commission in 2013. At the time, the company claimed to have over 160,000 recruits, but far more had already been defrauded. The FTC stated the scheme was designed so that at least 96% of investors *had to* lose money, which was transferred to earlier recruiters.[29]

I have deep and extensive knowledge and experience with the Ponzi charges brought against Pastor Bakker and the related lawsuits and prosecutions of the "business" of Amway and all others modeled on Amway, called "multi-level marketing" (MLM). I wrote two books on this "business model" famously characterized by each member recruiting others who do the same, creating a recruiting chain expanding *to infinity*, with money flowing up the entire chain from last to first.[30] The "infinite" recruiting chain is the basis for promoters to promise all recruits the opportunity to gain "unlimited" income.[31]

Behind the Ponzi promise is a metaphysical—religious—doctrine, which supersedes the mathematical impossibility. It is that God makes a destiny of wealth available to all through a form of prayer, a way of thinking and living—positive thinking. Market sizes and mathematical limits are dismissed as obstacles only for non-believers, negative thinkers, and doubters.

Delivered as both a viable business plan and a metaphysical prescription for living, the Amway program can evoke an explosive outpouring of hope indistinguishable from people experiencing "spontaneous conversion" and suddenly "speaking in tongues."

Delivered with great authority by trusted leaders who swear that their own great wealth was gained in this way, and *anyone can do it*, the promise can be so inspirational, so freeing, so redeeming, followers are known to give up careers, families, friends, and all they own in its pursuit.

I served as expert witness and consultant in dozens of court cases against Amway and other MLM enterprises that are clones of Amway. Most lawsuits charge that the MLM companies engage in pervasive deception and cause nearly all investors to lose money. As head of the consumer education group *Pyramid Scheme Alert*, I've heard countless stories from Amway followers, describing tragic losses of money, wasting years of their lives, and suffering debilitating disillusionment.[32]

It should, therefore, be unsurprising that the crime Jim Bakker was sent to prison for was selling "unlimited" numbers of "lifetime" benefits at Heritage, when there was, obviously, a limited capacity for Heritage to honor these agreements. Bakker was accused of running an "advanced fee" scheme, in which participants paid up front and continuously for wondrous future benefits promised by Bakker, which he did not and could not possibly deliver. To keep his scheme afloat, he used the funds of new investors to satisfy commitments to earlier ones, creating an unsustainable "endless" chain based on robbing Peter to pay Paul.[33]

Heaven on Earth in Charlotte

Dr. Eric Weinberg, whose earlier referenced work traced the connections of Bakker to Amway, also documented how Bakker's ministry and the later national explosion of megachurches, such as Elevation, meshed with emerging economic trends and political policies.

Fueling the explosive hopes that Bakker tapped into, he argues, are deep-seated and unfulfilled needs, and, for millions, a sense that their work and daily lives are bereft of substance or Soul. They came to Bakker for what had gone missing in their lives—community, connection, Place—while also getting reassurances that what the culture does offer—financial "success," consumer goods, insulated family life—constitute a heaven on earth, available to all with faith and prayerful, positive intentions. According to Weinberg:

> Bakker's religious message was ideally suited to suburban Sunbelt communities such as Charlotte. . . . Living in isolated suburbs, often feeling alienated and rootless, his followers were drawn to his promises of mental tranquility, family happiness, and material success. . . . Bakker provided a religion that matched the larger corporate vision. . . . [It] sanctified their lives and prepared them for competitive careers in which mental transformation and positive thinking were integral to success.[34]

The suburban communities in which Weinberg describes residents as alienated and rootless are the modern neighborhoods established as Charlotte changed from Place to Brand, a process occurring in many other cities and towns. Thousands of White residents moved out to these suburbs, at first to escape commercialization and congestion, and later to avoid school desegregation. Many working-class Whites were pushed out by "blockbusting" realtors fomenting racial fears.

Later, gentrification and skyrocketing housing costs drove others into new and distant developments, requiring them to make long commutes. And thousands more who relocated to Charlotte for corporate management jobs were directed to the recently constructed exurbs with the "best" schools, the greatest security, and a tranquil, family-supportive, and affluent lifestyle.

Many Black residents lost Sense of Place in Charlotte due to urban renewal demolitions, and later due to gentrification of the formerly White areas they had gained legal ability to buy into or rent. The crack cocaine epidemic had ravaged families during the 1980s, and policies of mass incarceration disrupted the lives of many younger men, further devastating family and community. The dream of an integrated and fair society was fading. In the later years, loss of neighborhood was accompanied by enduring and seemingly inescapable poverty and by the decline of activism in Black churches that had provided local attachment and identity.

Whereas Charlotte's brand managers demolish the present in favor of an imagined "world-class" future, Bakker's narrative lifted followers out of their current life conditions and delivered them to an imaginary, Seahaven-like past, where *"It's all true. It's all real. Nothing here is fake. . . It's merely controlled."*

As Weinberg explained, Bakker's theology mirrored Charlotte's New South vision quest in which "social disparities were minimized. . . racial conflict played no role . . . [and] leisure and prosperity abounded for all . . . who believed."

Bakker's ideal world manifested in Heritage USA, a Christian theme park. Like all theme parks, it was a "Non-Place" without history, inspiring no personal attachment. It featured gleaming towers, a "luxury" hotel, and family entertainment—a commercial paradise claiming spiritual purity.

Heritage was an expression of myths and unspoken emotions and longings. It was like a brand that promises fulfillment and authentic experience while offering only a commodity. Heritage was an abstraction of authentic life experience. Its "theme" was religious, but it mirrored a prevailing secular brand, that of Charlotte itself. Situated mythologically outside present time, Bakker's vision, Weinberg argues, *[is] embodied in the image of Charlotte put forth by its most aggressive boosters.*

The "heaven on earth" Bakker sold with "lifetime" memberships was modeled on the Amway Mecca of an "unlimited" income peddled by Dexter Yager, which was a modern adaptation of the Calvinist Lhasa of business booster George Babbitt. The prosperity gospel now preached by Steven Furtick in Charlotte's megachurch is the apotheosis of the sacred faith and fervent hope of Charlotte and, increasingly, America.

---

1 "Presby Power, Presbyterians' Influence Extends Far" by Tim Funk, *Charlotte Observer*, June 13, 1998

2 "Setting, Ball Theme Worry Some" by David Perlmutt, *Charlotte Observer*, Apr 17, 1990, and "Country Clubs Adopt Integration Policies" *Greensboro News & Record*, Dec 30, 1990, Updated Jan 23, 2015

3 Essay by historian Matthew Lassiter, included in the 2010 book, *Charlotte NC: The Global Evolution of a New South City*, published by the University of Georgia Press, 2012.

4 "Pawnshops Hurt by Credit System" by Harry Lloyd, *Charlotte Observer*, April 16, 1972

5 Despite the tiny and low-profile Jewish presence in Charlotte in the past, the city did have one authentic, high quality Jewish Deli, Leo's Delicatessen, owned by Leo and Helen Finman, whose family lived a block from where I grew up at the edge of Freedom Park. Son Ed and I were (and are) friends. Leo Finman opened the deli in 1948 and operated it until 1968 when the family sold it due to Leo's health. Leo Finman died in 1976. Leo's Deli was popular with locals of all faiths as well as among Charlotte's Jewish community, numbering about 600 at the time. See "Counter Culture" by Eric Ginsberg, *Our State Magazine*, July 25, 2022

6 https://billmoyers.com/content/preaching-the-prosperity-gospel/

7 "Grahams Prepare to Move Headquarters to Charlotte" by Associated Press, Nov. 16, 2001

8 When the PTL club went bankrupt, Graham's nephew acquired the house and moved it to the newly developed Library property, where it is a tourist attraction. See: "The Story Behind Billy Graham's Childhood Home" (https://billygrahamlibrary.org/blog-the-story-behind-billy-grahams-childhood-home/#:~:text=The%20Graham%20home%20in%20its,Library%20in%20Charlotte%2C%20North%20Carolina)

9 "Banking Lifts Charlotte, City on the Rise, to the Top" by Peter Applebome, *New York Times*, Aug. 24, 1991

10 https://www.facebook.com/MyersParkBaptistChurch/about_details

11 "Where Do We Go from Here?" A sermon delivered by Rev. Dr. Benjamin Boswell at Myers Park Baptist Church on November 10, 2024, (https://s3.amazonaws.com/account-media/27665/uploaded/s/0e18695564_1731357860_stxt-2024-11-10-ben-boswell-where-do-we-go-from-here.pdf)

12 https://thrivingcongregations.ptsem.edu/myers-park-baptist-church/#:~:text=Founded%20in%201943%2C%20Myers%20Park,five%20senior%20ministers%20before%20W

13 "Pastor Pushed out after Parishioners Complain about Focus on Racial Justice" by Frank Langfitt, *NPR, All Things Considered*, Feb. 4, 2025

14 "The House of Steven, Elevation Church" by Stuart Watson, Investigative Reporter, NBC Affiliate, *WCNC*, Jan 29, 2014 (https://www.youtube.com/watch?v=o6hGdohLCwM)

15 "Credit Card for Christ" by Michelle Boudin, *Charlotte Magazine*, November 22, 2010

16 "WCNC Parts Ways with Long-Time Investigative Reporter" by Mark Washburn, *Charlotte Observer*, January 11, 2015

17 The excerpt is published on the website of broadcast journalist, Bill Moyers, https://billmoyers.com/content/preaching-the-prosperity-gospel/

18 Amway's own (unaudited) disclosures show that retail-based direct selling accounted for only 18% of sales and the majority of Amway "distributors" never made even one sale. Virtually all "sales" are actually just purchases made by the "sales reps" themselves. (https://pyramidschemealert.org/wp-content/uploads/2018/08/SA4400.RetailSales.pdf)

19 *Creating Heaven on Earth: Jim Bakker and the Birth of a Sunbelt Pentecostalism* by Eric G. Weinberg, University of Kentucky, 2012, p. 184.

20 Doug Wead is another figure in the Charlotte/Bakker/Amway/Yager power group that extended Bakker's Charlotte-based influence right up to the White House. Wead's and Bakker's closest connections were with the two Bush presidencies, but also with Ronald Reagan. Wead was a former

Pentecostal minister. He was an Amway Diamond Distributor, a highly paid "motivation" speaker at Amway events and a promoter and beneficiary of Yager's "tools" scheme. Wead was a close associate and advisor of Bakker. He was paid a $75,000 advance by Bakker to write a book that claimed his innocence of criminal charges and claimed a conspiracy against him. See: "The Tangled Roots of Doug Wead" by Ward Harkavy, *Phoenix New Times*, June 10, 1992; "Behind the Secret Tapings of Bush, a Life Is Changed" by Robin Abcarian, *Los Angeles Times*, March 25, 2005, and "Opinion: Bush and the Bakker Connection on his Way to the White House, The Vice President Wooed The Preacher" by William Scott Malone, *Washington Post*, December 17, 1988

[21] The *Charlotte Observer* did an extensive investigative series on Dexter Yager's Amway business and its political connections in Charlotte. See: "Amway, the Yager Way" by Nancy Stancill and Jim Morrill, *Charlotte Observer*, March 19,1995

[22] Amway is currently charged by regulators in India of operating a $7 billion Ponzi scheme in India. The profits and commission payments Amway took out of India are defined by the regulators as "money laundering" in the charges. See https://www.pyramidschemealert.org/amway-charged-with-massive-money-laundering-scheme-in-india/

[23] See the Receiver's Report at https://web.archive.org/web/20090611231056/http://www.tlennonfor12dailypro.com/media/12DP_FirstInterimReport.pdf and "SEC Halts 'Paid Autosurf' Internet Ponzi Scheme", *SEC Press Release*, February 27, 2006, https://www.sec.gov/litigation/litreleases/lr-19579

[24] https://www.sec.gov/enforcement-litigation/litigation-releases/lr-19579

[25] See "'Autosurf' Sites Stir Fear of Fraud" by Mark Maremont, *Wall Street Journal*, reprinted in *Charlotte Observer*, Feb 11, 2006; "Pay to Surf Inquiry Continues" by Andrew Shain, *The Charlotte Observer*, Feb 17, 2006; "Deal to End 12DailyPro" by Andrew Shain, *Charlotte Observer*, Feb 27, 2006

[26] "Donald Trump Made Millions from Multilevel Marketing Firm" by James V. Grimaldi and Mark Maremont, *Wall Street Journal*, Aug. 13, 2015

[27] https://cdn.cnn.com/cnn/2019/images/01/31/doevtrumpcomplaint.pdf

[28] "Wife of Bank of America's Former CEO Admits to MLM Recruiting" *Pyramid Scheme Alert*, Aug 3, 2010 (https://www.pyramidschemealert.org/wife-of-bank-of-americas-former-ceo-admits-to-mlm-recruiting/)

[29] "Federal, State Regulators Shut Down Fortune Hi-Tech" by Jayne O'Donnell, *USA TODAY*, January 28, 2013

[30] *False Profits: Seeking Financial and Spiritual Deliverance in Multi-Level Marketing and Pyramid Schemes* by Joyce K. Reynolds and Robert L. FitzPatrick, paperback, 1997, Kindle, 2012; *Ponzinomics, the Untold Story of Multi-Level Marketing* by Robert L. FitzPatrick, 2020

[31] Amway's own data show, when costs are factored, and all recruits are counted, less than 1% gain any profit. In a news feature on *CBS 60 Minutes*

this astounding fact was dramatically presented by Bruce Craig, Asst. Attorney General of Wisconsin, which had sued Amway for false income claims. I have confirmed this data with my own published research. When an annual "churn" rate of 50% of Amway recruits quitting and being replaced each year is also factored, the percent of all who ever joined Amway gaining a net profit drops to a tiny fraction of one percent. Virtually no one ever gains the fabled income. (https://www.pyramidschemealert.org/amways-deceptions/)

[32] *Pyramid Scheme Alert* was founded in 2001 by me and two other consumer advocates and authors, Susanna Perkins and Jon M. Taylor. It is a nonprofit, privately supported (by memberships and donations), all-volunteer, non-commercial (no ads or corporate sponsors) consumer education resource. See: http://www.pyramidschemealert.org

[33] Eventually, I formulated a precise definition of "multi-level marketing", which required coining a new word, *Ponzinomics*, to capture both its financial trickery and evangelical claims of metaphysical truth. "Ponzinomics: noun / pän-zē-'nä-miks / a pseud-economic, all-encompassing, delusional belief system that promotes the swindle of a Ponzi or pyramid scheme as a valid economic model that promises believers a fulfilling and financially rewarding way of life, complete with mission, values, leadership and worldview. The societal spread of Ponzinomics is necessarily accompanied by governmental collusion," excerpted from *PONZINOMICS, The Untold Story of Multi-Level Marketing* by Robert L. FitzPatrick, 2020 (https://www.amazon.com/Ponzinomics-Untold-Story-Multi-Level-Marketing/dp/0578443511)

[34] *Creating Heaven On Earth: Jim Bakker And The Birth Of A Sunbelt Pentecostalism* by Eric G. Weinberg, University of Kentucky, 2012

XI. Omissions

For lack of knowledge or personal experience and due to obvious limits to the story's length, I consciously excluded some areas from my inquiry into Charlotte's Soul. One area that I did not make a search deserves explanation. It is commonly associated with Place and it is certainly present in Charlotte.

In many cities, home teams, local sports heroes, revered stadiums, and dramatic athletic victories and losses strongly contribute to Sense of Place. In recent decades, the hyper-commercialization of sports has diminished the connections between teams, ordinary citizens, and local identities. I had an old friend who used to say he never quite got over the Dodgers leaving Brooklyn for Los Angeles. It was an unforgiveable betrayal in his view, indicating how important the Dodgers were to Brooklyn's Soul back then and how sports can give substance to Place. European and Latin American football (soccer) clubs still contribute this kind of pride in local identity.

Charlotte has no such tradition or experience. The commercialization that eventually tarnished the sporting world in other American cities has been at full tilt in Charlotte from the moment it gained national franchises in football and basketball. For this reason, I did not look for the pulsating Soul of Charlotte in its professional sports scene, with one qualifier: Soccer is emerging in Charlotte, tapping into a different font of experience and tradition, and a different fan base. That sport and its fans may breathe a powerful new spirit into Charlotte, if given the chance.

Oligarchs and Team Spirit

Covered in Logos

The oldest, largest, and wealthiest sport in Charlotte, NASCAR stock car racing, arguably does not qualify as a public sport at all. Nonprofessionals cannot "play." In its modern form, stock car racing in Charlotte is vicarious spectacle and power fantasy, a display of mechanical and financial resources as much as driver skill on the racetrack. The deafening sound of the roaring engines of more than 40 cars vying for commanding positions and revved at full throttle literally pulsates through the bodies of the spectators. Fans sitting in rows closer to the track are showered with a fine rubberized dust from the tires and track. The air is pungent with oil, rubber, and gasoline, masking the toxic carbon monoxide hovering over the entire raceway. Each car with its enormous, finely-tuned engine and running at 150 miles per hour gets only 2-5 miles per gallon.

The "athletes" and their multimillion dollar "stock" cars are covered bumper-to-bumper in corporate logos. The NASCAR track, a gigantic open-air stadium on 2,000 acres, seating up to 100,000, hosts two major racing events: one named for Coca-Cola, the other for Bank of America. The facility is owned by one person. Even the governing body, NASCAR, that defines and oversees this international sport is a private company, owned by a single person.[1]

The stars of the sport are well known locally but not because most race attendees are local. Most residents will never set foot in the stadium. Rather, drivers, sponsors and other race-related businesspeople are renowned locally for their conspicuous wealth. For example, it was recently reported that what was likely the highest-priced residence in the Charlotte area went up for sale. The asking price: $12.5 million. The "castle," as it was called, has six bedrooms, seven full bathrooms, and three half-baths. At 13,124 square feet, the gated estate also has a guest house equipped with a "man cave," a gym, arcade, and golf simulator.

Local readers could easily guess, if not the exact identity of the owner, then at least the owner's occupation. It was owned by a former NASCAR driver. Before selling the castle, he had already purchased another house for $6.75 million and moved there a year earlier.[2]

The NASCAR culture and brand are popular among millions of people, but no one argues that NASCAR engenders loyalty or attachment to the city of Charlotte. What NASCAR does bring to Charlotte, though, is a lot of money. Charlotte campaigned and won the bidding to be the site of the NASCAR Hall of Fame, a tourist attraction and office building in the center city near the Levine Center for the Arts. The city owns the land, taken through urban renewal, and it paid $160 million to construct the facility, but it is operated independently by a tourism agency. Funds from a special tax on hotel guests in Charlotte are designated exclusively for the NASCAR facility. None of this revenue can be used for other city needs, like housing, or even for other tourism or sports facilities. Critics have noted that the designs of the NASCAR Hall and the adjacent convention center brought blank walls, loading docks, and ugly and scary blocks of "dead zone" into an area where retail and lively pedestrian activity could have developed.[3]

Any concerns regarding the NASCAR Hall of Fame's costs, design or effect on local city life were overshadowed by a single-minded focus on attracting tourist dollars. Boosters projected that 800,000 visitors a year would flock to the Hall of Fame, all bringing wads of money to spend in Charlotte. In its first year, the Hall attracted less than half that and immediately became a tax deficit. Attendance declined yearly after that. Located right across the street from the convention center, it has attracted on average only about 160,000 visitors a year. The Hall loses a million dollars a year on average. The loss would be greater but in 2015, the city of Charlotte forgave the Hall of $23 million of its debt. The city agreed to pay Bank of America and Wells Fargo, which held the debt, $5 million. The banks then wrote off nearly $18 million in debt

The disconnection of this "sport" from the city's Soul is about money, but not just taxes and tourist dollars. It is its mercenary relationship with the city and the public and the oligarchic character of the enterprise. This was demonstrated in an infamous episode involving the late Bruton Smith, the owner of Charlotte Motor Speedway, Charlotte's main connection to the stock car world. The gigantic track is located twelve miles from downtown Charlotte on 1,300 acres of land within the limits of the adjacent small township of Concord. Smith announced plans to build an additional race facility on the stadium property, a dragstrip racing track. It would bring frequent and intrusive noise and pollution to the residents living nearby. Concord had legal rights over the land use. The town council did not approve the drag racing track due to the harm it would cause its residents.

In response, Smith angrily threatened to demolish the entire stadium and move everything to another city, destroying Concord's tax base — as the town's finances had become dependent on the track — as well as inflicting harm to the economy of Charlotte.[4] Town of Concord officials were forced to capitulate to Smith and, for good measure, named a nearby street in his honor.

In another incident, Smith ordered the cutting down of hundreds of trees near the speedway track in violation of Charlotte codes. He then refused to pay damages or replant trees, claiming he owed the city nothing, not even adherence to its codes.[5]

Hoops, Hive and Honey Bees

The first "world-class" sport to come to Charlotte was pro basketball. The NBA preceded the NFL franchise for football by two decades and seemingly set the pattern for the relationship of the team to the city, players, and fans that was later followed by the NFL team owners. The arrival of the NBA franchise was a hugely celebrated event for a city hungering for a unifying connection. It was also a breakthrough moment for the "world-class" crusaders.

The prevailing narrative at the time, which is still in force, was that Charlotte would gain a heart and soul with just more "amenities" and a proper branding campaign.[6] The larger the amenity, the greater sense of civic unity and attachment, the theory went. At the time, the NBA team and home stadium were viewed as perhaps the ultimate amenity.

Understood more broadly, this "amenity" claim is a just a variation of the "lifestyle" sales pitch that philosopher Theodor Adorno warned of. Lifestyle, he wrote, is a commercial substitute for authentic human expressions of identity and community.[7] Lifestyle commodities may be *symbols* of real human expression— as hometown sports teams often are—but never a *replacement*.

In keeping with W. J. Cash's observation nearly a century ago of Charlotte's "gigantism," Charlotte built the largest NBA home team arena in America. It was located near the rapidly growing hub airport, another monumental achievement of Charlotte's quest for status and recognition. The arena, called the Coliseum, was a landmark viewed from the air by incoming and departing flights.

With a 24,000-seat capacity, the enormous facility was erected on high ground fifty-five feet above the street entrance. Leading directly from the road to the Coliseum was a sixty-foot wide, 1,500-foot-long grassy median, creating a dramatic entry view focused on the looming dome-shaped building above. Vast parking lots flanked the median strip. To consecrate the giant new facility, the city sought to place a dramatic work of environmental art on this long, straight median.

The arts commission had a budget of about $900,000 (in today's dollars). It issued a formal invitation for art submissions, and the process included public comment. In interviews with the three finalists, one artist called the Coliseum a "heroic building" symbolizing Charlotte's growth. Describing the long, ascending median, another said, "You couldn't ask for a better site."

In the end, the city commissioned the sculptor Maya Ying Lin, the artistic creator of the Vietnam Veterans Memorial in Washington, DC, and the Civil Rights Memorial in Montgomery, Alabama, to design and install the monumental art for Charlotte's "heroic coliseum."[8]

Lin's environmental art took advantage of the ascent of the long median, flanked by the large parking lots. Its main feature was a placement of ten-foot-high round shrubs that appear to roll down the hill.

> In between would be irregularly placed spheres shaped from juniper or cypress, planted so they would appear to float over the ground. They would be lighted from below. . . . A double row of willow oaks flanking the median would frame the playing field. . . . Lin said the park would be enjoyable from automobiles and also by pedestrians.[9]

George Shinn, who led the drive to bring the NBA franchise to Charlotte, is from a small textile town very near Charlotte. He made a fortune from buying, consolidating, and then selling off a network of private "business schools." The schools offered two-year programs and were attended by working-class students who could not afford or lacked proper grades for regular college or university, a modern version of the correspondence schools of the past.

In the late '80s, Shinn successfully got an NBA franchise, the Charlotte Hornets, with the giant new stadium provided by the city as its collateral and home court. For this achievement, Shinn received extraordinary adulation in Charlotte, even a parade. Adding to his popularity among Charlotte residents and leaders, Shinn presented himself as a pious, devout Christian. He arranged for the famous televangelist Pat Robertson to sit next to him at games. He was a model family man, according to his self-promotions.

To the surprise of many, the Hornets generated sell-out games, with 24,000 in attendance, and wins. Charlotte appeared to be building team loyalty and city spirit, like other cities that boasted of revered players, dramatic victories, and treasured home stadiums.

But then, as occurred later in eerily similar ways with team owner Jerry Richardson and the NFL franchise, an imperious commercial ambition began to smother the incubating team spirit and diminish civic connection. It revealed itself not in self-serving financial maneuvers, but in the crass behavior of the wealthy owner and of obsequious Charlotte officials desperate for the "world-class" recognition and perceived business benefits of professional sports.

In the eyes of many in Charlotte, the franchise owner George Shinn began to tarnish the spirit of the game when he ruthlessly forced out other investors to gain full financial control of the NBA enterprise. In another instance of callous and arbitrary behavior, Shinn fired the head coach the same day the coach's brother died. For team president, Shinn hired a longtime personal associate who had been disbarred from law practice and gone bankrupt in Florida, racking up debts of more than $400,000. Before that, he was indicted on a charge of conspiring to smuggle drugs into Florida. Shinn made this person the president of the Charlotte

Hornets for five years. Rancor among the players and the fans grew over Shinn's refusal to pay market pay rates to several popular players, who then left the team and Charlotte.

Shinn's arrogant behavior toward the city of Charlotte, which had built and paid for the stadium and thrown a parade in his honor, began to stress the relationship. Shinn threatened to move the team out of Charlotte over terms of lease renewal. He demanded a new stadium uptown but refused to pay even a modest portion of the costs. Team spirit, loyalty, and pride among people in Charlotte dropped, as did attendance. Soon the team was losing money for Shinn, who was increasingly depicted as a villain. Naturally, the negativity affected the local popularity of the team.

Shinn escalated his demand for a new stadium at the expense of the city with more aggressive threats to move the team away from Charlotte. He opened public negotiations with the city of New Orleans. The basis for Shinn's claim that the current arena was inadequate was not its size—as it was the largest in America—or even, primarily, its location—near the airport with abundant convenient parking. It was that it lacked lucrative luxury boxes for wealthy corporate patrons of the type that later provided a crucial source of revenue for the Bank of America NFL stadium. For team owners, that's where the real money was. Public seating for fans was secondary. Additionally, city leaders, despite having spent $134 million (today's dollars) just twelve years earlier to build the huge stadium near the airport, now wanted a new stadium in the center city to stimulate real estate development in the area, which was still deadened by urban renewal.

Desperate to keep the "world-class" NBA amenity, Charlotte's booster mayor, Pat McCrory, pushed a bond referendum to build the new "luxury" arena in the downtown that Shinn demanded. Charlotte's business leadership also backed the new stadium. A "world-class" city needed a center city with the energy of an NBA stadium![10]

Soul vs. Brand Rematch

Readers who have stayed with this story to this point may recall that it was at this time in Charlotte history that a grassroots citizen group called Helping Empower Local People (HELP) was formed. The group was led by a Saul Alinsky-affiliated community organizer and backed by some Charlotte churches. It was HELP that mobilized the opposition to building the downtown arena that Shinn demanded, the booster Mayor promoted, and "downtown" interests coveted.

The community organization highlighted local needs that members argued should be prioritized—Soul—over the downtown stadium and its luxury box seats—Brand. An issue that galvanized opposition to the stadium referendum was the city's refusal to pay a living wage to city employees, a decision supported by the same booster mayor pushing for the luxury stadium. This moment in the history of the battle for Charlotte's "Soul" harkens to my work twenty years earlier as a community organizer in North Charlotte, when Charlotte squashed an effort of unionized city workers to gain a living wage. In that era, the groups I organized successfully opposed plans to expand Charlotte's airport as part of its "world class" branding campaign.

The city knew that the public might balk at the idea of using tax funds for a luxury arena to replace a perfectly usable existing one. So the city sought to obscure the profligate expenditure and the naked subsidy to downtown developers by also pledging bond funds for a "world-class" arts district. It didn't work. The entire bond package was defeated by a margin of 57 percent to 43 percent:

> "People are concerned about a living wage and affordable housing in this city and not an arena," said Donnie Garris, a Baptist minister and spokesman for the group

Helping Empower Local People, which also opposed
the referendum.[11]

As these troubling events were unfolding, the economic and
political issues were overshadowed by a sex scandal that acti-
vated the flip side of Charlotte's character, *religious piety*. As this
story has shown in all areas examined, faith and finance are con-
flated in Charlotte.

Shinn, the self-proclaimed family man, devoted husband,
Christian, and philanthropist, was dragged into court on shocking charges of sexual assault. He narrowly escaped criminal
prosecution, but publicly admitted to sexual affairs outside his
marriage. The sordid story was covered daily in the local newspapers and on Court TV.

This scandal was followed by more charges from two other
women. A member of the Honey Bees who danced at Hornets
games and a Hornets office worker said that Shinn had frequently sexually harassed them. In a court document, they claimed,
among other examples of lascivious behavior, that "Shinn made
lewd comments and touched or grabbed them."[12] Once the hero,
Shinn became the goat, blamed for lost games, declining attendance, and waning team spirit in Charlotte. In the end, Shinn ig-
nominiously, in the view of the Charlotte media, moved the team
out of Charlotte to New Orleans. Before leaving for New Orleans,
he had even stopped attending Hornets home games.

In 2005, Charlotte's leaders found a way to build the new
downtown arena Shinn had wanted with tax funds, but without need of voter approval. The cost was $400 million (in to-
day's dollars). With the new arena as an enticement, the city
again was able to gain an NBA franchise. The new facility was
originally named Bobcat Arena for the team's new owner, Bob
Johnson. Later the arena naming rights were sold to Time Warner. Time Warner was acquired by another telecommunications

company, and the arena is now known (albeit not "affectionate-ly") as Spectrum Center. Spectrum has much less seating than the "coliseum" did, with a maximum capacity of 19,000, but it "boasts modern amenities such as luxury suites, club seats, and advanced technology."[13]

A decade or so later, Charlotte recovered its team's old name, Hornets. Despite the new stadium, the mascot restoration, and the ousting of George Shinn, Charlotte's NBA team has strug-gled. In 2012, it had the league's worst record. Though the popu-lation of Charlotte has more than doubled, average recent atten-dance is 30% lower than it was at the packed home games of the early seasons of the first Hornets team three decades ago. In 2023, the Hornets reported average attendance of about 16,000 at the Spectrum Center, with a 4 percent drop in the latest season. Sea-son ticket prices, however, increased by 15 percent. The average price of a single ticket is $74.

In 2007, two years after the opening of the downtown arena, 550 pounds of explosives were set off in the old landmark Col-iseum, the largest of its kind in America, affectionately known as "the Hive," which had been in use for less than 20 years. It was blasted into rubble. The massive property was left vacant for years to come. The sculpture by Maya Ling Yin, of Vietnam War memorial fame, that the city had commissioned was also demol-ished. Known as *Topo,* the environmental artwork never received its due in Charlotte and was ridiculed by local talk show hosts as "shrubs." City officials said the cost of moving the work was too high. It is no longer found in any lists of Lin's works.

Luxury Suites, Southern Gentleman

Then there is pro football. For me, growing up in Charlotte, professional football, basketball, and baseball—these were myth-ic and faraway phenomena. Famous players, great rivalries, beloved stadiums—in Charlotte, we watched in awe, from a great distance. College football was very popular, but there were no universities with major football teams in Charlotte.

In 1996, Charlotte got its first NFL franchise. The word "Charlotte" was not in the team's name. It was to be called the Carolina Panthers, and the market base to support the team includes both North and South Carolina. The choice of Panther as the mascot did not involve any public input or comment. It was reportedly made by the son of the team's first owner, Jerry Richardson. Richardson, a Charlotte native and former NFL player, is credited with getting the team for the region and building its home stadium in Charlotte.

From the start, the role of Charlotte residents in relation to the Carolina Panthers was limited to that of paying fans, part of a "market." With urban renewal powers, the city of Charlotte acquired and owns the 35-acres of land the stadium sits on. It leases the land to the stadium owners for $1 a year. The stadium does not pay property taxes on the land it leases. In 2019, the county determined the stadium to be valued at $572 million, but after an appeal by the owners, the County lowered the tax valuation to $215 million, saving Panthers $3.5 million per year on taxes.[14]

Though built on city-owned land that is effectively donated to the owners, the construction of the "uptown" stadium, home to the Panthers, was a very private affair, similar to the installation of the four "pillars" at the Square. The NFL franchise and the stadium were viewed primarily as assets to attract national and international companies. The stadium was funded and operated accordingly. About 160 luxury suites were sold with prices as high as $325,000 for multi-year rentals.[15] The city's impressive success in raising tens of millions from wealthy purchasers of private suites reportedly led other stadiums to follow its example. The successful marketing of the luxury suites, as much or more than potential fan support, was a key factor in Charlotte's winning the franchise.

The stadium "owner," Jerry Richardson, was a fast-food franchise operator with close ties to Bank of America CEO Hugh McColl. Richardson was instrumental in gaining the NFL franchise with money from Bank of America. "Hugh McColl has financed everything I've been involved in. . . . We know each other so well that we can communicate without talking," Richardson stated in an interview he gave when he and McColl jointly acquired the fast-food fried chicken franchisor Bojangles.[16] Bojangles at that time consisted of 386 units in 11 states and Latin America. Richardson was one of the largest Bojangles franchisees. McColl's investment company sold Bojangles four years later.[17] There are over 800 Bojangles restaurants today in 17 states, with 33 in Charlotte.

The stadium is situated on the site of Good Samaritan, the former African American community hospital demolished by the city to make room for the new stadium. The hospital, known for decades affectionately as "Good Sam," was situated almost exactly on the 40-yard line of today's stadium. The hospital was the first of its kind in the South and in 1903 established the first nurses training school accessible to African Americans.

In addition to its special role in serving thousands of Charlotte residents who were otherwise denied life-saving care under Jim Crow, the hospital was noted for two major events. A 1911 train accident in the town of Hamlet caused extensive injuries to a large number of African American passengers. They were forced at the time to ride in wooden train cars separated from White passengers who traveled in newer and better built iron ones. No White medical facility would treat African Americans. About 80 of the injured African Americas were transported 75 miles into Charlotte to Good Samaritan. The treatment put the under-staffed, under-resourced facility to an historic test. All but three of the injured were saved. The care that all received earned the hospital new prestige.

Local historians also unearthed the disturbing fact that Good Sam was the site of what was reportedly the first documented lynching in Mecklenburg County. In 1913, Joe McNeely, a nineteen-year-old African American, was forcibly taken from Good Samaritan Hospital and shot to death outside the hospital doors by a White mob.[18]

Seven years after the stadium was opened on the land occupied by Good Samaritan Hospital, the city installed a brass placard mounted on a post at the edge of stadium property. It commemorates Good Samaritan Hospital. It states that the hospital was "built exclusively for African Americans" rather than because existing hospitals were exclusively for Whites. No marker has been installed about the historic killing of Joe McNeely.[19]

Revered for bringing the NFL to Charlotte, Richardson reigned over pro-football in Charlotte. His ubiquitous presence overshadowed fans, players, wins or losses, and taxpayers. References to events or people that tie the stadium to Charlotte's history had little chance for recognition. This was especially true for a remembrance of a savage crime, though it held great meaning to many local people.

On his eightieth birthday, a thirteen-foot-tall statue of Richardson was installed at the stadium entrance. Often reverently referred to in the media as "old fashioned" and a "Southern gentleman," Richardson was reportedly called "mister" by all employees and players, who were advised never to contradict him. The statue placed larger-than-life Richardson between two enormous and ferocious panthers. He stood, bravely, resolutely, an outstretched arm holding a football.

In 2017, a lurid, detailed account in *Sports Illustrated* of Richardson's "inappropriate" sexual conduct and insulting and demeaning racial speech and behavior led to a sudden and hurried sale of the NFL enterprise by Richardson.[20] An NFL investigation resulted in Richardson paying a $2.75 million fine. Exposure of his behavior toward African Americans also led to Richardson becoming the target of social justice protests in Charlotte following the killing of George Floyd by police in Minneapolis. Richardson's statue was hastily and unceremoniously removed from the front of the stadium, never to return. The removal occurred despite a clause Richardson inserted into the sale contract that the statue could not be removed. A spokesman for the Panthers told the media:

> "We . . . are concerned there may be attempts to take it down. We are moving the statue in the interest of public safety."[21]

In 2024, the new owner of the Panthers, hedge fund manager David Tepper, who also owned the soccer club, called Charlotte FC, and the stadium, "requested" that city taxpayers spend $650 million for renovations and upgrades to his privately owned facility, now called Bank of America Stadium. Tepper has been ranked as the highest paid hedge fund owner in America, with annual earnings of more than $2 billion. Called the "richest man in New Jersey," Tepper reportedly purchased a home in New Jersey for $43.5 million and then *had it demolished*. On that property he constructed an "11,268 sq. ft. oceanfront palace."[22]

Regarding the massive renovation costs that Tepper demanded the city pay, a long-time sports columnist at the *Charlotte Observer* opined:

> Charlotte's controversial billionaire wants a whole lot of money. . . . Do you know what would happen if this proposal fails and everything goes sideways? The teams, eventually, will leave.[23]

As to why Charlotte's NFL franchise and current stadium owner is referred to as a "controversial" billionaire, an excerpt from *Wikipedia* partially explains:

> Since buying the Panthers in 2018, they have compiled a 31-68 record and 6 head coaches in that span. Tepper has been described as one of the NFL's worst owners, with the Panthers going into a downturn since his ownership began. In 2022, Tepper canceled the construction of a practice facility for the team in Rock Hill, South Carolina, after claiming that the city didn't hold up the end of their deal, had his real estate arm declare bankruptcy . . . and . . . demolish[ed] the half-built facility. [In] 2023, Tepper threw a drink at a fan. . . . He was fined $300,000 by the NFL for the incident.

In June 2024, the Charlotte City Council approved a stadium renovation plan in which the city will pay $650 million and, in return, Tepper agreed not to take the team out of Charlotte for the next two decades. Three of the ten councilmembers voted against the deal. Councilmember Tiawana Brown was one of those that voted no. She said:

> "It sounds real good until we get Mr. Tepper angry and then he might throw something at the city council," Brown said, a reference to Tepper throwing a drink on a fan during an away game last year. "The behavior of someone asking for $650 million is ridiculous."[24]

---

[1] NSACAR is the acronym for National Association for Stock Car Auto Racing, LLC. It was founded by Bill France Sr. in 1948. His son, Jim France, has served as CEO since 2018. The private company is based in Daytona Beach, Florida. NASCAR sanctions over 1,500 races throughout the US, as well as in Europe, Canada and South America.

[2] "South Charlotte Castle for Sale" by Alexis Clinton, *Axios Charlotte*, May 31, 2024

[3] "One Side of Street Is a Dead Zone for Pedestrians" by Steve Harrison, *The Charlotte Observer*, Jan 14, 2017

[4] "Owner of Charlotte Track Threatens Move," *Tuscon.com*, Oct. 5, 2007 (https://tucson.com/sports/motor-sports/owner-of-charlotte-track-threatens-move/article_c23284db-d91d-52f6-8b2b-49339d26a839.html)

[5] "Smith Says No Replanting" by Michelle Crouch, *Charlotte Observer*, July 29, 2004

[6] *Charlotte NC: The Global Evolution* …, University of Georgia Press, 2012.

[7] *The Culture Industry*, by Theodor W. Adorno (Author), J. M. Bernstein (Editor), 2001

[8] "Charlotte's History of Arts Controversies" by Andy Smith, *Charlotte Magazine*, November 6, 2016

[9] "Rolling Bushes, Flying Ribbons: Proposals for Coliseum Art Unveiled" by Richard Maschal, *Charlotte Observer*, Wed, Apr 19, 1989

[10] "The Rise and Fall of George Shinn and the Hornets" by Tim Povtak, *The Orlando Sentinel* (Orlando, Florida), Feb 6, 2002, Page B1

[11] "Charlotte Voters Reject Arena Project," *Associated Press*, June 6, 2001

[12] "Hornets Owner Under Fire Again\ George Shinn, Already Facing a Sexual Harassment Lawsuit, Is Accused of Making Sexual Advances by Two Former Employees of the Charlotte Hornets," *The Associated Press* Columbia, S.C., Oct 13, 1998

[13] https://sportshistorynetwork.com/multiple-sports/charlotte-hornets-arena-history/

[14] "Carolina Panthers Get a Big Tax Break on their Stadium following County Review" by Katie Peralta Soloff, *Axios Charlotte*, Feb 2, 2020

[15] https://sportsmarketanalytics.com/Resource-Center/Venues/Venue-Reports/Venue-Detail.aspx?id=181287#:~:text=Bank%20of%20America%20Stadium%20was,cost%2C%20or%20around%20%2465%20million

[16] "Richardson, McColl Take Over Bojangles" by Robert W. Dalton, *GoUpstate*, Sept. 14, 2007.

[17] https://www.businesswire.com/news/home/20110725005493/en/Falfurrias-Capital-Partners-Announces-Agreement-to-Sell-Bojangles'-Stake

[18] "Carolina Panthers Stadium Sits on Top of Charlotte's First Documented Lynching Site" by Tim Funk, *Charlotte Observer*, Oct. 05, 2018

[19] Though there is no public commemoration of the mob lynching of Joseph McNeely at Good Samaritan Hospital, the *Charlotte-Mecklenburg Remembrance Project* has created an extraordinary record of Mecklenburg County's lynchings through "spoken word, video and community engagement." The project is a collaboration with the Equal Justice Initiative (https://eji.org/about/), which "commemorates the legacy of racial violence against Black Americans through lynching." Using eye witness accounts and archived newspaper reports, the *Remembrance*

Project provides a terrifying hour-by-hour account of the lynching of Joseph McNeely. See: https://ithappenedhereclt.com/joe-mcneely/ The African American-owned *Charlotte Post* published an interview with Krista Terrell, the *Remembrance Project's* content and communications chair. She discussed why "light should be shone on one of Mecklenburg's darkest chapters." See "It Happened Here: the Legacy of Lynching in Charlotte" by Herbert L. White, *Charlotte Post*, September 23, 2024. (https://www.thecharlottepost.com/news/2024/09/23/local-state/it-happened-here-the-legacy-of-lynching-in-charlotte/)

[20] "Sources: Jerry Richardson, Panthers Have Made Multiple Confidential Payouts for Workplace Misconduct, Including Sexual Harassment and Use of a Racial Slur" by L. Jon Wertheim And Viv Bernstein, *Sports Illustrated*, Dec. 17, 2017

[21] "Panthers Move Jerry Richardson Statue from outside Stadium as Precaution" by David Newton, *ESPN*, Jun 10, 2020

[22] "N.J.'s Richest Man Razes Corzine's Ex-Wife's Mansion, Builds Bigger Mansion" by Jeff Goldman, *NJ Advance Media for NJ.com*, Sep 25, 2015

[23] David Tepper Wants $650 Million to Renovate Panthers' Stadium? Here's How to Handle that" by Scott Fowler, *Charlotte Observer*, June 15, 2024

[24] "Charlotte City Council OK's Panthers Stadium Renovation Plan," *Associated Press*, June 24, 2024

XII. Discoveries: Fireflies Of Soul

There is a philosophical joke about a guy looking for his lost keys under a streetlight. A friend comes along and asks him if this is where he thinks he dropped the keys. He answers that he has no idea where he dropped them, but this is the only area that's lit up.

In my search for Soul in Charlotte, I looked mostly where there was "light," so to speak, places familiar to me—downtown, parks, schools, arts, neighborhoods, and churches—and where I had direct experience or connections with others who did. Some of this book records historical events that I was closely involved in for several years. Other events I experienced, discussed, and researched over the many years I lived in Charlotte.

I did find instances of Soul in these better lit, familiar areas. Yet, even under the streetlight, the search involves probing in dimness. The light of Soul, I discovered, shows up mostly in struggle against dark forces or they generate their own luminosity. They are as fireflies: flashing, dimming, flashing again or disappearing, never constant and largely invisible to us except in contrast to the darkness.

There are many such flashes in Charlotte that I have not included, which deserved recognition. Though not named and described, hopefully they are honored in principle by the ones that I did investigate and describe now.

Upholding "Equality" in Separated Schools

In a nationally reported federal court battle, Charlotte's old, segregated school system was declared a systemic denial of human and civil rights. Racial segregation and educational deprivation were shown to have cruel consequences for victims that extend a lifetime and reverberate through future generations.

Nevertheless, today in Charlotte, as in many other cities, segregation of students is once again the general rule. Once extolled as the "city that made it work" regarding desegregation, Charlotte's is now the state's most segregated system. What had been declared inherently harmful and illegal has regained a legalized status.

Now, exorbitant home prices, widening income disparity, residential patterns, and new roads do the work of separation as efficiently as old Jim Crow. Schools are no longer explicitly identified as "Black" or "White," but are ranked as excelling or challenged and linked to zip codes, accomplishing much the same thing.

Beyond legal interpretations and politics, there remains the daily lived experience for children and parents within segregated schools. It is the same today as it always was, as education advocate, teacher, and author Jonathan Kozol recently wrote in *An End to Inequality, Breaking Down the Walls of Apartheid Education in America*:

> Separate is not equal. It never was. It isn't now. It won't be in another fifty years. Tests and punishments and scientific measurement and longer lists of incorrect behaviors are not going to "fix" it. Apartheid education isn't something you can "fix."

Kozol explains how the Jim Crow era justifications for separating students based on color have been recast as sophisticated educational theories for why children of color or of lower income families require different, separate schooling. For instance:

> [Some claim] that young children of color need a uniquely different course of training than white children because

of their allegedly inherent liabilities. . . . According to this thinking, Black and Latino children have different ways of understanding what we should expect of them than white and middle-class children do.[1]

In place of addressing the inherent inequities of a functionally segregated system, the schools are now subjected to a stream of reforms and programs to implement new teaching methods. In Charlotte these new theories and strategies are also accompanied by ever-changing school superintendents, eleven since 1991 when the "magnet" school plan was begun. Yet, even as leaders come and go, each with a new theory, and resources continue to erode, teachers and other advocates still raise high public education's tattered banner. They are among the brightest and bravest fireflies of Soul in Charlotte.

The reality is that beyond the *de facto* segregation of many schools, Charlotte's public school system is being abandoned, slowly but steadily, by affluent and, recently, middle-income families. Charlotte-Mecklenburg now has 103 private schools serving 20,857 children, or about one of every eight students. Of these private schools, 43 percent are religious. In 2022–23, private school enrollment grew 7 percent.[2] Average tuition is $16,000. At the most prestigious of the private high schools, Charlotte Latin School, tuition is over $31,000.[3]

At this time, there is no organized movement, no champions with a voice and clout in Charlotte upholding the ideals of equal education for all. As noted earlier, the word "integrated" was removed from the school system's mission statement. The daily injuries caused by segregation or its long-term effects are seldom documented, investigated, or discussed. The work of upholding a measure of "equality" in separated schools falls to thousands of brave teachers, heroic parents, committed administrators, and some sympathetic school board members.

Saving Treasured Trees

At what used to be Park Road Elementary, built in the 1950s, now Park Road Montessori school, two young students organized a petition to save the large and historic "treasure trees" on the school campus. The campus will be demolished soon, and the trees are at risk of being cut down. The huge trees are part of a nature preserve on the campus. Nearly a thousand people signed on to the petition.[4] Their effort is one of many, sometimes desperate, efforts to stem the tide of tree destruction in Charlotte.

I was personally involved in one of the most poignant of tree protection efforts, a successful grassroots campaign to save some of the city's most iconic trees. Japanese cherry trees, the same type that add life and beauty to otherwise institutional Washington, DC, are similarly loved and enjoyed in Charlotte. Since the 1960s, they have been the highlight of the city's beloved Freedom Park, announcing spring with the brilliant pinkish white blossoms.

Yet, seemingly, city and park administrators were not among those who realized the trees held special meaning—Soul—in Charlotte. They had determined that the older cherry trees should be cut down in order to give the park a more "uniform" look. The old cherry trees, which, as it turned out, had never been properly cared for or protected, had grown gnarly of trunk and uneven of branch. Some had dead limbs, though in March they all produced an explosion of blooms.

Charlotte's tree canopy is one of its true distinctions as a city—one that is not a fake historical narrative, not a brand, not a tourist attraction, and not a franchise. Preventing tree destruction in a place where development is mostly unfettered is a frustrating and nearly futile exercise. This makes efforts such as that of the students at the condemned Park Road Montessori or the residents who saved Freedom Park's springtime heralds special expressions of Soul.

The most prominent nonprofit group for tree advocacy in Charlotte does not focus on saving trees, but mostly on planting new trees to replace the thousands being cut down. Its study of the state of the trees in Charlotte revealed that in just six years, from 2012 to 2018, 8 percent of Charlotte's entire canopy was destroyed, equivalent to clear-cutting three football fields every day for six years.[5]

Most of the Charlotte's tree destruction has been for residential development. Vast acreage is clear-cut for instant new "neighborhoods." Infill—higher density construction within the city—leaves no room for the large old hardwoods. Replacing stately oaks or tall pines, developers introduced a plague of Bradford ornamental pear trees, a non-native species that is useless if not harmful to pollinating insects, birds, and other trees.

The ubiquitous Bradfords come as close as Charlotte can get to turning natural trees into branded commercial goods. The Bradfords grow rapidly—perfect to add some green to the barren, clear-cut lots—making them more sellable. Disease-resistant and prolific, they have spread like a virus to many areas where they were not cultivated or welcomed. Also important, from a commercial perspective, the Bradford Pear develops a consistent, pear-like shape, making them a favorite of landscape architects.[6] This unvaried "design" of the Bradfords, as if produced on an assembly line, is likely the real-estate standard that influenced Charlotte's park officials to try to destroy the old cherry trees. Those old trees were not "symmetrical," which, ironically, was why so many people cherished them.

The grassroots campaign not only saved the cherry trees but also pressed the city to grasp the larger value of Freedom Park, which today has gained a status in Charlotte similar to New York's Central Park. It is one of the last remaining areas where the varied faces, ages, and languages of Charlotte mix. It is an island of respite from bank advertising and commercial signage. Victory was gained through the traditional means of meetings, petitions, and expert testimony. Charlotte Arborist Patrick George attested to the tree's basic health after park officials claimed, without evidence, that the trees were sick and posed a danger of falling on park patrons!

As reported in an editorial in the *Charlotte Observer* on the citizen efforts:

> People love Freedom Park, and they love those Cherry trees. . . . As park neighbor Robert FitzPatrick said, "Trees are not just commodities. They have meaning." . . . Now, it's fair to say that organized protest in Charlotte is as rare here as a California redwood forest, so the sight of neighbors rallying around their park's trees and wielding democracy as a weapon was fully as inspiring as the trees themselves were in their spring finery last week. It worked. The Friends of Freedom Park generated enough concern to get the park department's attention.[7]

The campaign used art, photos, and poetry to illustrate the value and meaning of the cherry trees—and all trees—and how people emotionally (Soulfully) relate to them. Referring to the proposal to destroy the older trees, one local poet wrote:

> These plans make me nervous, give me pause,
> We destroy the young and discard the old.
> Aware of this body becoming wizened and gnarly,
> How soon will my gnarliness offend thee too?
>
> Be it diversity perverted or uniformity bland,
> Is this sufficient cause to wantonly
> Take a gnarly life so rightly rooted?
> Nay, let the cherry tree be!

I too want to be free to be gnarly,
I want to stand beside the stream,
To drink of the living waters,
And grow old and be fruitful still.

And another poem...

How mundane to treat our trees as such, a military dress,
With precision lines, matching form, and crew
cut evenness.
Whatever that's found not quite measuring up to one
kind of orderliness,
We'll lop it right off right at its roots, because, well, we
know what's best.

A managed domain leaves little room for chance to
find success
But a child prefers the chance dandelion over endless
grassiness.
Consider the artist's point of view, where the exception
is what is best.
Isn't a park's most pressing goal: visual interest?[8]

Holding Banktown Accountable

Paradoxically, while Charlotte's big banks and their executives are credited with the city's "transformation," many local people blame the banks for making Charlotte "a bland banker's paradise." Bank of America and Wells Fargo reign over Charlotte, and plan to install giant new signage atop their skyscrapers like imperial flags. The banks are the city's largest employers and the most radical of Charlotte's crusaders for development, growth, status, and wealth. To search for Charlotte's Soul inevitably leads into the banks' matrix of commercial values and political influence.

Whatever those bank values are, they are now Charlotte's, woven into the social character so tightly they are not recognized as a distinct private interest. The prevailing view in Charlotte is that what's good for the banks is good for Charlotte.[9] There is no other significant and identifiable voice or interest group in Charlotte that represents an alternative and cohesive set of policies. This dominant belief system, like a religious ideology that persists despite the failure of its prophesies, is upheld even after the catastrophe of 2008. No significant measures have been taken to prepare for a repeat or worse.

Yet, some few Charlotteans still dare to hold these giant institutions to some local accountability—a keystone of Sense of Place, its absence the definition of non-Place. An activist group, Third Act, composed mostly of older residents, quietly and peacefully demonstrates in front of Taj McColl, on a regular basis calling for the bank to divest from fossil fuel enterprises.[10]

The group's protests were inspired by a 2022 report, *Banking on Climate Chaos*, researched and compiled by seven major environmental organizations. The report showed that Wells Fargo and Bank of America's financing (lending and underwriting debt and equity issuances) of fossil fuel industries exceeded

$500 billion between 2016 and 2021. These two Charlotte icons were listed at No. 3 and No. 4 on the list of the world's "Dirty Dozen," the twelve banking institutions most heavily engaged in financing and profiting from fossil fuels.[11]

The significance of these small demonstrations of Charlotte residents in front of the largest bank, largely ignored by the media, can be recognized only if the numbing influence the banks cast over Charlotte is understood.

Bank "products" are invisible or indecipherable; their workforce is nonunion, amorphous, and voiceless as a group, with no distinct local identity; and their buildings are tightly secured and nondescript. Many bank employees work in complex teams, often remotely, seldom meeting in person. Many perform tasks too dispersed for any but a rare few to know what they are doing, making discussions with either colleagues or nonemployees about "work" pointless. Only a rare few inside the banks understand how these institutions actually make money, what their focus or direction is, or why the banks might suddenly, catastrophically, become insolvent as they did in 2008.

To most residents, the differences between the two big banks are imperceptible, despite a constant barrage of advertising attributing human-like images and personalities to the respective banks and claiming significant differentiation and competitive choice for consumers.

The complexity of banking also inhibits the banks from generating any genuine local pride, "Soul," or contribution to Sense of Place. A local tribute to the city's banking workforce is unimagined. Though the largest single employee group in the city, bank workers have no local recognition and no local organization.

The absence of any power over their work conditions and lack of recognition likely played a role in sparking recent efforts by a labor union to organize Charlotte bank employees. In April 2024, the *Charlotte Observer* reported that 20 union activists passed out flyers in uptown Charlotte informing Wells Fargo employees of their right to form a union. The flyers included news of a new union local formed by some Wells Fargo employees in Apex, North Carolina, the first in the state. There are now ten locals among Wells Fargo workers in seven states.

A union spokesperson said employees claim they are under-staffed and feel they are not getting paid enough. The spokesman also noted that "return-to-office mandates" are inciting bank workers and "stress to meet high expectations for sales."[12]

Beyond the tens of thousands with name tags on their belts, sometimes carrying laptops in backpacks as they walk the city streets, are the rarified bank executives, who need no name tag or briefcase of any kind. Charlotte residents see their faces online or in the newspaper, always smiling. The most frequently appearing and perplexing figure is that of Brian Moynihan, CEO of Bank of America. Moynihan's official, ubiquitous photo shows a closed mouth, controlled grin, the expression of a person holding special and advantageous information. Making some Charlotte businesspeople nervous about the durability of Charlotte's ties to the banks, Moynihan never moved to the city. He resides in Massachusetts. Wells Fargo, the other anchor bank, is headquartered in San Francisco and its CEO, Charles Scharf, lives in New York City.

Moynihan came into this top job after being made head of the ill-fated stock brokerage Merrill Lynch during the meltdown of 2007–2008. Bank of America's controversial acquisition of Merrill Lynch ruined the value of the bank's stock. The bank's stock went from a high value of $50 to as low as $5 between 2006 and 2009. It later paid $2.4 billion in restitution to shareholders in a damage lawsuit.

Moynihan's immediate predecessor, Ken Lewis (whose wife was involved in promoting a multi-level marketing pyramid scheme in Charlotte), was accused of withholding vital information from shareholders about the condition of Merrill Lynch. The acquisition cost American taxpayers over $20 billion in a bailout. Lewis later claimed he was forced to make the acquisition by federal officials and that his job as CEO had been threatened. Moynihan's current annual compensation is $29 million, the equivalent of $14,000 per hour or 370 times the average pay of branch managers. The CEO of Wells Fargo was given a $4.5 million raise in 2023, placing his pay at the same $29 million total.

Local sentiment toward the banks as dominant and pervasive local enterprises, to the degree any exists at all, is mostly an uncomfortable sense of *dependency*. How would Charlotte be affected by mass layoffs or a sudden revenue drop or share price crash? Will the city be left with empty office space from a possible decline or remote working or a decision to move headquarters? Since the 2008 financial crisis, there have been lingering concerns about the possibility of the banks' catastrophic failure, a wariness of overreliance on their philanthropy, and perhaps unspoken anxiety about the trustworthiness or competence of their executives.

This concern for the bank executives' trustworthiness is fueled by shocking revelations of dishonesty and fraud, damaging shareholders and customers. Yet the bankers somehow retain an official image of unimpeachable integrity and dedication to the public interest. In 2023, the Federal Reserve levied fines of nearly $100 million on Wells Fargo for outlawed transactions with foreign banks, which possibly violated sanctions or facilitated money laundering.[13] This abuse followed a far larger scandal affecting millions of ordinary customers and for which Wells Fargo paid $5 billion in fines and restitution:

> Wells Fargo will pay $1 billion to settle an investor lawsuit. . . . The settlement . . . brings the amount the banking giant has agreed to pay to close to $5 billion. . . . [T]he 2020 suit alleged . . . executives misled investors,

the media and Congress. . . Federal authorities found that Wells Fargo's aggressive sales goals led employees to open millions of fake accounts for customers to meet their targets. In many cases, they did this by creating false records or misappropriating customer identities, generating millions of dollars in fees and harming some customers' credit ratings.[14]

Bank of America was forced to pay a quarter billion dollars for "duping" its customers with similar abusive practices, including erroneously charging fees, not honoring credit card reward bonuses and opening accounts without customer consent. The bank was ordered to pay $100 million to duped customers, plus an additional $150 million in fines. The CFPB found that Bank of America violated laws including the Truth in Lending Act, the Fair Credit Reporting Act, and the Consumer Financial Protection Act of 2010.[15]

The most thorough book on the role of Charlotte-based banks in the global collapse of 2008 took the city's moniker "Banktown" as its title. It was written by a long-time business reporter for the *Charlotte Observer*, Rick Rothacker. It offers a genuinely local perspective, citing people, places, and events very familiar to Charlotte residents.

Despite the title, there is actually little in *Banktown* about the community of Charlotte or the impact of banking on city life.[16] The book does offer a wealth of details on the disastrous policy decisions that took the banks from supremacy to insolvency. *Banktown* also contains detailed portrayals of the characters in the executive suites, focusing on their careers, compensation packages, rivalries, and connections.

The book's treatment of bank executives tends toward hagiography—the usual mode in Charlotte when discussing the banks. But if one attempts to look past this filter to trace accountability for the crisis, the book recounts actions that can only be described as reckless, egotistical, and almost childlike:

> Bank of America's Hugh McColl, Jr., and First Union's Ed Crutchfield . . . pushed regulatory envelopes, jockeyed for acquisitions, and pursued an eat-or-be-eaten vision for the financial services industry. . . .

> This book is . . . the story of ambitious bankers like Hugh McColl, Ed Crutchfield, Ken Lewis, and Ken Thompson. . . . They forged giant banks that created huge profits in good times while also helping to fuel a debt-burdened economy that unraveled when high-stakes bets made in Charlotte and around the world went awry.

The book suggests that personal competition between the bank executives fueled rapid expansion, and that ego-rivalry even extended to the size of the banks' buildings:

> [B]ack-and-forth acquisitions fueled the suspicion among some that McColl and Crutchfield were engaged in an expensive game of one-upmanship. The rivalry extended to the banks' buildings as well. In 1988, Crutchfield opened a new 42-story headquarters in Charlotte. McColl responded with plans for a 60-story tower at the center of Uptown.

Banktown follows Charlotte's long-established pattern of placing concern for damage to the city's "image" before any reckoning for actual damage to people. Accordingly, the word "eviction" is not found anywhere in the book. "Foreclosure" appears only a half dozen times and is mostly sanitized as a balance sheet problem for bankers, not for the people losing their homes.

Many people came to an understanding of the 2008 disaster through the book and movie, *The Big Short*. It is a shocking story of "liar loans," "no-doc" mortgages, and millions of "toxic" mortgages hidden among credit-worthy loans in "tranches" and deviously sold into the securities market, fueling the stock market crash and destroying pension funds. The bankers' reckless speculation was supposedly secured by a form of insurance called "credit default swaps" that turned out to be unpayable.

In 2013, *The Nation* magazine reported:

> Since 2007, the foreclosure crisis has displaced at least 10 million people from more than 4 million homes across the country. . . . They add up to approximately the entire population of Michigan.[17]

Banktown characterizes the disaster as putting the "first significant dents" in Charlotte's "Teflon, can-do image." It reduces the "lingering question for Charlotte" to how the city could "replace the salaries of high-paying bank jobs" if regulators were to have responded to the crisis by limiting bank executives' bonuses or breaking up the banks:

> [Though] big bonuses for executives have been vilified in many quarters, these payouts form a significant chunk of the city's wages. . . . [P]ushing to break up giant banks, lawmakers could hurt the city by downsizing its corporate citizens.

In one anecdote, retired Bank of America CEO Hugh McColl defiantly rejects responsibility for the aggressive acquisition and borrowing policies that led to collapse, insolvency, and untold losses to the public:

> A student asked the retired CEO if he felt bad about creating a bank considered too big to fail.

> "I feel no regret about building a large company that spread across the United States," McColl replied. . . . But he said he "might have some regrets" about not building his bank larger—meaning the company should have socked away more capital in good times to help it weather downturns.

Written by a Charlotte journalist who covered the banks locally for many years, *Banktown* reflects the Charlotte "state of mind." It is a case study of the unspoken fact in Charlotte that there is only one operable perspective in the city: the banks'. Anything else is seen as "critical" and "negative."

It is this background that makes local citizens challenging the banks' energy investment policy in front of Taj McColl so significant. It is one of the rare but persistent displays of light to be seen in Charlotte.

The big banks may weigh down upon Charlotte's Soul but they are also, indisputably, the city's existential benefactor, the sustainer of livelihoods. This is reflected even in the writer of *Banktown's* own resumé. His *LinkedIn* page shows he no longer works as a journalist but now does Charlotte-based PR for US Bank, the fifth largest banking institution in the US.[18]

Defying Dirty Energy

Pre-dating the big banks' extraordinary influence over life in Charlotte is one other dominating and pervasive corporate entity. This is Duke Power as it is known to long-time Charlotte residents, now officially Duke Energy. In keeping with W. J. Cash's observation of Charlotte's "gigantism," Charlotte-based Duke has become the largest utility company in America.[19]

But sheer size has never been Duke's source of supremacy or the core of its corporate culture. It is *monopoly*. Duke is a utility monopoly in North Carolina, and it was created with a king's fortune gained from an earlier monopoly on North Carolina's cigarette industry, controlled by Duke's founding family. It may be said that entitlement, unaccountability, control, and exclusion of other stakeholders—the innate hallmarks of monopolies— are in Duke's DNA.

When local residents dare to oppose or even question Duke's actions and policies—an extremely rare phenomenon—their efforts must be counted among the brilliant flashes of Charlotte Soul. In recent years, a sustained, organized movement coalesced around resisting Duke's plans to deliver greater profits to its shareholders by producing more "dirty energy" and raising rates to pay for this expansion.

To understand the effect of such policies on Charlotte's Soul and the powerlessness of ordinary people in the face of an omnipresent monopoly requires a brief reflection on Duke's corporate history and culture. Duke is not only a gigantic, publicly traded company, but one with decades of experience protecting its monopoly status. This necessarily involves controlling public opinion and "capturing" government regulators and lawmakers.

In Charlotte, Duke's approach to doing business and view of the world are treated by local government, business boosters, and the media not as imposed policies but as the *natural order*. Duke's influence is literally stamped upon the land and water. Beyond ownership or control over vast acreages for energy production and powerline right-of-way, Duke dammed the Catawba River, creating Lake Norman, just north of Charlotte, the largest artificial body of water in the state. It is named after a president of Duke. In flooding vast sections of private land, Duke gained ownership of much of the land along the newly established shores, which suddenly rose in value as "lakefront" property. One body of water created by Duke, Lake James, is named for James B. Duke, company founder, and another, Lake Wylie, for the president of the company that Duke acquired at its start. In Charlotte, the former home of James B. Duke, known locally as the Duke Mansion, is a historic landmark. The state's most prestigious university and hospital are named after the family.

In keeping with the broader trend of financialization of utilities, Duke's core business has increasingly shifted from energy to finance. Its mission has become less about bringing low-cost power to the public than low-risk profit to shareholders, which are themselves increasingly abstract entities. Duke's largest shareholder is the investment firm Vanguard. Until 2016, Charlotte's Duke Energy operated businesses in Peru, Chile, Ecuador, Guatemala, El Salvador, and Argentina, and it is currently a partner in a joint venture with a Saudi Arabian company to produce methanol and methyl tertiary butyl ether (MTBE), a gasoline additive. Duke's CEO received $21 million in compensation in 2023.

Charlotte's intrepid and upstart protestors faced not only this increasingly abstract financial institution but an entrenched one-hundred-year-old monopoly. As there are no market levers available to consumers under a monopoly, the only chance for Charlotte's activists to bring about change was to influence popular opinion. However, public attitudes have been shaped by years of Duke PR and by the favorable views of Duke held by local and state government, the result of years of influence-buying. Charlotte's longest serving mayor, Pat McCrory, was an employee of Duke.

Beginning in 1890, the Dukes began manufacturing cigarettes and within a few years gained control over virtually the entire cigarette industry. Public opinion became increasingly hostile toward the cigarette monopoly. The public came to see monopolies as harmful and to demand enforcement of antitrust law. The Cigarette Trust, officially called the American Tobacco Company, was broken up in 1911 into smaller and supposedly competitive companies: Liggett-Myers, P. Lorillard, Philip Morris, Brown and Williamson, and R. J. Reynolds. James B. Duke immediately exited the tobacco business, and with his cigarette-based fortune he began development of hydroelectric energy, primarily to power new textile mills along Carolina rivers. Tobacco money produced Duke, which in turn produced textile fortunes.

Despite assiduous effort of Charlotte's brand managers to expunge them from modern "narratives," the ghosts of these two foundational industries—tobacco and textiles—haunt the culture of Duke Energy and reveal themselves in its "dirty energy" policies. Astute observers cannot help but discern those old corporate cultures in Duke's patronizing, secretive, and polluting ways.

And so it happened that beleaguered Charlotte citizens, concerned about rate hikes and environmental degradation, united and mobilized against the energy icon. They were guided by a professional community organizer in Charlotte working for the activist group Green Peace. The organizer, Monica Mariko Embrey, documented the main issues, principles, and strategies of the campaign in the booklet she wrote and published in 2016, *New Dawn for Energy Justice in North Carolina.*[20]

Specifically, the citizen campaign in Charlotte protested Duke's proposed 17 percent hike and plans to build more coal-fired power plants. Citizens demanded the removal of coal-ash "ponds," structures used to store the toxic products of coal combustion, some of which are close to residential areas and adjacent to Charlotte's main source of city water. Duke's "dirty" energy policies involved continuing use of energy technologies as outmoded as old textile machinery and as harmful as smoking cigarettes. The movement charged the policies with poisoning the air, soil, and water as well as financially harming millions of households who would be forced to pay for the increased pollution in their monthly bills.

Embrey's booklet tells of the key role played by one soulful North Carolinian, Beth Henry, a retired lawyer and avid gardener, in opposing Duke. It was in her garden that Beth Henry saw firsthand the reality of a warming climate, leading her to study the climate crisis and the effects of burning coal on human health. On hearing that Duke planned a huge new coal-fired plant about an hour from where she lived, she helped mobilize the first protest at a Duke Energy annual meeting held in Charlotte, an almost sacred, perfunctory ritual treated in the media as relevant only to Duke's shareholders. Duke was one of the last utilities in the US to seek more coal-fired power for future energy needs. The campaign did succeed in getting one rate hike that Duke originally sought cut in half, among other victories.

My wife, Terry Thirion, and I were both active in these efforts, including participating in demonstrations at the annual shareholders meeting at Duke headquarters in downtown Charlotte.

Revealing how Duke and Charlotte officials were unused to and frightened by any local opposition to Duke Energy policies, one year, Charlotte's police declared our upcoming protests an "extraordinary event." An "extraordinary event" is a special "crowd control" status to combat or prevent mass violence and terrorism by allowing the police to impose far greater restrictions on free speech and assembly. We gathered in front of the headquarters building at midday. Most of our small band of protesters were seniors and women, longtime Charlotte residents, holding homemade signs about "dirty energy." We were literally outnumbered by heavily armed police protecting the shareholders, presumably from us. A helicopter hovered above.

Seeing how Duke dismissed other protests as limited to "environmentalists," the strategy of the Charlotte-based effort attacked Duke's entire business model. The protests connected the interests of rate payers, especially lower-income residents, with Wall Street investors, as well as with those concerned with personal health, climate change, and environmental pollution. The normally exclusive annual meeting became a public showcase of Duke's "dirty" policies, but also it exposed how Duke's profits were generated, reported, and "regulated," under a peculiar accounting system that almost no one among the public was aware of.

At a public rally against the rate hikes, a speaker asked the crowd, "How does Duke Energy make money?" Various people answered with their version of "selling electricity." Perplexingly, he rejected the answers, saying this is not the basis of Duke's business. The speaker's explanation of how Duke actually makes money shocked the audience. It seemed to bring light and clarity to Duke's overall business model and policies, which many people could otherwise see only as irrational and intransigent.

A recent newsletter of the Southern Environmental Law Center offered a succinct restatement of what was revealed at that meeting. The newsletter reported the insights of journalist and activist David Neal, who explained the regulatory history and strange accounting behind Duke's "dirty" policies. Neal showed that more than a hundred years ago, when energy monopolies first developed, the public sought protection from unlimited rate hikes. The first regulatory commissions devised the plan in which,

> [Utilities] could not set their own prices on power. Instead, their profits were based on the costs of the infrastructure they built—power plants, poles, wires—plus a return. The more they built, and the more expensive the infrastructure they built, the more money they could earn."[21]

Under this system, the crucial role of regulators was to "make sure that utilities did not . . . overbuild just to earn a larger return for their shareholders." The system worked reasonably well, he wrote, partly because energy needs were rapidly expanding and utilities built more and larger plants to meet the demand. The price to users declined or rose very little for many years—until recently.

Neal explained that demand for energy plateaued about 20 years ago. Now, "many clean energy solutions don't necessarily require costly, enormous, utility-owned infrastructure."

In the new economy, that old model, based on profiting from building more infrastructure suddenly limited utility company profits. Larger plants were no longer justified, and the new renewable technologies enabled consumers to generate electricity from their roofs, which, along with conservation measures, further reduced demand. "Those things are very good . . . for everyone, except the utility," he wrote.

Neal concludes that this explains Duke's seemingly irrational and destructive opposition to consumers generating their own solar power. Duke's profit model explains its insistence on constructing more high-pollution coal plants despite climate change, its promotion of projects to build unneeded and exorbitantly expensive nuclear plants, and its laxity in maintenance of toxic sites. He said Duke's policies are still based on exploiting an obsolete model that serves Duke's profit needs at the expense of users, communities, and nature: "The bigger projects add to the base on which profits are based."

Charlotte's unprecedented campaign of opposition to Duke's "dirty" and "unfair" policies gained additional momentum after an all-too-predictable disaster. Some of the protestors discovered the school system planned to move a school close to an older, high-pollution coal-fired power plant that included an unlined "coal ash pond," a highly toxic by-product of coal burning. Some neighbors suspected the plant and the toxic waste dump contributed to a strange pattern of cancers in their areas.

Duke maintained thirty-six "dumps" of coal ash near fourteen of its coal plants in North Carlina. Many of these dumps were rated "high hazard" by the Environmental Protection Agency, meaning that failure of the infrastructure containing the coal ash would be likely to result in loss of human life. Duke insisted the "ponds" were safe and secure.

On February 2, 2014, a disaster occurred that made the hazard "potential" an immediate reality. A pipe burst at a Duke plant in Virginia, spilling 39,000 tons of toxic coal ash and 27 million gallons of contaminated water into the Dan River in one night. It flowed downstream to the town of Danville a few hours later.

On the ten-year anniversary of the catastrophe, a Danville television station aired a segment reflecting on the event:

> Brian Williams with the Dan River Basin Association said the thick layer of coal ash coated the river floor, covering anything living on the bottom. . . . Coal ash contains heavy metals like arsenic, selenium, and cadmium, which can be toxic to humans and animals if ingested in large amounts. The Dan River Basin Association says coal ash remains mixed in with the sediments of the river today, as the EPA was only able to remove

about 7% of the spill. . . [so] they recommend using caution when eating fish out of the Dan River. "We really just don't know. It may be 20 years out before we know the full effects of this. We may never know the full effects of it, but we know it's still in the river," said Williams.

Prompted by the disaster, many groups joined the citizen campaign to change Duke's "dirty energy" policies. Their efforts culminated in the Coal Ash Management Act of 2014, passed by the North Carolina State legislature.

According to a local news report, as of 2024, Duke Energy reported that it had removed 3.3 million tons, or twenty percent, of the toxic materials at one plant near Charlotte, with 13.8 million tons remaining. Duke has agreed to finish removal of toxic material from that plant by the end of 2035.[22]

---

[1] *An End to Inequality, Breaking Down the Walls of Apartheid Education in America* by Jonathan Kozol, The New Press, p.140, Kindle Edition, 2024

[2] "NC Private-school Enrollment has Grown 24% in Four Years, New Data Show" by Ann Doss Helms, *WFAE*, August 1, 2023. The pattern of abandonment by affluent and now also middle-income White families was discussed in my conversation with former school board member, Jennifer De La Jara, as part of research for this book.

[3] https://www.privateschoolreview.com/north-carolina/charlotte#:~:text=How%20much%20do%20private%20schools,average%20tuition%20cost%20of%20%2410%2C347

[4] "Two Park Road Montessori Students Fight to Save 'Treasure Trees'" by Ann Doss Helms, *WFAE*, May 16, 2024

[5] Some Experts Skeptical of Latest Tree Study in Charlotte" by Gavin Off, *Charlotte Observer*, Dec 06, 2023

[6] "Bradford Pear Trees Are Banned in a Few States. More Are Looking to Replace, Eradicate Them" by Mike Snider, *USA Today*, March 25, 2024

[7] "Saved from the Ax", Opinion of Editorial Staff, *Charlotte Observer*, April 7, 2004

[8] The art initiative of the citizen campaign to save the cherry trees in Freedom Park was led mostly by artist Terry Thirion, my spouse. She gathered petitions in the park while doing *pleine aire* paintings of the trees. See https://terrythirion.com/saving-the-cherry-trees-in-freedom-park/. The two poems were presented at public meetings by the authors, respectively, George G. Rose and Marc Kool

[9] This prevalent view in Charlotte reveals how the conflating of public interest with private monopoly interests that was common in the 1950s persists in Charlotte now. The iconic quote, "What's good for General Motors is good for America," was said by Charles Wilson, CEO of General Motors during hearings for his appointment as US Secretary of Defense in 1953. Asked if he could support policies good for America but potentially harmful to GM stockholder share value, Wilson said he could but added that he thought that "what was good for our country was good for General Motors, and vice versa. The difference did not exist. Our company is too big. It goes with the welfare of the country."

[10] "Elder-led Protesters Want Banks to Stop Financing Fossil Fuels" by David Boraks, *WFAE*, March 21, 2023

[11] The 2022 Report, "Banking on Climate Chaos," shows only J. P. Morgan and Citi with greater levels of investments than Wells Fargo and Bank of America. See https://www.bankingonclimatechaos.org//wp-content/themes/bocc-2021/inc/bcc-data-2022/BOCC_2022_vSPREAD.pdf

[12] "Union with Little Inroads at Banks Tries to Organize Wells Fargo Workers In Charlotte" by Chase Jordan, *Charlotte Observer*, April 29, 2024. The union leading the organizing effort is Communications Workers of America.

[13] https://www.federalreserve.gov/newsevents/pressreleases/enforcement20230330a.htm

[14] "Wells Fargo $1 Billion Accord over Fake Accounts Approved" by Chris Dolmetsch, *Bloomberg News*, September 8, 2023, and "Wells Fargo Fake Accounts Settlements Nears $5 Billion Mark," *PYMNTS Intelligence*, Sept. 10, 2023, and "Wells Fargo Agrees to Pay $3 Billion to Resolve Criminal and Civil Investigations into Sales Practices Involving the Opening of Millions of Accounts without Customer Authorization," *Office of Public Affairs of U.S. Dept. of Justice*, February 21, 2020

[15] "Bank of America to Pay $150 Million in Fines for Bad Consumer Practices," by Dawn Papandrea, *Investopedia*, July 11, 2023. Also see the news releases of the *Consumer Financial Protection Bureau*, "CFPB Takes Action Against Bank of America for Illegally Charging Junk Fees, Withholding Credit Card Rewards, and Opening Fake Accounts," July 11, 2023.

[16] *Banktown: The Rise and Struggles of Charlotte's Big Banks* by Rick Rothacker, John F. Blair, Publisher, Kindle Edition, 2010

[17] "The Great Eviction, the Landscape of Wall Street's Creative Destruction" by Laura Gottesdiener, *The Nation*, August 2013

[18] https://www.linkedin.com/in/rickrothacker/

[19] Duke Energy is the nation's largest utility company by revenue, which is over $29 billion. See https://www.statista.com/statistics/224212/the-largest-gas-and-electric-utilities-in-the-us-based-on-revenue/#:~:text=Duke%20Energy%20was%20ranked%20as,in%20the%20financial%20year%202023

[20] The text is part of an academic publication, New Dawn for Energy Justice in North Carolina, edited by Jeff Crane and Char Miller, University Press of Colorado, 2017, available through the academic publisher, Project Muse, See: https://muse.jhu.edu/pub/173/edited_volume/chapter/2271225/pdf

[21] "Utility Monopolies Still Reign in the South," *Southern Environmental Law Center*, January 27, 2024 (https://www.southernenvironment.org/news/utility-monopolies-still-reign-in-the-south/)

[22] "Duke Energy Ahead of Schedule on Lake Norman Coal Ash Basin Closure" by Zachary Turner, *WFAE*, July 16, 2024

XIII. Conclusions

When I returned to Charlotte in the late '90s after living in Florida for eighteen years, I encountered the "transformation" that Charlotte was already becoming famous for. On previous visits I only saw the main highlights of Charlotte's new construction boom. Now I had time to see the full spectrum and contemplate the extraordinary phenomenon.

I saw the vast and affluent White exurbs, but I was not amazed. Charlotte was already sprawling before I left. The Taj McColl tower "uptown," just fifty feet shorter than the Empire State Building, did not qualify as *transformative*. As W. J. Cash had noted, Charlotte was flaunting "skyscrapers" a hundred years earlier. The transit center, which shifted the poor bus riders away from the new bank's grand entrance, looked to me more like a removal than an addition. The four monumental pillar statues appeared oversized, out of place, and pretentious in a downtown that had been gutted by urban renewal's rampage. The luxury condos, NBA franchise, and Bank of America-branded stadium were impressive, but mostly mimics of the cities Charlotte emulated, Atlanta in particular. I took flights to and from Charlotte's constantly expanding hub airport, but I certainly did not find Soul there. The megachurches with millionaire preachers promising prosperity to their paying congregants didn't feel soulful or connecting. There are nearly exact replicas of such churches in many other cities.

The renamed and continuously redeveloping "uptown" did not feel like home. The newly gentrified neighborhoods, some of which I used to live in or had organized the residents of years ago, now feel like real estate commercials.

Charlotte's many new restaurants, clubs, coffee houses, and entertainment venues definitely add flavor to the city. But they are mostly in gentrified areas and hardly qualify as creating character or uniqueness.

Over time, I did find Soul, flashing brightly and often briefly here and there in neighborhood preservation efforts and non-profit art centers and projects often led by individual artists.[1] I found Soul among residents and small businesses resisting the onslaught of urban renewal, flipping, and land speculation. I saw flashes of Soul at churches engaged in meeting social as well as spiritual needs, some serving public housing residents, and in local citizen groups daring to defy Charlotte's icons of power, the big banks and Duke Energy. Most of these soulful struggles are barely acknowledged in the media, almost never lauded, and usually dismissed as marginal. They tend to be quickly forgotten and redacted from Charlotte's happy official history.

The identifying markers of Soul in Charlotte, and likely in any city today, I learned, are not wealth, gentrification, growth, or even success, which are often soulless and can be soul-killing. They are struggle and resistance, and the active participation of ordinary people in preserving and improving the places where they live.

With that realization, the strongest and most inspiring expressions of Soul I found in Charlotte are among the members of the community with the longest and most arduous struggles for freedom against discrimination and the legacies of enslavement and apartheid. And, I found hope for Charlotte's Soul in its newest community bursting with aspiration yet facing the threats of discrimination, expulsion, and exile.

Must Be Greek or Sump'n

While the signs of "boom" upon my return to Charlotte did not dazzle, I was astounded by one change never before experienced in Charlotte. I heard voices and saw signage in Spanish! Thousands of Latinos were now in Charlotte, mostly from Mexico, many without documentation, and the city was seemingly welcoming them. Now, that was a transformation!

There were also many Vietnamese and Indians, among other nationalities, colors, and cultures. One large older apartment complex close to where I had once lived housed a community of Bosnians and nearby was a little boutique grocer with European specialty foods.[2] In Charlotte! Just one year before I came back to Charlotte, Serbian-aligned forces massacred 8,000 Bosnian men and boys in Srebrenica. Now, refugees who escaped this violence are walking the streets of Charlotte, making Charlotte home. I could only imagine the traumas, journeys, and aspirations of these new Charlotte residents.

So bereft of diverse cultures and language was the Charlotte I had left that, as a kid, I used to be embarrassed by my father's "accent." Born in Lawrence, Massachusetts, he never lost his New Englandish speech, though he came to the South when he was just thirteen. He must have also incorporated a bit of the speech patterns of his own father, my grandfather, who died before I was born. Thomas Bernard FitzPatrick was born in Bradford, England, of Irish parents who fled the potato famine, so he likely had some Yorkshire accent added to an Irish brogue, which may have also showed up in my father's speech. My mother's father, Anthony Frank, who also passed away before I was born, was born in Italy and spoke with a distinct Italian accent, I am told. The family of my mother's mother, Katherine Hieber, were German. My mother heard Italian and German in her childhood home. She had a passable Southern accent from earlier years in

Birmingham and Asheville and then Charlotte. We looked like our neighbors and most White people in Charlotte, but my father's speech gave us away. We did not fully qualify.

In most of the South of that not-too-distant time, and especially so in Charlotte, foreign languages, foreign accents, and even non-Southern regional American accents were true oddities. When another language was heard, or a "foreign" accent, someone might wonder out loud where the speaker might be from or what language they were speaking. A common response in Charlotte, spoken matter-of-factly and not as a joke, was, "*I don't know, must be Greek or sump'n.*" There was little curiosity and no point in knowing the actual national origin. There were no "ethnicities" in Charlotte or in most other Southern cities. Historically, there was no wave of immigrants as in the Northeast, Great Lakes, or West Coast. Charlotte did have a smattering of actual people from Greece who often spoke Greek among themselves and most attended the Greek Orthodox church. They operated many restaurants in Charlotte, but these restaurants were not called Greek or even Mediterranean. Most were classic Southern diners that—though many customers found this odd—offered baklava as a dessert. Thus, for classifying a strange accent or incomprehensible tongue, *Greek or sump'n* sufficed.

Not Black or White Any More

Ethnicity is a source of personal and family identity, closely tied to honor of ancestors and respect for home. As a source of connectedness, ethnic identity is recognizable as an expression of "Soul." Ethnicity is real history. It is authentic culture that manifests in joy, grief, and art. It can be commercialized through the marketing of styles, music, and other "ethnic" products or services, but it is inherently noncommercial. Ethnicity is a central element of Sense of Place, even when people are far from a "homeland." It provides a perspective from which to view the world, at least as a starting point. It is a link for connecting to wherever people live.

It follows that wherever ethnicity is absent or suppressed, as was true for generations in Charlotte, Soul is handicapped. In its place, social patterns of enforced conformity and divisions based on social class or racism grow. Surrogate ideologies—commercial, political, and religious—dominate. These surrogate ideologies produce *restrictions* on personal freedom and self-expression. For instance, as discussed earlier, Thoreau regarded civilization disconnected from Nature as restricting freedom, while Theodor Adorno made the same claim about the entrapments of "lifestyle." Poet Deborah Tall recognized "avoidance of ties to a place" as self-destructive.

Historically, there were two groups in Charlotte, and neither was "ethnic" by local standards of the day. The majority was "White." Recently, "White" is being depicted as a distinct ethnic group. If a claim of White ethnicity had validity, Charlotte would be one of its cultural centers. But "White" is not and never was an ethnicity, not in the way Italian, Irish, Latino, Lithuanian, Kenyan, Caribbean, Chinese, Polynesian, etc., are. The Protestant Scottish people who were sent to Catholic Ireland as colonial settlers and then migrated or were sent to America were heavily represented in Charlotte. However, they exhibited few cultural distinctions that stand out from the larger "White" society, and few knew much of their heritage.

As historians, sociologists and anthropologists have sought to document, "White" is an invented classification that connotes *social status*, not genetics, common history, culture, language, or territory. Historically, it has not even reliably corresponded to skin color. It is a *socially* constructed idea. The "White" status is that of power and privilege over others who are "non-White" — nothing more.

Historian Noel Ignatiev persuasively demonstrated that the Irish, who were among the lightest-skinned people in America, were not accepted or treated as "Whites" when they first arrived in large numbers as immigrants. They gained their "White" status, he argued, only after they rejected the petitions of their Irish brethren back in Ireland—who were fighting for their own freedom—to side with abolitionists in America.

When the Irish immigrants demonstrated their willingness to join conventional American society that largely accepted racial hierarchy, Ignatiev argued, they were able to gain "White" status with all its perks and security.[3] Subsequently, many Irish in America became champions of "whiteness" and were slow to accept Italians or Greeks as "White."[4]

As "White" is not an ethnicity but an *invented* social status of power and privilege, "Black," back then, was also not an ethnicity but an *imposed* status signifying *lack* of power and privilege. Authentic Black ethnicity exists, of course. Like all ethnicities, it is rooted in heritage, language, religion and tradition. It derives from customs in Africa and centuries of unique experience in America. All of that was suppressed in Charlotte in a way that was similar to how other ethnicities were overshadowed by the dominance of the "White–Black" social system, but more extreme. Italian, German, Irish, Scandinavian, or Polish heritage, for example, were prudently not promoted or publicly celebrated in Charlotte, except in superficial ways (on St. Patrick's Day, "everyone" is Irish). There was nothing to be gained, and potentially much to lose. The "White" status required conformity, unity, and compliance with Jim Crow laws, customs, and beliefs, which linger today.

Until very recently, it was socially taboo for African Americans in Charlotte to publicly acknowledge and celebrate their African heritage. Appreciation for African heritage endured underground at historically Black colleges such as Johnson C. Smith in Charlotte, or other niches of academia, in churches, in food preparation, at family reunions, and in marginal political movements. The term "Black" was seldom used in those times and, if it was, it was pejorative. The preferred social terms were "Negro" and "colored," which meant, above all, "not White." This was a social standing applied to people defined by the dominating White powers as excluded from "White" status.

Charlotte's bipolar social system, though it was composed of both White and Black people, could not be called "diverse." Diversity, usually involving more than only two groups, is based on general equality of opportunity and rights. Prejudices may never disappear in a diverse city but are not rigidly and institutionally enforced. Real diversity unleashes aspirations, reduces resentment and conflict, and unlocks opportunities for everyone's talents and ambitions to be realized.

Before my return in the '90s, Charlotte was not ethnically diverse. It was Black and White. When I returned, I could see that had all changed, and that this remarkable change had the potential to breathe enriching and energizing Soul into Charlotte, if only given the chance.

The Souls of Charlotte Folk

Perhaps the greatest story of the quest for Soul in America is W. E. B. Du Bois's *The Souls of Black Folk*. Written in 1903, Du Bois's masterpiece is part memoir, part historical tract, and part bold philosophical declaration. Du Bois, an African American, was one of the founders of the NAACP and one of the greatest intellectuals in American history. He died on August 27, 1963, the day before the great March on Washington, attended by more than 250,000 people, where Martin Luther King delivered his famous "I Have a Dream" speech.

As any story of the Soul of a people must be, Du Bois's treatise is addressed simultaneously to those longing to express their freedom and those who obstruct it. One group seeks a "place" in America. In preventing this, the other group suppresses their awareness of their own place in society and history, concocting myths of a "lost cause," racial superiority, or absurd and empty pretenses of racial harmony. It is a story of America through the "dark veil," as Du Bois called the institution of racism. It is also, as Du Bois makes clear with his many references to other cultures and historic freedom struggles, a universal and timeless tale of the human spirit.

Charlotte's struggle with Soul is but one more of the tales of a people—voiceless, their story officially invalidated—who seek to express their truth and have that truth recognized. They must overcome the dark and restrictive "veil" of Charlotte's hyper-commercialism and shallow salesmanship, a force akin to Jim Crow in its insinuation and controlling influence over every aspect of city life: recreation, worship, civic participation, education, livelihood, and personal identity.

Also, as with Jim Crow, the greatest impact of the hyper-commercial veil is to persuade those who question it or choose another path that their longings are illegitimate, unnatural, and impossible. When they persist, the pretenses to benevolence by those behind the veil fall away, revealing a system of strict regulation, delivering unwelcome consequences for resistance.

In *The Souls of Black Folk,* Du Bois faces the reality that liberation for Black folk will not come without major change among White folk. One group sought rightful opportunity that could not be realized until the other gained, if not empathy, then at least awareness. He also saw that the dark veil crushed the Souls of both White and Black people. Charlotte's "boom" was enabled only with the dismantling of Jim Crow.

Du Bois lived most of his life under the terror of Jim Crow. He also faced legal threats and government prosecution. Yet, as activist and voice for change, over his lifetime he witnessed tangible progress and he never succumbed to despair or bitterness. Written long before the struggle for civil rights could be called a mass movement, *The Souls of Black Folk* is a magnificent testimony to the power of vision and hope. Addressing White readers, Du Bois wrote that he hoped their "ears would tingle with truth." Imagining a new awareness in America that would sweep away the forces of ignorance and myth, he looked to "infinite reason [to] turn the tangle straight" and anticipated that "in due time the country will come to its senses."

Many souls in Charlotte seek greater freedom and opportunities for self-expression, and to make Charlotte a more humane place to call home. Local and national media, artists, writers, community activists and other commentators have at various times pointed to Charlotte's arid and characterless center city, the trampling of local history, erasure of long-established communities. They have lamented the destruction of natural beauty, declining and segregated schools, homes valued for flipping rather than living, inadequate and neglected parks, lack of mass transit, maddening traffic gridlock, diminished artistic community, and materialistic religious institutions. Perhaps the most tragic consequence of Charlotte's commercial culture is the brutal denial of opportunity for those of lower income to gain a better life in Charlotte, what is politely called a lack of "social mobility."

Each of these wounds to the city's Soul has been acknowledged and some have triggered real concern among Charlotte leaders, especially when they attracted national attention. Yet, unlike the veil of racism that relies on myth and ignorance that can be debunked and refuted, Charlotte's veil that suppresses Soul and diminishes Place has deeper and more intractable roots. Philosopher Wendell Berry noted the "dominant tendency" in American history "to take, to exploit, to use up, and to move on." As noted earlier in this book, there is no clearly articulated alternative to the growth-and-profit crusade. The seekers of Soul have no NAACP that unites them, and no national voices like Du Bois or Dr. King.

There is official awareness that something important is missing in Charlotte that stadiums, towers, and convention centers can never provide. But this awareness has not led to redirection or even self-reflection. Rather it has prompted journeys down the Yellow Brick Road in search of the mysterious missing element, comically expressed in periodic junkets taken by delegates of the chamber of commerce or visitors bureau and members of the city council to learn of another city's branding wizardry. Like the Tin Man, Cowardly Lion, and the Scarecrow, the Charlotte delegates go in search for what could put heart, wisdom, and soul into Charlotte. Each publicized mission to other cities is accompanied by media commentary on public discontent: not with policy, but with the city's current slogan.

Officials of host cities have sometimes advised Charlotte to accept what the city is already known and respected for, its status as a money town. Charlotte came close to it in earlier decades with the slogan "Charlotte, a Good Place to Make Money." The motto was intended to boast of economic opportunity, but was heard as evoking a cultural wasteland, reducing the city to a tacky shopping mall, and conjuring the pathos of Willy Loman.

In a 2019 essay, the city's slogan, "Charlotte's Got a Lot," (Char-lot, get it?) was reexamined and derided as past slogans have been, this time by a local writer who specializes in tracking Charlotte's blitzkrieg "development," i.e., demolitions and new construction. His statement featured in the *Charlotte Observer* called for yet another slogan:

> The city just doesn't have "a lot." Plenty of cities have a lot more breweries, taco restaurants, and a lot more of the beige boxes [apartments] that seemingly are becoming the city's identity. There is so little left of what makes a city great, like remnants of its history, and we lose more and more of it every year, replacing it with things that are more "Instagrammable."[5]

The article also noted that, though Charlotte no longer boasts openly about "making money," the current slogan, when it was adopted in 2008, subliminally sought to convey the same thing. The columnist reminded readers of the economic and cultural climate when the current slogan was adopted, just before the mighty banks collapsed like a house of cards:

> Donald Trump was promising to build a new tallest building on South Tryon Street, and banks were too big to fail. . . . [A] developer promised 20 future residents a free Porsche to buy an obscenely expensive condo, with a car elevator. . . . Everyone was a "home flipper" all of a sudden, and everyone wanted a slice of "The New South."

In March 2007, Charlotte media had reported that Donald Trump, the star of *Celebrity Apprentice*, who was at that point in the national and local news almost daily for insulting comedian Rosie O'Donnell, was negotiating to acquire property in the center of Charlotte. The property would be the site of a tower that would surpass the Bank of America headquarters in height. The news created a storm of excitement.[6]

A 2021 news article recalling that forgotten moment of near-glory for Charlotte explained that, at that time, *"Trump Charlotte* was touted as a symbol of Charlotte's status as a 'world-class' city, something residents could be proud of."[7]

Trump Charlotte was never built, and no one knows if the project was anything more than a publicity stunt, but it lives on as a symbol of what the current slogan, "Charlotte's Got a Lot" was actually all about. Yet, even if Charlotte adopted a new slogan evoking loftier values, it is doubtful that Charlotte will ever shake its reputation for an on-the-make, venal, one-dimensional culture, a "banker's paradise." There is no plausible indicator that the policies and practices that earned Charlotte this reputation will change.

From Venal to Venerable

One reason there is little prospect of change is that the dishonor of Charlotte's reputation for venality has lessened in recent years. Many other cities are now taking on the same character and adopting similar "narratives."

This development—that Charlotte's mercenary character and relentless self-promotion are being venerated and emulated by other cities—seems to fulfill W. J. Cash's prophetic view about Charlotte's "secret" power. He wrote that the city's culture elevates obsessive commercialism to a moral crusade, pursued with missionary zeal. Above all, he noted,

> "The thing works . . . and it pays. Yesterday and today,
> it has made and makes uniformly for the prosperity and
> security of those who rule in Charlotte."[8]

Now, this commercial religion is spreading, and Charlotte is an elder in the Church of the Profits, sitting in the pews ahead of the ultimate "world-class" city: New York, New York! A 2001 *New York Times* story described the Big Apple's flirtation with promotional "branding" campaigns that threatened to overshadow New York's renowned authenticity and undermine the city's famous reputation for not caring what others think. Charlotte, North Carolina is referenced six times in the story as the model of what "old" New York is now having to become.

The article addressed why it was that the most identifiable, storied, and historic city in America, the fullest expression of a sophisticated, globalized metropolis, is now competing with mid-size cities—like Charlotte, North Carolina—to attract companies, conventions, and capital. It quoted Marshall Blonsky, a professor of communications, at New York University, as saying: "I don't know why . . . we're imitating second-rate cities [that are] pretending to be first rate. It's really quite curious." The article then presented some insights that address the professor's quandary.[9]

New York is home of Wall Street. It's the city that doesn't sleep. "Making it there" means being able to "make it anywhere," and even time is measured differently in "New York minutes." Yet the article placed middling Charlotte as New York's new peer, even an example for New York to follow:

> For most of its history New York has hardly been a lofty sanctuary for artistes and littérateurs, but the world's most tenacious capital of commerce and avarice, a place where Charlotte's cut-to-the-chase, mid-70's civic slogan, "Charlotte—A Good Place to Make Money," would not have been inappropriate.

The article quotes Phillip Lopate, an author and academic, who explains that "cities are now selling images as much as realities":

> Cities have to position themselves as cultural flytraps and to market themselves based on images; the image of city life becomes a product of the city.

The jeopardy to New York in this strategy, the *Times* article explained, is that New York will lose its famed lack of fakery, becoming a false and empty avatar. Public policy would come to be shaped by the invented image, not real needs and wants of New Yorkers.

Charlotte's history has plainly shown that when an image becomes the city's product, the city's character passes from real substance to fictional brand. Authenticity, originality, and freedom are sacrificed to maintain a "narrative" that supersedes the needs of the city's residents.

From the perspective of Soul, this is a discouraging trend, bolstering the soul-deadening twin forces pervasive in Charlotte, pretense and profit, which put image above substance and the dollar above all. Yet, the trend may be difficult for other cities to escape.

Acting as a "cultural flytrap" has been Charlotte's hallmark for many decades. Charlotte's long experience in approaching every aspect of life "like a business" accounts for its phenomenal success in attracting capital and corporate headquarters. Charlotte's "secret" power, which J. W. Cash described satirically and derisively, is now the very proclivity other cities are trying to cultivate.

It is also the root source of constant searches by Charlotte boosters for a missing core element of the city's identity. This subordination of all aspects of life to commercial logic is why many residents long for Charlotte to become a more worthy place to call home. It is why Charlotte is referred to as both booming and soulless.

Soul Imported

The current trend of exporting Charlotte's obsessions with growth, profit, and "image" portends no local change of culture. However, there is another trend that may uncover that elusive quality Charlotte's boosters perpetually search for. This is the arrival of new residents from faraway lands and the return of the descendants of those who had gone into exile from Charlotte and the South generations ago. In attracting both, Charlotte is *importing* Soul. This represents a development with a cultural potential that W. E. B. Du Bois, or any visionary of his era could not have imagined, an external force entering the city that could lift the "veil."

Charlotte is now regularly referred to as a "Black mecca," a term with profound meaning but possibly unfamiliar to White readers. Black mecca is a long-standing legend, a utopian ideal of deliverance generated by horrific history. Moving from city to city, or to another state, seeking a home where roots can spread, investments planted, and a happy life nurtured is a pattern among African Americans, beginning not long after the Civil War. It continues today.

Much has been written about the Great Migration, officially dated from 1910 to 1970, when more than six million African Americans left the South for northern and western urban centers. They fled lynchings, Jim Crow laws, educational restrictions, and innumerable, insidious barriers to building a better life. The Great Migration followed the end of federally protected Reconstruction, a short period of great hope and ferment, tragically followed by what some Southern Whites called the "Redemption," state-sponsored terror aimed at suppressing legal rights, safety and economic gains of African Americans.

The earliest movement of the Great Migration was to the state of Kansas. Kansas, the home of abolitionist John Brown, was perceived during the Civil War and the years immediately afterward as a promised land for new beginnings, where farm skills and experience could be put to good use. So significant was the flight to Kansas that a formal investigation was conducted by the US Senate. Some White landowners claimed Northern "agitators" were deliberately "luring" away the Black labor force for political purposes.[10]

Soon, the pattern of migration shifted toward Northern states. The flight to New York of the family of Charlotte's most famous artist, Romare Bearden, referenced earlier, is but one example. New York was the most popular destination for migrants from North Carolina. Family and neighbors reunited in Harlem, among other parts of the city and state. But now many of these migrants or their descendants are coming back to the South, and Charlotte is a major destination.

Citing data and testimonies, *The Charlotte Observer* noted the modern resettlement of African Americans into Charlotte in the 2023 article "Why Some Are Calling Charlotte a 'Black Mecca'":

> The largest growth in pure numbers of Black residents since 2010 hasn't taken place in popular cities like Atlanta or Houston, but rather in Charlotte during a period where there is a mass exodus of Black people leaving America's largest industrial hubs like New York and Chicago for the South. In 1970, . . . the city's Black population stood at 72,938 people. . . . By 2020, . . . Charlotte's Black population swelled to 307,858. Currently, Black residents account for 35.2% of Charlotte's population.[11]

An accompanying chart of census data showed that in the fifty-year span, from 1970 to 2020, the Black population of Charlotte increased 400 percent. Even more significantly, the Black population as a percentage of the total population increased by 16 percent.

The influx of Latino immigrants to Charlotte has also been tracked and discussed in hard numbers. However, there has been little analysis of longer-term effects on city life, apart from mentions of ethnic restaurants and some cultural festivals, as though this population were a new "amenity." From 2020 to 2023, the *Charlotte Observer* reported that the Latino population of Charlotte-Mecklenburg grew 9 percent, while White residents increased by less than 2 percent. In the previous year, Latinos accounted for 30 percent of total population increase.[12]

The new Black and Latino residents and immigrants from other countries and continents—eastern Europe, Africa, India, Korea, China, Vietnam—are young. Their engagement with Charlotte is forward-looking, and likely to be long-term. Charlotte is not where they were "transferred" by their employer, or a stopping off place on a career trajectory. They are not seeking to replicate where they came from in a familiar franchise-like "borough." Few have the option or the desire to opt out of the public schools. These new residents buy cars, homes, start businesses and make other local investments. And whereas for the last few decades to say you were a native of Charlotte marked you as a rarity, the children of these new residents may establish Charlotte as their hometown for generations to come.

Like previous groups who have moved to Charlotte, the newly arriving residents are drawn to Charlotte for economic reasons, but with a major difference. They are looking for new opportunity, not merely to continue or advance current careers. As they congregate, they will also build businesses to meet needs within their own ethnic communities, learn new skills, and build equity. They are not coming to Charlotte just to get jobs, but, in many cases, to create them.

Though it is impossible to verify or document with data, it is reasonable to believe and strongly supported by my own experience that these newcomers bring a different mindset and values than the previous waves of job-seekers, who came from nearby smaller towns or as part corporate moves and expansions in Charlotte. The international and young African American arrivals have stronger and more extended family ties, more respect for older family members and ancestors, and a greater sense of ethnic identity, all of which offset the commercially saturated Charlotte culture. Previous newcomers quickly internalized Charlotte's pervasive business orientation. If they did not already hold compatible views, they soon adopted them. The new arrivals have the potential of changing Charlotte, even as Charlotte will inevitably change them.

The international newcomers are even breathing Soul into Charlotte's oligarch-oppressed professional sports. A veteran sportswriter for the *Charlotte Observer* took special note of the refreshing new influence of world-class "soccer" in Charlotte. In August of 2024, 62,617 fans packed into Charlotte's Bank of America stadium, home to the Carolina Panthers, and the venue where the infamous statue of previous owner Jerry Richardson had been hastily removed in a shroud of scandal.

The match was between two famous Euro teams, Real Madrid and Chelsea FC, with most of the Charlotte crowd favoring the team from Spain. The news report on the huge crowd noted that, whereas at NFL games corporate blocks of tickets are counted as attendees even when the seats are empty, at this game each member of the audience had paid $75 or more a ticket. Also, the game was played on real grass, not the NFL fake turf. A match earlier in the season between Uruguay and Colombia drew more than 70,000, comparable to or surpassing crowd sizes at pro-football games. According to the *Charlotte Observer*, "Charlotte is feeling like a soccer town," and "*futbol* is having a moment in Charlotte."

Fresh energy and optimism are also palpable at the new arts enclave in Charlotte, the Visual and Performing Arts Center, where African American and Latino artists are creating new styles and reflecting international movements and perspectives with great feeling and boldness.

Will the aspirations and energy of this generation of new residents be allowed to flourish in Charlotte the way other immigrant communities have in other American cities? There have been some ominous signs of control and suppression, and despite a large population, the Latino community, in particular, has not gained what could be called a foothold on political power in Charlotte. Nearly a third of public school students are Latino, but only recently has the first Latin American school board member been elected.

Gentrification, high rents, and inflated home pricing, among other factors, have prevented a geographically concentrated ethnic community in Charlotte, such as *Pequeña Habana* in Miami, Little Ethiopia in Washington, DC, or a Chinatown as in New York or Honolulu. A declining but very famous enclosed mall in Charlotte, Eastland Mall, in an area where many Latino residents had concentrated, showed some possibility of evolving into a unifying—culturally and commercially—Latino and international market with independent vendors, churches and educational facilities filling spaces vacated by large chains. In 2012, the City of Charlotte purchased the mall for $13 million and spent another $800,000 the next year to demolish it. The 80-acre site remained vacant for the next ten years.

The *Charlotte Observer* article that documented the unprecedented growth of the Latino population notes that much of the increase is not within the Charlotte city limits, where home pricing is prohibitive to young and working people, but near and over the border with South Carolina where land and homes are still relatively affordable.

The force that most threatens the Latino population is not local neglect or discrimination, but virulent, often racist anti-immigration sentiment. Anti-immigration sentiment is expressed mostly at the national level, but the earliest and ugliest voices against immigration came straight out of Charlotte, North Carolina. Deportation programs originated with Charlotte's own congressional representative, Sue Myrick, and with the Charlotte-based county sheriff, James Pendergraph. Myrick, as discussed previously, was a former mayor and heavily supported by money from the pyramid selling scheme, Amway.

Myrick made loud and unfounded claims in Congress and to the national media of links between newly arriving Latino immigrants and domestic terrorism, including Islamic groups. She used the death of a pedestrian in Charlotte who was accidentally hit by a Latino driver to introduce national legislation giving greater power to police in checking citizenship status of drivers.

In 1996, Myrick was among those backing the inclusion of the 287(g) provision of the Illegal Immigration Reform and Immigrant Responsibility Act of 1996. This national law deputized local police to carry out functions previously reserved for federal agents regarding immigrants. The first sheriff in America to use the provision was James Pendergraph in Charlotte, but his policies soon spread to many other cities, though some later abandoned the program.

Thousands of immigrants in Charlotte who were detained because of minor issues, such as broken taillights on a car, were arrested and turned over to federal agents for deportation procedures. Families were traumatically divided. US-born or naturalized Latinos were harassed and mistreated as suspected "illegals" or even as possible "terrorists." The policy spread fear throughout Charlotte's new immigrant population. Under 287(g) Pendergraph claimed his office identified more than 3,000 undocumented immigrants to federal officials. Pendergraph and Congressperson Myrick tied their deportation policy to efforts at getting for-profit prisons into the Charlotte area, a plan that local officials rejected.[13]

Pendergraph's aggressive actions in Charlotte led to his appointment by President George W. Bush to a high profile position with US Homeland Security coordinating local law enforcement with US Immigration and Customs Enforcement (ICE). In Washington, Pendergraph quickly gained national attention by telling a national gathering of local police that if they "did not have enough evidence" to bring a criminal charge against an immigrant in custody, his office "can make him disappear."[14]

Pendergaph resigned from Homeland Security within a year following a dispute with a North Carolina congressman who charged his office was not focused on criminals but on arresting immigrants in workplace raids. Pendergraph called the criticisms "political correctness."[15]

And so it was that just as I arrived back to Charlotte and felt amazement and hope at seeing the new "diversity," hearing other languages, and witnessing the unprecedented infusion of new cultures into Charlotte life, Charlotte was leading a national movement to demonize immigrants and criminalize their presence, closing off paths to citizenship or work permits.

During my first years back in Charlotte, I refreshed the Spanish I had learned in Florida and Mexico. I did this by taking free classes at International House, a center to support people moving to Charlotte from other countries. I also volunteered at the immigrant support organization, Mi Casa Su Casa, operating in offices provided by a local church. I saw the joy and hope immigrants once felt turning to fear and despair. Victims of crimes were afraid to seek police protection. Driving, shopping, getting medical attention or attending church became frightening experiences, as people would have to watch for police or undercover agents.

The election of a new sheriff who opposed the use of local deputies for federal immigration law enforcement reduced the level of panic and desperation in Charlotte, but deportation remains a daily threat.

Younger African Americans in Charlotte, including some who recently arrived from Atlanta and New York as part of the reverse migration trend, were also met with frightening resistance when they raised their voices.

In June 2020, hundreds of protestors assembled in Charlotte, as in many other cities, to protest the police killing of George Floyd in Minneapolis. Charlotte regularly boasts of its calm restraint in responding to civil rights protests, even claiming a "Charlotte Way" of building trust and finding a just resolution. The young protestors, marching peacefully, thought they had little reason to fear a repressive or violent response from Charlotte officials.

On June 2, after several days of protest, the group marching in the center city realized that the people toward the front were suddenly running back into their ranks in panic. Heavily armed police had arrived on a city bus in riot gear and began firing tear gas canisters and throwing flash-bang devices into the marchers.

A local journalist who was livestreaming the events told national news media, "They closed the whole group in between a line of riot officers and a wall of tear gas. They blocked all the exits with tear gas, and nobody was going to just run through the tear gas, because if you did, you were getting shot with pepper bullets."

Another journalist who was also filming reported that police snipers on an upper level of a parking garage fired pepper balls at the crowd. "Not only we were getting hit from both sides, we were getting hit from the top as well," he said. "I felt sick to my stomach out of fear."[16]

Charlotte police appeared to be employing a special entrapment and control maneuver called "kettling." It involves encircling protestors, leaving no exit, and then subjecting them to tear gas, beatings, and pepper bullets.

The incident focused negative attention from national media on Charlotte, but the mayor and police chief, both of whom were African American, publicly denied the use of kettling. The use of sudden and extreme violence toward peaceful protestors has been interpreted as a message from officials that in the future strong voices of protest would also meet this same kind of response.

The 2020 protests in Charlotte were part of the Black Lives Matter movement, which amplified new calls for justice and opportunity. It was a new and younger voice within the African American community, and many participants were part of the new migration into Charlotte. They were awakened to the reality that Charlotte, like other places that gained the legendary status of "Black mecca," has far to go to earn the title.

New waves of immigrants and the returning descendants of previous residents are looking for a "home" where they can be safe and feel included. They are looking for a place to identify with, and where they can exercise their fullest potential in building a life. Many more people in America, in different ways, are on that same quest.

If Charlotte's newcomers become the force that shifts this "booming" city toward Sense of Place and Soul, Charlotte will find its new slogan. It won't be a claim about what Charlotte's "got" or a boast about making money, but simply, *Charlotte, a place to call Home.*

---

[1] Two activist artists, Bunny Gregory and Rosalía Torres-Weiner, deserve recognition for taking art into the community, especially to children who may not have opportunities otherwise. See "Charlotte Artist's Dream of Mobile Studio for Kids will Soon Hit the Road" by Dashiell Coleman, *WFAE*, May 2, 2021, and "Meet Charlotte's "Artivist" Rosalía Torres-Weiner" (https://www.youtube.com/watch?v=h1V1s0UuEuk)

[2] The apartment complex, called Morningside Apartments, was built after World War II as affordable housing. On 26 acres, it consisted of 42 buildings containing a total of 336 one, two, and three-bedroom units. Originally restricted both by race and income with now-illegal deed restrictions, the

complex later became celebrated for diversity, livability, and affordability, including for LBGTQ residents, Africans, East Europeans, Latinos, and African Americans. The Charlotte Landmark Commissions surveyed the complex, stating, "Morningside Apartments possess special historical, social, and cultural significance." The entire complex was demolished in 2007, just before the housing crash and all 26 acres lay vacant for a decade. In 2017, The Village at Commonwealth was constructed on part of the site. Tiny studio apartments were available for rent for $1,666, and two-bedrooms for $2,572. The complex is advertised as "Resort Inspired Living."

[3] *How the Irish Became White,* by Noel Ignatiev, Routledge, 2008

[4] For this citation I need only anecdotes within my own family between the Irish and Italian lineages.

[5] "Charlotte Needs a New, Non-Crappy Slogan that Reminds Us to Work to Be Great" by Clayton Sealey, *Charlotte Observer*, October 13, 2019

[6] "New Neighbor Awaits Trump" by Doug Smith, *Charlotte Observer*, March 29, 2007

[7] "The Time Trump Almost Built Charlotte's Tallest Skyscraper" by Emma Way, *Axios Charlotte*, Jan 19, 2021, and

[8] "Close View of a Calvinist Lhasa" by W. J. Cash, *The American Mercury*, Edited by H. L. Mencken, April 1933

[9] "Those Little Town Blues, in Old New York?" by Peter Applebome, *New York Times*, April 29, 2001

[10] "Exodus to Kansas, the 1880 Senate Investigation of the Beginnings of the African American Migration from the South" by Damani Davis, *Prologue Magazine,* Summer 2008: Vol. 40, No. 2

[11] "'All the Things a City Can Have.' Here's Why Some Are Calling Charlotte a 'Black Mecca'" by Kendrick Marshall, *Charlotte Observer*, March 1, 2023

[12] "In the Charlotte Area, a Slice of South Carolina Helped Boost the Hispanic Growth Rate" by Desiree Mathurin and Gavin Off, *Charlotte Observer,* July 22, 2024

[13] "Pendergraph Ties to Prison Industry Raise Questions" by John Grooms, *Creative Loafing*, October 26, 2010

[14] America's Secret ICE Castles"by Jacqueline Stevens, *The Nation*, December 16, 2009

[15] "Pendergraph Quits Federal Position" by Franco Ordoñez and Gary Wright, *Charlotte Observer*, Aug 25, 2008

[16] "Ambushed by the Cops: When Police Deliberately Trap Peaceful Protesters, *An Intercept* and *Situ* Reconstruction of an Incident in North Carolina Last June Shows Police Intentionally Trapped and Tear-Gassed Hundreds of Peaceful Protesters" by Alice Speri, Situ Research and Travis Mannon, *The Intercept*, June 2, 2021

A Postscript And A Prophecy

My friend Hank and I have not taken a driving tour through Charlotte lately but we continue to trade memories and reflections. In his own neighborhood miles from "uptown," new hotels, movie theaters, shopping centers and big box stores seemingly sprang out of the ground after he and his wife purchased their home, not very long ago. It is a quintessential neighborhood in modern Charlotte—brand new, convenient amenities, rising in price, with most residents recently moved to the Charlotte area.

Like other similar new suburbs in Charlotte, longer term residents would likely not know it exists, thinking perhaps it is still a rural landscape and still calling the area by an archaic term associated with a creek or a church or a long forgotten family name. Few would ever see the gleaming new neighborhood if they did not live there or have friends or relatives who do. It is without history and there is little reason to believe that it will create any before another wave of development replaces its current identity.

For my part, my wife and I moved from our house near the center city to a small town in the mountains of Western North Carolina, not far from Asheville, about 150 miles from Charlotte. Our house in Charlotte, built before World War II and on a very busy street, stigmas in an earlier era, had tripled in value, along with taxes. Homes all around us were being demolished, trees felled and entire lots filled with five-thousand plus square foot behemoths inhabited by couples or even singles. Local stores disappeared, replaced by franchises. One young neighbor who purchased the house next to us immediately built a high privacy fence separating our back yards without a gate. Where we used to see and speak to the children and pets of previous owners, all social contact was blockaded. The talk of our area was all about home sales, renovations, tear-downs and mortgage interest rates. Strangely, though the area is among the most crime-free in the city, there is an obsessive worry about home invasions and a high alert for "strangers," though few know even their next door neighbors.[1]

I had formulated a de facto rule of residence in the new Charlotte: *If you can't afford to buy the house you now live in at its current market value, it is probably time to go.* We had a comfortable and convenient shelter but felt displaced from home and community. We did not belong any more.

As part of our mutual interests, one evening Hank and I met uptown to attend a unique, one-person tribute to "old Charlotte." The performance was in a small theater, located up a long escalator ride and at the back of the cavernous Bank of America lobby called "Founders Hall."

Like many other long-time residents of Charlotte, we hardly ever went into the city, and the rate at which the city was changing made any trip there seem like visiting a new, unexplored place. But what struck us both this particular evening was not what was new but what was absent.

COVID and remote work had seemingly sucked life out of the uptown that the city and boosters had spent decades respirating. Walking from a huge but nearly empty and unattended parking garage, past blank walls devoid of commercial activity into the bank building, we immediately noticed the disappearance of the many small shops that used to be patronized by office workers. We were told the shops had gone out of business and the city was now talking about converting the building's retail spaces into residences. It struck us as implausible but we doubted our own eyes. What was possible or impossible in Charlotte, real versus narrative, true or false, we weren't sure any more.

Amidst new construction, amenities, and rising home equity in our neighborhoods, Hank and I experienced isolation, invisibility and a sense of exile. Ironically, the most visible and most talked about residents of Charlotte were those without any home at all. More than the splendiferous mansions in gentrified old neighborhoods or the majestic chateaus of NASCAR drivers on Lake Norman, the communities that more people took notice of were the tent cities of homeless people in the center city. In 2021, the city issued an order to force the tent city residents out of their "homes."

Now, the homeless are invisible though still present. The city officially reported a total of 2,839 people living without shelter in 2024, possibly a significant undercount, but still a community about three-quarters the size of my own in Charlotte before I moved. The report, "Charlotte-Mecklenburg Housing & Homelessness Data Factsheet 2024," said this homeless community number grew 3% over the previous year,[2] almost double the rate of growth of the city in the same time frame.[3]

Of course, and especially since their places of shelter have been outlawed, the homeless are never described as a "community." They literally have no Place in Charlotte. They exist as "data" or a condition. A community designation would give them faces and economically connect them to the rest of us, occupying one rung on the same economic ladder we all cling to or climb. Most importantly, it would mean that the larger economic system, including local tax priorities, the education system, bank loan policies for housing, and the job market would have to take responsibility for the existence of this community just as it takes credit for the prosperous ones.

The city's formal study that identified about 3,000 homeless does put them into some larger context, showing how close to being homeless huge numbers of people in Charlotte are. It shows that fifty percent of renter households and twenty-two percent of owners—150,000 households in all—pay more than 30 percent of their total incomes to keep a roof over their heads. About 4,000 eviction notices were filed *every month* in the Charlotte area. According to the report, at federal minimum wage, a Charlotte resident would have to work 147 hours a week to afford a 1-bedroom apartment.

Famed urban sociologist Jane Jacobs had long ago argued that a local economy, if it is functioning properly, should facilitate "unslumming," transforming poor people to middle class, less educated to skilled and newcomers to "competent citizens." But she noted that "unslumming was frequently halted by the "ultimate discouragement—destruction."

Charlotte no longer has what were called "slums." Urban renewal and gentrification have eliminated them. The "abatement order" against the homeless in 2021 extended the destruction.

Few would connect the sense of exile and loss of Place that Hank and I experience with the sad spectacle of tents in booming "uptown." The tents, the evictions, and absurd disparity between wages and housing costs are not officially linked in Charlotte's narrative of "New South" and "booming."

It remains only for artists to make sense of the contradictions. In a recently published essay, "The Home Within, A Call to Black Artists on the Experience of Homelessness and Belonging," Charlotte artist Dasia Hood explored the connections of the homeless to the larger community and traced the roots of the tragedy. She cited author, James Baldwin, *"Perhaps home is not a place but simply an irrevocable condition"*

"If that is true", she concluded, "then home is what we make of each other . . . The challenge is to go beyond calling attention to homelessness as an issue and instead forge deeper connections . . . In other words, how do we reach out and let our [homeless] people know they are not alone?"[4]

Economics, Icons and Idols

Since the early 60s when the wrecking ball and bulldozers of urban renewal began their work, the primary tenet of Charlotte's "transformation" has been that the center city, a.k.a. downtown, a.k.a. uptown, is the city's *economic* wellspring, the vortex of Charlotte's viability as well as that of its residents.

Based on that belief, Charlotte completely erased its old downtown, and all that it had meant to locals, including thousands whose homes and churches were wiped away. Charlotte's boosters created a new identity symbolized by banking office towers. History was not only deleted but maligned as an inconvenient obstacle to modern branding.

To justify this extreme government intervention over allowing the center city to develop organically and respecting the rights of existing residents, the invisible hand of the market and abiding economic principles were authoritatively cited. Economic orthodoxy was said to justify government seizure of private property on the promise it would increase the tax base. Then, a version of this rationale was reversed to justify locating public and tax-exempt facilities—government offices, museums, arenas, convention centers—in the largely vacant center city to "stimulate" tax-paying development.

Despite the contradictions and unfulfilled promises, the appeals to economic logic worked very effectively to rebuff and exclude citizens who challenged the decisions of Charlotte's business and political elite. Neighborhood activists, senior citizen groups, small retailers, and other voices called for more money and attention to be directed to local civic needs. They petitioned for investment in public transit, antipoverty programs, neighborhood stability, sidewalks, historical preservation, education, affordable housing, parks, and healthcare services. Their views were skillfully dispatched as uninformed, misguided, naïve, and, worst, un-economic.

In recent years, Charlotte boosters took the center city narrative to a new height. They began referring to Charlotte's office tower skyline as *iconic*, like San Antonio's Alamo, St. Louis's Arch, Seattle's Space Needle, and San Francisco's Golden Gate Bridge.

Unlike those and other urban icons, which are unique and can be visited and experienced, Charlotte's skyline is not nationally recognizable or unique. Every major city has one. A skyline, any skyline, is something of an illusion. It is an impressionistic image that can be glimpsed only from a distance and is best viewed in dim light or darkness. As one moves closer, the image disappears, replaced, in Charlotte, with the mundane reality of concrete canyons lined with undistinguished structures, office worker compounds, and streets with strangely little auto or pedestrian traffic. At street level, one can see the still bare ruins of urban renewal and arid acres of commuter parking lots.

As an imagined icon, even if relatively undistinguished, Charlotte's silhouette of banking towers is said to symbolize enduring economic power, validation of Charlotte's growth-and-status crusade. As the physical manifestation of the boosterism dream quest and culmination of a mythic journey to world class status, the center city is described as *monumental*. The questions remain, a monument to what? To whom? What, exactly, does this monument symbolize? At what costs to city life was it erected? Was it a golden calf, the people's own wealth and well being made into a graven idol?

Recent developments are calling into question not only Charlotte's civic priorities but the validity of the economic beliefs and claims that sustained the "uptown-first" policy for almost fifty years. New economic conditions are challenging the towers as possibly unsustainable and illusory, not unlike the loan policies and merger and acquisition frenzy that brought the banks down in 2008. The very purpose of Charlotte's towers is now in *economic* question.

Dogma and Heresy

The economic dogma behind the fixation on the center city has at times—if only hesitantly and on rare occasions—been taken to task for its possible connections to entrenched poverty, homelessness, congestion, declining schools, unaffordable housing, and the loss of character and history. These urban woes are inevitably dismissed as the unavoidable price of Charlotte's renowned economic security and stability.

The possibility that any other viable strategy exists is almost never entertained in Charlotte. Any notion that more could be done to alleviate the "price" born by ordinary residents is dismissed as fuzzy-headed idealism, possibly socialism.

A direct challenge to Charlotte's economic dogma—questioning if it might be folly, a delusion, a quixotic quest, or an economic house of cards—is regarded as an act of heresy. As booster-in-chief Hugh McColl framed it, the choice for Charlotte is between constant growth and certain death.[5]

Despite these sanctions and city leaders' dogmatic appeals to economic "law," the possibility that the approach of always putting Profit over Place could be flawed was alarmingly raised when Charlotte's two big banks—anchors of "uptown"—suddenly crumbled in 2008. The warning was ignored. Today, Bank of America and Wells Fargo still control the city's fate. Their combined workforce makes up about 40% of the people employed by the city's top five employers.[6] The concentration of the banks' assets and workers in the center city makes any shift in priorities unthinkable to government officials or the local media.

A recurrence of the sudden and little understood 2008 crash remains a dreaded prospect for Charlotte, but a new threat has arisen that is more—in a word—concrete, and it is already causing trouble. *Charlotte office space is 25 percent vacant.* Thomas Birnbaum of the Cultural Landscape Foundation blamed urban renewal for causing "desertion" and "dereliction" in Charlotte's formerly vibrant and iconic Square. The new threat is of desertion at a much greater scale.

Urban Doom Loop

The term for the new threat is "urban doom loop," a theory of the devaluation and declining usefulness of large office buildings in the center city, which leads to either higher residential taxes or reduced public services. The urban doom loop was identified and named by Stijn Van Nieuwerburgh, a professor of real estate at Columbia Business School. He described the phenomenon in 2022, following the COVID-19 pandemic, which accelerated the shift toward remote working.[7]

Remote working might have initiated the doom loop, but digital technology is the root cause. Videoconferencing and integrated workflow software facilitated real-time connectivity and enabled employees to be more productive when working flexibly or remotely.[8] Though some dispute the productivity measures, what is not disputed are the benefits to employees. The flexible option provides employees with more time freedom. It relieves difficulties associated with child care, reduces time and money spent commuting, and decreases spending on clothing and other needs associated with working in an office. Fully remote work allows people to live where they choose, an extraordinary benefit. The other undisputed benefit accrues to employers: reduced office space to lease.

To the earlier forces driving remote work and reduced office space needs must now be added artificial intelligence (AI). Remote work and communications software reduce need for center city offices. AI will eliminate the need for many of the workers. Another technology driver of reduced need for office workers and office space is blockchain technology.

Blockchain is commonly associated with cryptocurrencies, but the technology has other, more practical, uses, particularly in the financial industry.[9] It is a comprehensive and secure digital ledger that eliminates redundant record keeping, archiving, and security measures on vast numbers of transactions between departments and institutions. Those eliminated tasks currently constitute a large portion of employee functions. As explained in an essay included in Stanford University's Cryptocurrencies and Blockchain Technologies certificate program, blockchain "allows for . . . turning each financial institution away from cost- and labor-intensive recordkeeping and toward an automated workflow."[10]

AI and blockchain are the equivalents for white collar work of the robots on factory floors that have ravaged manufacturing jobs. Reflecting the effects of these technology and workflow changes already implemented, since 2020, Bank of America's revenue increased nearly 20 percent without adding a single new position to total employment.[11]

A report on Charlotte's office rental market at the end of 2024 by Savills Research and Data Services showed an overall vacancy rate above 25 percent, and above 28 percent uptown.[12] The national average is 20 percent.

A feature article in the *Charlotte Observer* mentioned one large office building in the center city that recently sold for less than half its previous purchase price. It was 50 percent empty. Several new buildings opened with no major tenants and another large office building was foreclosed on with an outstanding $90 million mortgage. A pillar office building on the Square, One Independence, is reportedly 44 percent vacant, even after a major renovation to help it compete against newer buildings. Thirty percent of all uptown office buildings were delinquent on mortgage payments as of 2024, according to a source quoted in the *Observer* article.[13]

One South, the office tower formerly known as Bank of America Plaza, inspired many of the towers built later. It was the bank's headquarters and for a time was the tallest building in the state. Erected on the ruins of a department store and other retailers on land taken by the city with urban renewal, the front plaza area is the site of Charlotte's *Il Grande Disco*. Currently, One South, a.k.a. Bank of America Plaza, stands half empty.

Another giant in the pantheon of office towers is One Wells Fargo. This building went through numerous name changes as banks were acquired or collapsed. Most recently, it was the East Coast headquarters of Wells Fargo. Now, Wells Fargo is consolidating its operations into the large newer building built by Wachovia just before it collapsed and was taken over by Wells Fargo. Construction was begun in 2006 and completed 2010 at a cost of $880 million. The new building was originally intended to anchor Charlotte's "culture campus." Now, it is where the giant new Wells Fargo signs, fifty-four feet high, are being installed, one on each side of the tower.

Before the relocation of Wells Fargo employees into the new building, One Wells Fargo was speculatively flipped by successive new owners in rapid sales. It is now 66 percent empty. Overall, about 14 million square feet of office space in Charlotte was reported vacant in mid-2024, producing a revenue loss approaching half a billion dollars. Charlotte's rate of commercial vacancies is in the top one-third of urban markets. In the Southeast, it is at the very top, along with Atlanta.[14]

This raises the specter of loan defaults threatening the banks. But even more significantly, the defaults, delinquencies, and lowered values of office properties ultimately point toward reduced tax valuations on center city real estate.[15]

Postscript

The postscript to Charlotte's tale of transformation must be that the "iconic" center city—which boosters called Charlotte's economic engine and where so much tax money was spent—*is losing value.* A devaluation of Charlotte's greatest asset, measured by costs, public policy, and investments, is akin to a city's main industry facing an external threat from competition, disinvestment, foreign relocation, or obsolescence.

In Charlotte, about 40 percent of revenue from all property taxes is from commercial real estate. A significant drop in uptown's commercial property values would cause a shortfall in revenue needed to operate the city and meet debt obligations. Such a deficit could be recouped only with increased property taxes on homes, condos, and apartments, or by reducing city services.

The *Observer* article noted that city officials are already ginning up plans and political explanations for a new round of government intervention to alleviate unsustainable vacancy rates. Some of the vacated properties are being called "vintage"; in fact, nearly all of Charlotte's "vintage" center city office buildings were demolished long ago. Of Charlotte's twenty-nine largest office buildings the oldest was built in 1972; twenty-five were built after 1980.[16]

The first policy response under consideration is Charlotte's old stand-by: "incentives like a demolition fund for buildings that are not worth saving."[17] This time, though, the city cannot claim the center city is "blighted" or that demolitions of older buildings are part of a grand new vision. The immediate economic goal is merely to sustain the taxable and market values of newer buildings through demolitions or tax-subsidized renovations of older ones. Vacancies, dilapidation, and discounted rentals among the older office buildings drag down all valuations, as they would in a residential area.

A more inspiring narrative with a larger vision was clearly needed to gain public support. A new rationale had to be found to justify spending yet more public money to rehabilitate Charlotte's uptown, just when it had seemingly reached its apex, and its skyline was being declared the very symbol of Charlotte.

And so, Charlotte residents are no longer hearing the old familiar lectures about sound economic principles that mandate prioritizing the center city over other civic needs. Fewer voices are raised now claiming that uptown is an economic dynamo that sustains the city. Instead, the city is raising a banner that for fifty years it has trampled and dismissed with dogmatic economic arguments. The new rationale for spending more tax money on the center city is *honoring local history!*

Redefining "Historic"

A feature article in the *Charlotte Business Journal* described the new narrative. The director of Charlotte's Historic Landmarks Commission, Stewart Gray, stated that federal and state tax credits should be used for Charlotte's older office buildings uptown.[18]

> "We need to look at these skyscrapers and see what is eligible," he said. "It looks like some office space in uptown Charlotte is in trouble, and when we see a building being auctioned or sold at a much lower cost, it appears that these buildings need to be rethought."

Gaining the designation of "historic" offers significant financial benefit. Federal tax credit equal to 20 percent of renovation costs is available. An even greater percent of renovation costs is offered as a credit against state income taxes. Locally designated historic properties can also seek 50 percent property tax deferrals.[19]

An obvious question is: how could these nondescript office buildings, sites not of consequential events, but of routine daily work, and which are just decades old, qualify as "historic landmarks"? To this, Gray offered a classic Charlotte ploy. The meaning of historic will be redefined. Charlotte made history, he argued, by wiping out nearly all remnants of its past "downtown." The modern buildings constructed on the site of the old city center and demolished African American communities are "historic" symbols of Charlotte's great transformation.

This is an escalation of the narratives that accompany gentrification when actual historic communities are demolished and their names and history erased. The new development, with a new name, is then called "historic," as if the old community had been preserved. In the new uptown narrative, the act of demolition and erasure is itself called historic and the replacement buildings declared the monuments of this event.

> "The case to be made for these buildings is that they are the historical evidence of the incredible development of uptown Charlotte during the 1970s that turned the place into a financial center," he said.

Prophetic Voices

As national stories in other cities report, measures are being taken by large companies around the country to require office workers to return to their cubicles, commute to uptown, pay to park their cars, purchase lunch, arrange child-care, and dress for success. A Charlotte news feature reported that Bank of America and Truist Bank in uptown are now requiring employees to come to work at the office more often. It also acknowledged that the uptown they are returning to had changed. Many small retailers and restaurants had disappeared from uptown due to fewer workers on site. It referred to the huge new office buildings of Wells Fargo and Duke Energy that "expanded the Uptown skyline, [while] also leaving older, larger buildings without a major tenant, which has led to foreclosures."

The story also noted that plans were underway to extensively renovate some older buildings or convert some empty office space to residences or hotel rooms, but it qualified these possible remedies as "long-term projects that come with a steep price tag."[20]

This local feature and similar articles offer a vision for an uptown revival, combatting urban doom loop. It is difficult, though, not to view that vision like calls to get shoppers to return to stores or young people to put down their cell phones. The forces of new technologies and the activities they produce or replace seem irreversible.

Despite the vacancies and potential threat to the tax base, almost no one in positions of authority or in the local media will yet dare to question "uptown" as the locus of the city's identity and the highest priority for tax spending and infrastructure development. Yet, as recounted in the search for Soul in the neighborhoods, coalitions of local neighborhood organizations did make such unspeakable challenges decades ago. In calling attention to more pressing local and human needs, they rejected and delayed plans to make Charlotte's airport a national hub. Later, another uprising of neighborhoods raised the same banner of Place and Soul, temporarily stopping the construction of a stadium in the center city and the demolition of the existing stadium, which was less than twenty years old and the largest of its type in the country. Their courageous critiques struck at the economic assumptions guiding Charlotte's grand plan and shaping the city's social character. The neighborhood groups called the downtown scheme a "white elephant," an economic folly that would ultimately place a greater burden on residents who would gain little or no benefit, and whose vital and immediate needs would be neglected.

Their claims that fundamental aspects of city life that make a city a livable Place, a home, were declining in Charlotte were ignored, even derided. Now, the deteriorating vacancy and devaluations of the city center, which could trigger greater residential taxes and yet more costs to "renew," at the expense of meeting real needs of local residents, may make their rejected petitions prophetic.

---

[1] Amidst the disruptions of gentrification in our old neighborhood, we found one beautiful respite, which we soon joined on a regular basis. Neighbors gathered in one family's backyard around a firepit to share drinks, snacks and thoughts. Keeping safe distance during the pandemic period, neighbors made or maintained connections. When restrictions lifted, the gatherings continued with greater social contact. Most of the participants were older residents. Such gatherings occurred spontaneously in other areas, some sparked by Covid restrictions, like revived spirits of how neighbors used to connect.

[2] *Charlotte-Mecklenburg Housing & Homelessness Data Factsheet | 2024* (https:// mecklenburghousingdata.org/wp-content/uploads/2020/06/2024-Charlotte-Mecklenburg-Housing-Data-Factsheet.pdf)

[3] https://charlotteregion.com/news/charlotte-among-fastest-growing-cities-in-the-u-s/#:~:text=15%20most%20populous%20city%20in,Texas%20saw%20larger%20population%20increases.

[4] "The Home Within, a Call to Black Artists on the Experience of Homelessness and Belonging" by Dasia Hood, *Queen City Nerve*, Feb. 12, 2025

[5] "You're either growing or dying. There's no middle ground," quoted in *PBS Frontline*, "Breaking the Bank," June. 16, 2009, full transcript at https://www.pbs.org/wgbh/pages/frontline/breakingthebank/etc/script.html

[6] "Largest Charlotte-Area Employers Ranked by Total Local Employment" by Amy Shapiro, *Charlotte Business Journal*, June 30, 2023

[7] See "'Urban Doom Loop' Could Threaten Charlotte's Commercial Real Estate Sector," by Zach Rounceville, *Carolina Journal*, Sept. 2023, and "Whatever Happened to the Urban Doom Loop?" by Rogé Karma, *The Atlantic*, March 22, 2024.

[8] "Opinion | Where Are You More Productive, in the Office or Working Remotely? The Verdict Is In …" by Gleb Tsipursky, Contributing Columnist, *Toronto Star*, updated June 6, 2024

9 "Blockchain Technology and Modern Banking Systems" by Amelia Matthewson, *FinTech Magazine*, August 02, 2024

10 "Popular blockchain use cases across industries" See: https://online.stanford.edu/popular-blockchain-use-cases-across-industries

11 Bank of America has total annual revenue of more than $100 billion and 213,000 employees as reported in 2025, the same number of employees reported in 2020 when the company posted $85 billion in total revenue: https://www.macrotrends.net/stocks/charts/BAC/bank-of-america/number-of-employees and https://newsroom.bankofamerica.com/content/newsroom/company-overview/bank-of-america-fast-facts.html#:~:text=Overall,15%2C000%20ATMs%20in%20the%20U.S. and https://finance.yahoo.com/news/bank-america-corp-bac-q4-070250839.html#:~:text=Net%20Income%3A%20%246.7%20billion%20for,for%20the%20full%20year%202024

12 https://pdf.euro.savills.co.uk/usa/market-reports/charlotte-mim-office-q4-2024.pdf

13 "Charlotte's Office Vacancies Are Stabilizing" by Desiree Mathurin, *Charlotte Observer*, October 31, 2024

14 "Here's How Much Empty Office Space Is Costing Charlotte" by Elise Franco and Joanne Drilling, *Charlotte Business Journal*, Nov 19, 2024, updated Dec 3, 2024

15 "Nearly a Quarter of Charlotte's Offices Are Vacant. Will the Trend Get Worse in 2025?" by Desiree Mathurin, *Charlotte Observer*, updated January 15, 2025

16 "Charlotte's Largest Office Buildings" by Amy Shapiro, *Charlotte Business Journal*, Oct 25, 2024

17 "Nearly a Quarter of Charlotte's Offices," *Charlotte Observer*, January 15, 2025

18 "Tower Turnaround: The Remake of a Historic Uptown Office Building Could Be a Model for More" by Elise Franco, *Charlotte Business Journal*, Jan 31, 2025

19 'Historic Landmarks' Pay 50% of their Local Property Tax" by Lucie Smul, *Axios Charlotte*, Jan 10, 2017

20 "A Quarter of Uptown Charlotte Offices Remain Vacant 5 Years Later" by Taylor Young, *Queen City News*, Jan. 15, 2025 (https://www.qcnews.com/charlotte/a-quarter-of-uptown-charlotte-offices-remain-vacant-5-years-later/#:~:text=Last%20year%2C%20city%20leaders%20discussed,the%20country%20for%20company%20headquarters)

www.ingramcontent.com/pod-product-compliance
Lightning Source LLC
Chambersburg PA
CBHW052120270326
41930CB00012B/2693